Passing Through
Shady Side

Passing Through
Shady Side

Ann Widdifield

authorHOUSE®

AuthorHouse™
1663 Liberty Drive
Bloomington, IN 47403
www.authorhouse.com
Phone: 1-800-839-8640

Published by AuthorHouse   01/03/2013

ISBN: 978-1-4772-8441-4 (sc)
ISBN: 978-1-4772-8440-7 (hc)
ISBN: 978-1-4772-8439-1 (e)

Library of Congress Control Number: 2012920483

Contents

Chapter 1:   Location and Place 1

Chapter 2:   A Celebration of Life 25

Chapter 3:   Eliza Dennis, Miss Doll Baby 32

Chapter 4:   Shady Side School Stories 49

Chapter 5:   Boarding Houses and Post Offices 77

Chapter 6:   Nick Families 94

Chapter 7:   Watermen and Water Stories 107

Chapter 8:   Chuck Gross 138

Chapter 9:   Stores and Businesses 146

Chapter 10: Crowner Families 160

Chapter 11: Buddy Holland 199

Chapter 12: Hog Stories 219

Chapter 13: Shady Side Neighborhoods 227

Chapter 14: Athletics and Recreation in Shady Side 244

Chapter 15: Matthews Families 251

Chapter 16: Thompson Families 268

Chapter 17: "The Little Church Beside the Road" 285

Chapter 18: Neighboring Methodist Churches 300

Chapter 19: Serving in the Military 316

Chapter 20: April 2011 343

DEDICATION

To the Glory of God

And

To my greatest blessing,

Noel, my husband and best friend

ACKNOWLEDGMENTS

W HEN ASKED WHY I did this work, I answered truthfully that it was something that God put on my heart. As appointments weren't kept and phone calls not returned, I questioned whether I was on the wrong path: Maybe the idea was from *me* rather than from God after all. I told my husband, Noel, that maybe I should stop. We prayed about it at dinner, and during the meal I received a cheerful phone call from a precious lady whose choice of words was my sign to continue. To Miss Jean Matthews Johnson and so many others, I am indebted for their kindness, love, encouragement, patience, humor, repeated explanations, and pictures and for welcoming me into their homes. This four-year journey has turned into one of the best things I have ever done.

Reading transcripts at the Miss Ethel Memorial Library at the Captain Avery Museum started me on my way. Oral and video interviews conducted by volunteers in 1984 gave me stories and leads to other files and individuals. Particularly helpful was the work of George and Mavis Daly. Nancy Bauer directed me to the Dennis will. During the process librarian Janet George and her dedicated library volunteers; Susy Smith, chairman of the board; Melanie Turner, follow-on chairman of the board; and Vicki Peterson, museum director, partnered with me to reach the production goal. June Hall and Mavis Daly were silent cheerleaders. Prue Hoppin, present chairman of the board, stepped in at the last minute and made sure we crossed the finish line. It was always my intent to give the book to the museum for its programs, and it gives me great joy to do so.

The congregation of St. Matthew's United Methodist Church, under the leadership of Rev. Theresa Robinson, welcomed me from the beginning, and I have worshipped there ever since. I cherish the fellowship of love, testimonies, and singing.

Eliza "Doll Baby" Dennis was my first interviewee, and her willingness encouraged me. Olivia Scott Gray befriended me and shared her time, stories, and pictures. Doris Crowner Brown, my champion, and Mr. Leon, too, pointed me in the right historical directions and dug for pictures. Doris's aunt Helen Crowner Gorham had more pictures and marvelous stories, and her sister, Daisy Crowner Thompson, added quiet sweetness. Ron and "Buddy" Holland added so much depth to the water stories, and they were unfailingly patient with my questions and interests. Surely they had some laughs beyond my hearing, and their wives became weary with my calls.

I am indebted to sisters Delores Harley and Connie Nick, who knew the family names and relationships and clarified my questions. They are my pew buddies. Their sister, Carla Gross, and niece, Chantal Gross Banks, are especially close to my heart, and we all miss Chantal's beloved "Daddy Chuck" Gross. Their sharing was exceptional. Besides taking Chantal and me on a graveyard walk, O. T. Turner answered my questions and provided guidance.

Judy Cabral, former director of the Kunta Kinte-Alex Haley Foundation and librarian of the Sojourner-Douglass College, culled materials for me and gave priceless guidance to sources. Dr. Joni Jones, director of the Banneker-Douglass Museum pointed me to Philip Brown's book.

Being less specific, I wish to recognize and especially thank Lucille Matthews Brown, Jean Yvonne Johnson, Jean Matthews Johnson, Yvonne Holland Matthews, Alexander and Credella Matthews, Thelma Matthews

Holland, Mary Holland, John and Teresa Fountain, Diane Blunt and her father, Titus Blunt, June Smith, Robert Taylor, Gerald Taylor, "J. R." Pinkney, Kathleen Thompson Hicks, Tyra Dunscomb, Bessie Thompson, Jant Thompson, Douglas Thompson, Florine Booze Thompson, Debbie Thompson, Darlene Matthews, Darlene Thompson Washington, Victor Smith, Donna Brown Hicks, Gayle Thompson, Paul Turner, Nina Turner Bullock, DeWayne Salisbury, Cordell Salisbury, Mohan Grover, LeRoy Battle, Alice Holt Battle, Dr. Lisa Battle Singletary, Carmelia Nick Hicks, Marshall Nick, Sr., Jackie Andrews Grace and her father, Derwill Andrews, Tommy Nick, Cate Greene, Mike Dunn, Barry Cornwall, Bruce Cornwall, Steve Gauss, Glen Trott, Doug Hinton, Brenda Early, Susie and Bill LesCallett, Beebe and Jack Castro, Vickie Marsh, Wanda Hall, Rev. Edward Schell, and Irma Lashley. I apologize to the people I may have missed listing here. In addition to the unintentional errors in the story, the graver mistake was not having your name here. I am so sorry and hope you will give me the opportunity to thank you in person. One person specifically told me to *not* mention his name—see, I didn't.

For those of you who know that God has great plans for us, it will not be a surprise to learn that my friend and a professional editor is also my next-door neighbor. Jackie Fox Ibrahim volunteered to edit my project and faithfully carried through on her offer. Not only did Jackie edit the "manuscript," smoothing out the bumps and crashes, but she also early on suggested current excellent books that I read. They appear in the story and bibliography. She saved my life by helping me organize myself for keeping order in researching and in recording names to keep genealogies straight. Jackie has been an editor and publisher of books and scholarly journals for professional associations and for the Oxford University Press for forty years. Currently she is the Director of Communications and Publications for the Center for Biosecurity of UPMC in Baltimore.

Our daughter, Julie Widdifield Sanders, and her dad, Noel, have done all of the icky, sticky parts of seeing me through to my goal. Julie helped me find my voice in the earliest drafts and kindly asked when I was going to tell "the story" when I was on a tangent. In spite of having the responsibility for thousands of seventh grade students' writings, she found time to proofread for me. My husband, Noel, did not read any of my stories and waited for the completed book. He wanted it all to be mine alone. In the meantime he regularly backed up my computer files, bought me equipment to make the writing easier, taught me Word shortcuts, found lost files, copied pictures, coached me on potential problems, told me to "stop researching and write," encouraged my writing by giving me time minus pressure, and finally told me it was time to "just stop; just end it." I know how fortunate I am, and I am truly grateful that he knows me so well and takes turns cooking.

Finally, thank you, Granddaughter Katherine "Katie" Marie Wisor for designing the book's cover. I love it!

Ann Widdifield,
Shady Side, Maryland
August 13, 2012

INTRODUCTION

A Place to Call Home

F AMILIES OF BOTH EUROPEAN and African descent inhabit the Shady Side peninsula, and several residents can trace their family lines back to some of the earliest settlers who lived here long before the village itself had a name. The peninsula's location and environment have drawn visitors and newcomers to join the families who have called the area home for generations.

The surrounding waters and the fertile land of the peninsula made a hospitable place for farmers and watermen, although the work to support families was demanding. Livelihoods have changed and businesses have come and gone as the Bay life has declined. Improved roads and transportation made traveling to and from the peninsula more accessible. Shady Side is within easy distance from Annapolis, Baltimore, and Washington, DC, and these large cities became sources of jobs and the peninsula became an escape from the city.

From the beginning different experiences were being lived out by the two groups. One group came willingly, the other under duress. One group had opportunity for a future, while the other had only the past and present while in the throes of slavery. Although blacks and whites worshipped together during slavery, the practice didn't last, and two side-by-side Methodist church buildings reflect the separation today. Educational opportunity—or lack of it—was a glaring, intolerable divide lasting for decades, even into the latter part of the twentieth century.

Blacks and whites fought in all of America's wars, starting with the American Revolution, but their experiences were uneven and different. Even the law of the land disenfranchised people of African descent, and historical accounts seemed to sideline them as if they were invisible and nonproductive.

Virginia Fitz wrote *The Shady Side Peninsula* in 1984, documenting historical facts of the area and the people living on the peninsula. White residents were cited most frequently, and white women and their activities were discussed. Although the book contained information about African Americans, it lacked details about their daily lives and work and their interaction with the rest of the community. African American women, in particular, were minimally represented—mainly in a list of people buried in the St. Matthew's cemetery.

Because the Jacob Dennis family was freed early in the nineteenth century, and Jacob Dennis owned land before the Civil War, more records existed about him, his wife, and his eight children. Mrs. Fitz gave readers a fresh look at the economics of the family. She also interviewed one of Jacob's grandsons, then in his late eighties, for her book.

One of Jacob's four daughters was named Eliza Dennis. Her brother, Joshua, named his daughter after Eliza, the child's aunt. Later Edith and Ira Dennis named their last child, a daughter, after the second Eliza, Ira's sister. The third Eliza Dennis, born in August 1930, turned 81 in 2011. From the shadows of the earlier Elizas and the presence of Miss Eliza Dennis today, a historical picture can be drawn to capture the lives of the African American women and men who have lived in Shady Side. Gifted with a remarkable memory for dates and names, Miss Eliza, better known as Miss Doll Baby, agreed to be interviewed for this project. Her relatives, neighbors, church family, and contemporaries (white and black) shared experiences and stories to provide a broader view of African Americans living in Shady Side.

In Shady Side the two groups have gotten along well through the generations, and the few unsettling problems have come mainly from the outside or from thoughtless, divisive troublemakers. While a nearby town was inhospitable and threatening to blacks, residents of Shady Side built black and white friendships one on one. Stories of the past reveal the quiet cooperation and concern for one another. Not perfect nor ideal, Shady Side was still desirable for both races and a place to call home.

Virginia Fitz's work became the impetus for the founding of the Shady Side Rural Heritage Society. The society opened the Captain Avery Museum in 1984, and members and volunteers have recorded oral histories and compiled collections of memoirs, artifacts, pictures, and vertical files in the museum's library.

By researching available museum information and interviewing local residents, this account attempts to fill in some of the missing stories of the African Americans' experiences and lives passing through Shady Side up to 2011.

Ann Widdifield, June 2011

CHAPTER 1

LOCATION AND PLACE

TODAY, AFTER PASSING UNDER the stoplight at the Churchton intersection of Routes 468 and 256, travelers head northeast along Shady Side Road to reach the village of Shady Side, Maryland, which sits on a peninsula. If it is an early morning in October, then chances are that school buses are already making their daily trek to Shady Side Elementary School. Small houses are spaced in clusters or dot either side of the road, and a bus stops at homes and lanes to pick up children headed for school. Traffic headed away from the peninsula is steady, too, because workers have been passing along since before sunup to get to jobs in Annapolis, Washington, DC, and Baltimore. A cloudless blue sky complements the oranges, yellows, browns, and reds of maples, sycamores, green pines, and the ubiquitous red poison oak.

Heading toward Shady Side, Brown's Way is on the right, Holly Lane on the left, Deep Cove Road appears on the right, and a sign welcomes visitors to the Shady Side Peninsula. As the first curve leads past Ira and Sugar Lanes, rumble strips send a slight shudder through the vehicle. There is no labeled sign to caution a driver that Dead Man's Curve is straight ahead, but any native, police officer, or fire or rescue driver knows where to go if they hear "Dead Man's Curve" on their radio. The road curves to the right, passing Dent Road and more houses on the right; Nick Road is on the left as posted signs on Route 468 announce the speed limit is now 30 miles per hour. Scott Town Road appears on the left, and to the right is Columbia Beach Road. Miss Eliza Dennis's bungalow faces Columbia Beach Road not too far down on the left and across from the woods. A little way back in those woods but further down the road on the right is the grave of Miss Eliza's great-grandmother, Elizabeth Dennis, and others.

Shady Side Road is the only road in and out of town. Fleeing bank robbers would have to think twice before a staging a holdup in Shady Side (except there is no bank). There are two grocery stores, a gas station, a mechanic's garage, four churches, three restaurants, a few local tradesmen, several boat yards, a fire station—and a few surprises for the uninformed.

Facing Shady Side Road are a framing business and a restaurant building, which sit on opposite corners of Cedarhurst Road. Two doctors and two dentists have offices further up on the right. The Shady Side post office pops up on the left, with West River Road just beyond it. Renno's Market, the gas station, and the mechanic's garage are next, with two United Methodist churches further up on the left and Lula G. Scott school across the road. Just beyond the churches is the fire station.

Roll up the road; remove modern transportation, and the fire engines disappear. Automobiles? Whisking cars and motorcycle roars could only be a made-up story to scare the children in the Shady Side of the past.

> Quietness shouts,
> Stillness expands.
> Across fields or
> > In the village
> > Living out life,
> > Working each day.
> > > Lives passing through
> > > Lives passing through
> > > Lives passing through.

To understand the present Shady Side, one needs a perspective of the past and how the town fit into the wider world. The land and its inhabitants were shaped by historical events, and these measures helped define the heritage and story of blacks on the peninsula and the town eventually known as Shady Side.

The Setting

In the beginning it was so: water, marshes, fertile soil, vegetation, and living creatures—insects, shellfish, fish, birds, reptiles, amphibians, and mammals inhabiting the peninsula. Changing seasons, tides, weather, and climate influenced each species interacting with the natural resources, forms, and features of the peninsula. Shady Side's absolute location is 38° 83.7" N and 76° 51.1" W, and its relative location is often described as west of the Chesapeake Bay, wrapped by the West River to its north and northwest, south of Annapolis and Baltimore, east of Washington, DC, north of Calvert County.

The Chesapeake Bay and its rivers, creeks, and streams were formed during the last great ice melt, when the Susquehanna River flooded its valley over 12,000 years ago. The Bay, called an estuary because of the mixture of fresh water and saltwater, has tides falling and rising twice daily and is very shallow compared to the oceans.[1] Teeming with life, the Bay was especially blessed by its oyster bars. Indians came and left behind oyster shell piles and scattered arrowheads as evidence of their presence on the peninsula.

Lying on Maryland's coastal plain, the Shady Side peninsula is about ten feet above sea level and flat. Over time the West River expanded and eroded shorelines, causing some land features, such as an island off Wagner's Point, the Three Islands near Curtis Point, and Columbia Beach sand, to disappear. During Capt. Salem Avery's lifetime, his home, now incorporated into the Captain Avery Museum, was physically moved back three times because of erosion and the spreading river, according to an unpublished script for museum house tours. A local tradesman reported that a flooded farm lies across the river from the Avery house at the mouth of the Rhode River. In earlier centuries the peninsula was practically cut off from the rest of the county; thus, water transportation was the best, most efficient way to travel.

The peninsula was known as "The Great Swamp," and maps and deeds of the peninsula labeled it as such. Shady Side's postal zone is about 2 miles wide at its widest point and about 4 miles long from Wagner's Point to Dent Road, where Churchton's postal zone begins. In 1860 it was known simply as "The Swamp" or "Sedgefield," because of a type of marsh grass that grew in abundance. Inhabitants were referred to as "Swampers" as opposed to the "Highlanders," who lived in such places as the Lothian area, where the elevation is higher.

Edward Parrish and the Village

Parrish Creek, which opens into the south side of the West River, was named after Edward Parrish, the first known settler on the peninsula. First an indentured servant on the Isle of Kent, Parrish and his wife, Magdalene, began life on 250 acres of the peninsula embraced by the West River. Like many English men and women, including Magdalene, Parrish agreed to servitude to pay his transportation costs to reach Maryland. Other settlers came to the other English colonies in this way. Getting one's start as an indentured servant was neither unusual nor a social stigma. Many successful colonists arrived under such conditions before they were released from their three-, five-, or even seven-year indenture.

The first Edward Parrish arrived in the Chesapeake region from England in 1655, making the trip in eight to ten weeks if he experienced normal sailing conditions. He would have received rations and would have been allowed above deck. Reaching Kent Island, the captain most likely would have sold his indenture to an eager purchaser. Laborers

4

were sorely needed for building the colony and providing an agricultural workforce. If Parrish were already skilled or talented in some area, his value would have been greater. Thus, the captain was reimbursed for the passage, and the buyer had a worker to serve him in any way he wished for the agreed time period. At the end of the time period, the servant was entitled to items customary to the colony, including clothing, tools useful for a trade, farming tools, or, as in Edward Parrish's case, the right to survey land and receive a land grant. Parrish's land grant came from none other than the second Lord Baltimore, Cecil Calvert.

Parrish's first tract was called "Parrish's Park." He acquired at least five other tracts during his lifetime. All the land around present-day Parrish Creek was his, as was land near South Creek and Deep Creek. Other planters arrived to seat land that had been granted to them, and later generations of their families benefited from these first settlers' accomplishments. [2]

Earliest English Settlements

With Virginia's second successful attempt to establish Jamestown in 1607 and the arrival of the Pilgrims at Plymouth Rock in 1620, the English had a strong presence in the New World. These two settlements started as "joint-stock" companies. Maryland was the first of three proprietary colonies. (Pennsylvania and Delaware were the others.) Joint stock companies were owned by multiple people, and proprietary colonies were owned by a single individual.

Cecil Calvert, a Catholic, received a land grant, or charter, from Charles I in 1632. Calvert, the second Lord Baltimore, was the proprietor of the land north of Virginia. At the time, Catholics were being persecuted by the Church of England and were not free to participate in government, so Calvert established a colony where freedom of religion would be allowed. He could rule it like a king as long as he paid the required dues of two Indian arrows a year and one fifth of any precious metals found. Cecil Calvert stayed in England to protect his rights and sent his younger brother, Leonard, on the *Ark* and the *Dove* in 1634 to settle his land. Leonard led about an equal number of Catholics and Protestants to Maryland, which was named for Henrietta Maria, King Charles's Catholic wife. Anne Arundel County was named for Cecil Calvert's beloved wife, Anne Arundell.

The Maryland colonists on the *Ark* spent some weeks resting in Barbados and were rejoined again by the *Dove,* from which they had been separated earlier in the voyage. It was here, in 1634, that Mathias Sousa joined the group and became the first black man to arrive as an indentured servant in Maryland. It is historically interesting to note that Sousa, also a sailor, became a landowner once his indenture ended and was a voting individual in the government of St. Mary's City, the first capital of Maryland.

Edward Parrish of Anne Arundel County made at least one trip to St. Mary's City to represent a man named Thomas Taylor in court in 1678. Taylor, the plaintiff, was suing for 14,600 pounds of tobacco in repayment for William Ball's taking Taylor's cattle. [3]

About 30 years later, Governor Francis Nickelson wanted the colony's capital to be more centrally located and to minimize the Catholic influence in St. Mary's City. He chose the town of Providence on the Severn River for the location but renamed it Annapolis, city of Anne, for Princess Anne, who was later crowned Queen of England. (The very first Anne Arundel settlers probably came up from Virginia, but Edward Parrish was the first on the Shady Side peninsula.)

Indentured Servants and Slavery

England also sent convicts to Maryland for indenture. During the early period of the colony's settlement, the English lowered their prison population by shipping undesirables to the colonies. Unlike the indentured servants, these prisoners would have to remain chained below deck during the crossing. They had longer periods of servitude and might be bound for a lifetime. In some cases prisoners chose death over crossing the Atlantic Ocean and an unknown future. Although many had committed petty crimes, others were seasoned criminals. A purchaser of these indentured servants needed to beware! After the American Revolution, the practice of sending prisoners away from England continued, but the destination became Australia.

In effect, the British colonies were a dumping ground for England's poor, unemployed, and felons. Until the 1700s these individuals produced most of the labor for Maryland and other Chesapeake colonies. The English colonists were unsuccessful in enslaving the local Indian populations to grow tobacco and work as farm laborers.

An unquenchable thirst for laborers in the Americas was creating an expanding market for workers, and this demand began the terrible slide into the horrendous practice that would stain the growing country for generations to come. The third group of laborers, who came from Africa, worked as indentured servants for only a brief period of time. Their treatment and opportunities were like the waves that carried them on the ships—hopes rising to an apex then falling in a trench of despair.

Although Jamestown, Virginia, already had about 30 people of African descent, it was the arrival of 20 Angolans in 1619 that marked the arrival of blacks to the Chesapeake. These Angolans were part of a much larger group of slaves that had been headed for New Spain, or Mexico, on a Portuguese slaver. A Dutch warship attacked the slaver, taking some of the human cargo. Stopping in Jamestown for supplies, the Dutch captain traded 17 men and 3 women for provisions. Unlike Portugal and Spain, England had no laws about slavery. The 20 people had Christian names; therefore, lacking laws, the English defaulted to custom and decided the group would not be enslaved. Once they worked off their purchase price, they regained their freedom just as indentured servants did. The English adopted the Spanish word "negro," meaning "black." [4]

In the earliest years, all indentured field servants in the North American colonies, white and black, worked side by side in the fields, living and sleeping together. Tobacco was the labor-intensive, backbreaking, and tediously unforgiving cash crop. Owners intended to get every ounce of work from their servants, but when the indenture was over, race made no difference in the release. At one time white indentured servants outnumbered blacks three to one. Freed black servants had the same status as freed white servants. Free black men could own land, lend money, farm, sue in court, vote, and serve on juries.[5] The parallels and intersection of the two races occurred for only a short time during the 17th century.

Distinctions already embedded in English thinking about class and race influenced the fledgling colonies. The English class hierarchy had definite separations among royalty, gentry, merchants, tradesmen, commoners, and the ever-present unfit drudges among them. Any group that was different in culture or appearance, such as the nearby Irish or the distant American Indian, was thought to be inferior to the Englishman. Additionally, a strong precedent of enslaving Africans already existed in the British Caribbean sugar colonies.

In the North American colonies, differences could be seen between indentured blacks and whites: For example, an African woman went to the fields while a white woman worked as a domestic. Black servants did not have surnames like whites, and early census reports separated the two races. Local Anglican priests said that people of African descent could not become Christian. According to English common law, a child's status was that of the father, but bills of sale began to appear that made it clear that the child of a black female servant was a servant for life. By the 1640s courts began to infer that people of African descent would serve owners for a lifetime. Slave codes from 1640 to 1710 empowered slave owners with more control to exploit their enslaved Africans. The child of a slave was declared a slave at his or her birth, making slavery self-perpetuating. The Maryland Statute on Negroes and Other Slaves in 1664 established that all blacks, as well as their children and their families, would be slaves *durante vita,* or for their entire lives. (Source: Browne) People of African descent had been reduced legally to the status of domestic animals. [6]

Slavery dates from before 2000 **B.C.E.** to the Sumerians. (Source William H. Browne, ed. Archives of Maryland, Baltimore: Maryland Historical Society, 1883, pp.533-34.) Islamic nations and African kingdoms had been involved in the Islamic slave trade for centuries. White slaves were imported from Europe; forest Africans, usually women and children, were exported to North Africa and southwest Asia. When the Portuguese first reached the Guinea Coast, they were interested in trading for gold, pepper, and ivory. Soon enough Christopher Columbus's discoveries created a market for young men for agricultural labor in the New World, and the Atlantic slave trade surpassed the trans-Sahara slave trade by the early 1600s. [7]

The 1700s

More than a half million Africans traveled over 3,000 miles across the Atlantic Ocean to reach British North America, only to face a living death of separation, humiliation, servitude, and anguish. This trip, called the Middle Passage, has been documented in historical records, logs, and adult and children's books and dramatized in films such as *Amistad* and *Roots.* A chart showing the estimated slave imports by destination from 1451 to 1870 totaled over 11 million slaves, with Brazil importing the highest number at 4 million, Spanish America with 2½ million, and the Dutch Caribbean tying North America with half a million each. [8] Fewer than 4 percent of the Africans taken from Africa were brought to the United States. The rest went to the Caribbean and Latin America.[9]

All of the original 13 colonies had slaves at some time. Slavery in the colonies north of the Chesapeake colonies developed differently for two major reasons: There were plenty of white laborers who could work in a diversified economy, and the climate was cooler and wouldn't support a staple crop such as tobacco or rice.[10] South of the Chesapeake tobacco colonies, the Carolinas and Georgia grew rice as the staple crop. The West Indian plantation system was stronger in the rice colonies, and black people never experienced indentured servitude there. In 1740 the slave population was 90 percent of the total population in the region of Charleston, South Carolina. Before the American Revolution, the northern colonies' black people made up 4.5 percent of the total population; in the South, blacks were 40 percent of the population. Across the country, the black population varied from place to place. [11]

In the years leading up to the American Revolution, Maryland was the second largest slaveholding colony in British North America. By 1770, a total of 80,000 Africans were working in tobacco colonies. [12] Anne Arundel County was the most northerly of Maryland's five tobacco counties. By 1750, a total of 144,852 slaves lived in Maryland and Virginia. At the start of the 1700s, 2,000 slaves resided in Anne Arundel County. By the end of the American Revolution, its slave population had grown to more than 9,000 slaves. (The numbers include importation and natural increase.) [13]

A later Edward Parrish, a descendant of the original settler, was listed in the first U.S. Census in 1790. At that time there were 3,893,635 people counted in the United States, and 319,728 people lived in Maryland. Of that number 101,264 were slaves. In Anne Arundel County, the total population was 22,598 people with a total slave population of 10,130, according to the Maryland Population Data Base found on the Internet.

The first direct federal tax of the country in 1798 listed five plantation owners living on the area now known as the Shady Side peninsula. Four of the five owners were women, and two of the four were widows. Other families paid rent to these owners, so they could live and farm on the properties. Free blacks and slaves were also living on the peninsula.[14]

Nineteen dwellings and other outbuildings made the beginnings of a village in 1799 near Parrish Creek. [15]

A historic event occurred at West River in 1762 near present-day Galesville. George Fox, the English founder of the Society of Friends, also called Quakers, held the first General Meeting in the province. The Society of Friends had made a definite break from the established Church of England (Anglicans). The Friends stressed individuality and rejected ritual and a priesthood, violence, and slavery. Perhaps the edict against ownership of slaves weakened the Quaker church in the West River area, because some members had left the Quakers and rejoined the Anglican Church by the time of the Revolution.[16] In the meantime, Sarah Norris freed two of her slaves in 1759.[17] Her strong convictions and choices made a lasting imprint on the history of the Shady Side peninsula.

Evidence that African Americans slaves were on the peninsula appeared in the inventory of Edward Parrish II, dated August 1723: Jeremy, about 20, Sam, 17, Bess, 18, Murreeur, 15, and Maria, 7, were listed. Three other male slaves were listed for a second plantation. No surnames were given. Two indentured servants were also noted, including surnames and reference to severance due at their release time.[18] This clearly shows the different status and value placed on slaves and indentured servants on the peninsula.

In the Chesapeake region, individual slaves gained freedom either for their service or because their masters had embraced Enlightenment principles. During the Revolution, Maryland was the only colony to allow slaves to serve in return for freedom. [19]

In 1783, the American Revolution officially ended at the Annapolis State House with the ratification of the Treaty of Paris.

The Maryland legislature was saturated with slaveholding sentiments, since all but a few assemblymen held slaves. Together the legislators owned 3,000 slaves, nearly 4 percent of the state's entire population. Charles Carroll of Carrollton, a signer of the Declaration of Independence and himself the largest planter in Maryland and the owner of 400 slaves, introduced a bill in committee to abolish slavery over a period of time, but the pro-slavery interests squelched the idea, voting to keep the bill in committee. Three more generations of blacks were denied freedom and remained as chattel. [20]

However, on the peninsula some slaves were being given their freedom. Like their sister, Sarah Norris, Thomas Norris and Mary Norris were among the first to free their slaves. Where once only first names were given, last names began to appear in some documents. The following were listed in manumission documents: Tom Bugg, 24, is absolutely free in 1795; Phillip Crowner, between 25 and 30 years, in 1807 is free after his mistress's death; James Davis, 28, in 1809; William Offer, near the age of 40, in 1810; Sarah Offer in 1812; and Benjamin Offer in 1819. [21]

For a short period of time after the Revolution, there was a marked increase in manumission in Maryland in the "spirit of liberty" and the "natural rights of man." One person who espoused this spirit was the writer of the *Star Spangled Banner*, Francis Scott Key, who manumitted his slaves.[22] Freedom could be granted by means of the last will and testament of the owner provided the manumitted slave was under the age of 45 and able to work. If a female was declared to be free and had a child, or issue, it must have been stated that the issue was also free or the child or children remained in slavery. [23]

Francis Scott Key and others like him wondered if the freedman could make it on his own. There were many handicaps the newly free had to overcome: finding a job, not having past savings, a debt if he bought his or a family member's freedom, and the maze of laws themselves. Despite these hurdles, the new freedmen did find occupations in the free society and became an integral part of local and county life. [24]

In 1795 and again in 1799, Sarah Norris, whose plantation was called Rural Felicity [25] freed slaves. Appearing among the names in the 1820 census are John Parrish, Mary Parrish, and Sarah Norris. Sane Dennis,

Philip Crowner, and Henry Mathews also appear in this census, but their relationship to the present families living in Shady Side is uncertain because all of the names listed were under District 1, which included other villages such as Galesville.

From the Revolution to 1790, the number of Maryland's free blacks jumped from 3,000 to 8,000, and from 1790 to the Civil War, the number rose to 84,000, giving Maryland the largest free black population in the country. [26]

The 1800s

Despite setbacks, individual manumission continued for 2,100 black individuals by last wills and testaments and for 3,000 more by deeds of manumission in Anne Arundel County. Before the Civil War, the number of free blacks grew from 800 to 5,000, and the number of slaves fell by more than 3,000. In all of Maryland, 50,000 were removed from slavery, a record that no other state could match. [27]

In 1824 Sarah Norris began freeing the Dennis family.[28] Virginia Fitz's book, *The Shady Side Peninsula,* states that Sarah Norris freed the Jacob Dennis family with a Certificate of Freedom in 1824. The family members were Jacob Dennis, about 24, Charlotte, James, Joshua, Leonard, Rachel, John, Mariah, and Eliza Dennis. Their deed of manumission was dated 1824, but actual freedom varied for each person. According to the listing in Maryland Freedom Papers, Jacob Denniss was physically free on December 4, 1833; Charlotte and Leonard Dennis on July 21, 1838; and Joshua Dennis on October 10, 1840. Another entry was listed thus:

> **Eliza Dennis** 21 July 1838, DOM recorded by Sarah Norris
> 2 Aug 1824. Age about 24; 5'3 ¾"; yellow complexion; no
> marks or scars; raised in AA Co.

Fourteen years after the deed of manumission was filed, Eliza Dennis was released.

A deed of manumission was like a commitment made in advance, with the owner's intentions written on paper, because there were many reasons why owners chose the timing of the actual release. The event might happen at an owner's death, when the slave reached a certain age, when a family member bought the relative's freedom, when an owner had fathered a child, or for any other reason the owner decided. Deeds of manumission had to be executed by the slave owner and recorded among the records of the county clerk. In most counties, such deeds were entered among the land records.[29] The fee for a certificate of freedom was fifty cents.[30] Rules applied to lost certificates and to free Negroes traveling out of the county. For those who were to have freedom after the passage of time, a rule stated that the person could not in the meantime be sold out of state.

The famous Nat Turner rebellion in Southampton, Virginia, in 1831 so frightened and shocked whites in Maryland that manumission suffered a severe setback. A law passed in 1832 stated that any future freed black would have to leave the state or be placed back in slavery. Manumission fell by a third. Free blacks took up the burden of manumission, often to buy and free their own relatives.[31] Most free black families in the county had a close relative in bondage. In 1860, 87,000 Marylanders were enslaved, and 7,000 of these were in Anne Arundel County.[32]

The largest number of free blacks lived in rural Anne Arundel County. There were nearly 900 family units, with a free black householder heading three-fourths of the independent units. Of the eighty black farms in the county, five-eighths had land titles to their farms while the remainder were tenants of white owners.[33]

In 1859 two black men, George Handy and Solomon Evans, bought lots from the Peter Evans tract that was within "Parrishes Park Resurveyed."[34] Solomon Evans, age 50, was listed as an oysterman in the 1870 census, and his wife, Susan, 50, was described as keeping house.

William Evans, age 35, listed as a black sailor in the 1870 census, was counted in family #68, which was the family number for the Capt. Salem Avery family. A speculation is that he was working for Capt. Salem Avery, who was a buy-boat captain of two schooners and owned two farms. The name S. Evans appears on the Hopkins Atlas of 1878.

In the 1860 census, Maryland's population was 687,034, and in the 1870 census, its population was 780,894. In those ten years, from 1861 to 1865, the Civil War was fought.

There were both Southern and Northern sympathizers, but there was no major impact on the way of life on the Shady Side peninsula. When the Union Army's Enrolling Officer for Anne Arundel County, District No. 6, compiled a list of male citizens aged 18 to 45 in 1862, he recorded that of the 255 enrolled, 170 were exempt. Twenty-eight had gone south to join the Confederacy, so that left only 27 men to possibly serve in the Union Army. This small group of men was mostly oystermen, mariners, farmers, and merchants.

Farming was the number one occupation for Anne Arundel County's males, followed by maritime jobs. Tobacco was Maryland's staple and the export crop on which the economy rested. It could be grown profitably on large and small plantations. Corn was planted in mid-April, with three to four kernels placed in each corn hill; the plants were weeded in April and May and hills rebuilt if necessary, and the crop was harvested in October. Corn was vital for feeding animals and humans.

Wheat required less attention once fields were cleared of weeds and obstructions. Seed was scattered on the surface rather than planted in hills. Farmers required extra help only at harvest, when demands for tobacco and corn were low.

Other occupations were: carpenter, teacher, hotelkeeper, blacksmith, bricklayer, mechanic, well digger, harness maker, shoemaker, overseer, postmaster, painter, plasterer, physician, and justice of the peace. [35]

In Annapolis of 1860, there were 826 free blacks out of a population of 4,000. St John's College and the Naval Academy employed free blacks and slaves as laborers and domestics. Usually both husband and wife in black families worked, but in white families it was just the husband. Whites were paid more than blacks for the same job. A black day laborer earned $.87 a day with board, $1.12 a day without board, and farm hands made $8.00 a month plus board. [36]

At the turn of the 18th century, people from Africa and Europe resided on the Shady Side peninsula and throughout Anne Arundel County. The American Revolution had come and gone, but as it brought political and economic freedom to white Americans, it also brought the whole issue of slavery into question. "In the light of reason, it [slavery] appeared to be inefficient, barbaric, and oppressive."[37] However, planters wanted a slave labor force for economic reasons. [38]

Not surprisingly, on Shady Side peninsula as in the rest of the county, farming was the predominant occupation, followed by maritime jobs. There were few professional men, and one would have to go to Annapolis or Baltimore to hire a lawyer. [39]

★　★　★

As early as 1800, free blacks in Anne Arundel County owned five properties. The number grew slowly until there were twenty in 1830, but the number dropped back to eleven by 1840. According to the 1840 census, Jacob Dennis was listed as head of household, free, and colored; also in the household were one male under 10, one male under 36, one female under 10, one female under 36, and one person aged 55-100.

About two hundred county slaves were able to escape during the 1850s with the help of the Underground Railroad. The value of slaves in Texas was three times that of slaves in Maryland, so there was the constant threat to slaves of being sold south.[40] Because many free blacks had close kinship with enslaved individuals, they tended not to move out of state.

By 1850 the United States had won the Mexican War, gold had been discovered in California, and Frederick Douglass was publishing the *North Star*. The Fugitive Slave Law of 1850 increased the disputes over slavery and heightened the danger for blacks. Dred Scott, a southern slave whose master took him to a free state, appealed to the Supreme Court but was returned to slavery.

Abraham Lincoln was elected president in 1860. Shady Side family names appearing in the 1860 census were listed as free inhabitants, District 8, under the Tracey's Landing Post Office. Post office locations changed between the ten-year census years. Familiar black family names such as Coates, Crowner, Dennis, Gross, Holland, Matthews, and Scott were listed along with white family names: Atwell, Crandall, Lee, Weems, and Woodfield. The political thinking of the day can be inferred from the records, because there is no "W" recorded under the column for color for whites in the census, although a "B" records a black individual. (The heading specifies color: white, black, or mulatto. In the 1870 census, the heading requests the enumerator to record under color: white (W), black (B), mulatto (M), Chinese (C), or Italian (I).)

The 1860 census lists: Jacob Dennis, 49, male, black, farmer, real estate $1,200, personal $700; Elizabeth, 38, female, black; John, 19, male, black; Henrietta, 16, female, black; Elizabeth, 14, female, black; James, 12, male, black; Joshua, 9, male, black; Serena, 4, female, black. This census was taken on the cusp of the Civil War (1861-1865), and it is encouraging to see a free African American family on the peninsula with sizable real estate and significant personal finances. [41]

The Jacob Dennis property was labeled on the Martenet Map of 1860. His nearest neighbor, Mrs. Parrott, lived to the south of his land, and north of Jacob Dennis was William White. Scott, another African American family name, is shown south of South Creek in what would be the Churchton area. North of the Scotts and west of the Dennis family was Captain Smith. West of Parrish Creek appeared the names Evans, Leatherbury, Capt. Avery, Woodfield, and Lee. To the east of

Parrish Creek, two Parrishes controlled the northern peninsula at Curtis Point. Hartge, the area's wealthiest family, owned all the land along the West River from Cedar Point to South Creek, which included West Shady Side and Avalon Shores.

It is a fair guess that Jacob Dennis's crops were wheat, corn, and maybe a little tobacco, but tobacco did not grow very well in the Swamp. He would probably have had a productive garden, some fruit trees, ducks, geese, and chickens for eggs and meat, hogs for slaughter, and perhaps a cow, horse, mules, or oxen. The woods provided squirrels, rabbits, and deer, and surrounding waters provided ducks, fish, oysters, and crabs from the Bay. The Dennis family and their neighbors, black and white, worked from sun-up to sundown to provide for their families and to survive. Darkness in the Swamp would be total except for moonlight and glowing lamps or candles in tiny homes.

Blacks in Anne Arundel County made greater economic progress in the two generations following the Civil War than those living in cities.[42] Certainly Jacob Dennis is an example of this progress.

Both black and white families on the peninsula tended to be large. Families often included extended family members, boarders, or someone taken in to live with the family. It is not until the 1870 census that black families have their full names, birthdays, parents' names, children's names, and occupations listed.[43]

Social Implications

Other social, economic, and political events occurred beyond the isolated peninsula, and the events had an impact on Shady Side residents, white and black child, black and white adult, the unborn and the dead.

The process of separating the two races had plenty of historical precedents. For example, in the 1830s Thomas Rice, a white actor from New York, created a blackface minstrel act of song and dance called "Jump Jim Crow" to ridicule black people. He dressed in ragged clothes and acted like a handicapped black stableman as he entertained the advantaged at the expense of the disadvantaged. (In 1860 Thomas Rice died penniless of a health disorder that limited his speech and movements in his last years.) In 1841 Massachusetts set aside a "Jim Crow" railroad car for colored passengers only. Soon "Jim Crow" became a disparaging term used in other forms of racial segregation to bar colored people through practices and laws and all things related to them. After the Civil War and during Reconstruction, northerners enacted laws to improve life and conditions for the southern colored people. The Fourteenth Amendment of July 28, 1868, granted the right to due process and equal protection to anyone born in the United States. The Federal Civil Rights Act of 1875 clearly outlawed segregation of any sort. The Fifteenth Amendment in 1880 guaranteed all men the right to vote; however, the northerners were departing, leaving the South free to undo the short 30 years of progressive improvements of civil rights for the black population.

In 1896 the U.S. Supreme Court, in an 8-1 decision in *Plessy v. Ferguson,* paved the way to crippling the Fourteenth Amendment. Homer A. Plessy, who was seventh-eighths Caucasian and one-eighth of African blood, traveled by rail with a first-class ticket from Louisiana, but he was arrested because he had taken an empty seat in a white-only car and refused to move when threatened with the new state law for being in a place "which by race he does not belong." This case established the Supreme Court's ruling of "separate but equal," and it ushered in 60 years—a lifetime—of prohibitions between the races. Hundreds of laws were passed to separate the races, particularly in the South; however, the northern states maintained more subtle economic and social roadblocks.

Washington, DC, was a dividing border city between the free North and the segregated South during Reconstruction in the 1870s. If a black man traveled by train from Boston, he could sit anywhere he wished. If he continued south, he had to move to the Jim Crow car up front behind the engine to be sure he would be separated from the whites when the train crossed into Virginia.[44] When LeRoy Battle (see Chapter 23) headed south for training at Tuskegee Institute in 1943, he found himself in that very Jim Crow car, choking on soot.[45] It took almost ten years after the Civil Rights Act of 1964 to get the message across to those who chose not to recognize blacks' rights.[46]

In theory the end of the Civil War brought political freedom and the possibilities of social and economic improvements for African Americans, but in practice life was one of minimal gain and immense disappointment. Freedom gained did not translate into economic progress. In fact, it was harder for the black man to make progress than it had been 40 years earlier.[47]

Baltimore was one destination for many Anne Arundel blacks who were seeking better work opportunities. The black county population that once outnumbered the whites by 2 percent began to fall, and the white population increased to a 62% majority by the turn of the century.[48]

The 1900s

Travel away from the peninsula was often by boat to reach Galesville, Annapolis, or Baltimore, because the road leading out was a struggle. Once in Annapolis, the railroad had special cars to transport blacks to Baltimore, Washington, DC, and Philadelphia.[49] In the meantime, everyone was working hard each day, and people stayed close to home. Dennis family members and their neighbors traversed muddy paths and lanes, or roads thick with dust if it were dry, to reach other homes or church. If someone were going from point A to point B, she or he was walking.

★　★　★

In the early 1900s, most white people believed that black people were capable only of manual labor and entitled to only the most basic legal rights.[50] African Americans and their leaders disagreed on how to gain the opportunities that were so accessible to the white population. Dr. Booker T. Washington, a conservative leader, had access to and influence among white leaders. Known as "the Wizard of Tuskegee," his conciliatory approach endorsed the idea of teaching trades in high schools for African Americans.

W.E.B. Du Bois, perhaps the greatest scholar-activist in American history, opposed this thinking.[51] Having grown up free in Massachusetts with a great-grandfather who fought in the American Revolution, Du Bois was 12 years younger than Booker T. Washington, who was born a plantation slave and had little formal schooling. Du Bois wanted to confront disfranchisement, Jim Crow, and lynching. "Across the South, someone was hanged or burned alive every four days from 1889 to 1929," according to the 1933 book *The Tragedy of Lynching,* for alleged crimes such as "stealing hogs, horse-stealing, poisoning mules, . . . boastful remarks or 'trying to act like a white person.'"[52] Impatient with black people who were unwilling to demand their rights, Du Bois believed education was the key to advancement and that the "Talented Tenth," or upper 10 percent of black Americans, should lead the way.

"Statutes only served to worsen race relations, alienating one group from the other and removing the few informal interactions that might have helped both sides see the potential good and humanity in the other. With slavery, a white owner might have protected a financial investment, but after slavery there was no vested interest in the freed people, no intimate ties to ease harsh circumstances or to protect them from the whims of sheriffs, . . . or poor whites taking out their resentment at their unwitting competitors for work. They were losing ground and sinking lower in status with each passing day."[53]

Impossible as it seems, West African heritage survived in spite of the odds against it. A short list of surviving traditions includes family structure, a strong kinship, vocabulary, music, dance, musical instruments, food, cooking, religious concepts of the sacred, the unity of nature, and the medicinal use of herbs and roots.[54]

As previously mentioned, Virginia Fitz wrote *The Shady Side Peninsula* in 1984. She also wrote *Captain Salem Avery House, Its History: 1860-1990* about the waterman's home, when the house became a clubhouse for mostly Jewish masons from Washington, DC. The club belonged to the National Masonic Fishing and Country Club, renamed Our Place, for 66 years. Later they sold the house that became the home of the Shady Side Rural Heritage Society. Virginia Fitz was elected the first president of the society. Her writing and work were invaluable to the community and an enlightening resource for newcomers.

In *Miss Ethel Remembers*, published in 1991 by The Shady Side Rural Heritage Society, Mrs. Ethel Andrews talked about the blacks working at the Andrews Hotel. She was very definite in pointing out the importance of those who worked in the running of the hotel and most explicit in conveying her love for Carrie Nick, who "was part of our household for forty years. We just could not have made it without her." In her 1989 interview with researchers from Anne Arundel Community College, Mrs. Andrews, then aged 101, had this to say: "The blacks? They were like brothers and sisters. There were no quarrels, no fights. We just lived together, because they had the same privileges as a white man in Shady Side. Boating, and whatever they could do on land. They were just near and dear to each other." Born in Shady Side in 1888, she lived all but a few years of her life less than a mile from the intersection of Shady Side and Snug Harbor Roads.

Shady Side was probably one of the better places for blacks to live when compared to other regions of the county and country, but the peninsula was not self-sufficient. Beyond its boundaries were unfair laws, Jim Crow rules, destructive attitudes, and hateful people who made Miss Ethel's observation of "same privileges as a white man" a farce. For example, colored people had to stay outside on the deck of the *Emma Giles* (See Chapter 6); they could not sit down, order to eat in (Aida Hogg's, then later) Jimmy's Country Kitchen, attend the same elementary school, go to the white movie theater near Parrish Creek, or travel in the same railroad cars when going to and from Baltimore and Annapolis.

The *Capital* newspaper eventually began to make some corrections in dealing with its treatment of black citizens. According to a an article written in September 26, 2004, by Tom Marquardt, executive editor of the *Capital*, the newspaper was discriminating against African Americans until 1968 when Phil Merrill bought the paper. Until then whites received free space for obituaries, while African Americans had to buy space for death notices. An obituary was printed if an African American had committed a crime; African Americans were neither featured in society pages nor were their weddings announced. Meeting with African American funeral directors, Mr. Merrill learned of the discrepancy in the treatment of the two races.

Marquardt's article was headlined, "Archives search shows evolution of racial coverage." Editor Marquardt reported that in 1954, the *Evening Capital* had front page stories covering the possibility of the University of Maryland's admitting blacks to its undergraduate program, and the local NAACP chapter wanted to end segregation at Sandy Point State Park. No editorials commented on either subject. Also lacking was any report in 1957 that Congress had passed the Voting Rights Bill, which "was the first major civil rights legislation in more than 75 years; [however,] the front page [had coverage] of Ford's introduction of the Edsel."

By 1963 the newspaper gave "extensive coverage" to the March on Washington where Rev. Martin Luther King gave his "I Have a Dream" speech. The day after Rev. King's assassination on April 4, 1968, the newspaper had "extensive coverage . . . including a front-page editorial calling for justice and pleading for calm in the community."

In a video recording, "Voices of Shady Side," made in 1991, Woody Avery was asked what his hope was for the future. He replied that he hoped that things would be "uniform for us all. It's not equal, and it makes it very disturbing for the village. It is very much out of balance and not getting any better in the governing of the county and village. There are pros and cons, but it is not equal. I'd better not say any more about it."

During the centuries of slavery, black Americans, who were kept from reading and writing, had little opportunity to leave any written history about their lives. In the 1830s the Carnegie Corporation, a philanthropic foundation, sponsored a major study of black life. From that study, *An American Dilemma* was finally published in 1944. This book revealed how racism undermined the progress of African Americans.[55] It wasn't until the late 1960s that a major textbook, Ron Karenga's *Introduction to Black Studies*, was published.[56] Black history month, begun in 1960 and celebrated in February, helped to elevate awareness and to educate the American public about missing contributions and untold lives of African Americans.

There have been three types of individuals who have passed through Shady Side: those born here who never left, those born here who left, and those born elsewhere who visited and returned to live in Shady Side. All three groups have interacted throughout the years and place a value on Shady Side living. Interestingly, those who have moved to Shady Side have been the ones most likely to record its history. Many board directors and members of the original Shady Side Rural Heritage Society, more recognizably renamed the Capt. Avery Museum in 2011, are in the latter group and have worked tirelessly to record, collect, and exhibit the lives of Shady Side throughout its generations.

The pages that follow address some gaps in the stories of several African American families who were born here, stayed, and lived productive lives on the Shady Side peninsula.

Chapter 2

A Celebration of Life

ON A BEAUTIFUL SPRING day in the middle of April 2010, temperatures reached the upper 80s and the predicted rain refused to mar the day when the community, both black and white, said goodbye to its beloved citizen, Chuck Gross. A shiny white hearse sat in front of Franklin United Methodist Church, which was rapidly filling up more than an hour before the "Celebration of Life" service scheduled for noon. Half of the pews on the right side of the sanctuary were reserved for the family, and the front left row was reserved for the pallbearers. "Miss Doll Baby," Eliza Dennis, who had just dropped off food at St. Matthew's for the repast, smiled, greeted, and hugged neighbors, friends, and church members and joined the seated congregation, while a stream of people continued to find seats.

The number of cars and people arriving for the memorial service matched the numbers that had attended Chuck's viewing two days earlier at Hope St. Mark United Methodist Church on Muddy Creek Road near Edgewater.

At the viewing, cars overflowed the parking lot and spread up and down Route 468 in both directions. Men and women, black and white, young and old, entered the church where Chuck's brother-in-law, Rev.

Eddie Smith, was pastor. Friends, gathered in small clusters, talked outside the church, and inside more people occupied the pews. A guest book was near the entry for callers to sign. At the front of the sanctuary, Chuck lay in an open bronze and silver casket, the bottom half covered with a blanket of yellow roses. Chuck's siblings, mother, and family members sat in the front pews, and his daughter, Chantal Banks, her mother, Carla Gross, other family members and funeral staff stood near Chuck. "He looks like he is asleep," said a loved one. Truly, he looked like he could get up, but touching his hard, cold body startled the living. A man of small stature but with the energy, willingness, and strength of three was at rest. Oh, how strong the loss his death was for those who bore witness to Chuck's integrity, generosity, kindness, and decency. By his own hand, he had removed a friendly wave, silenced a particular voice and a special laugh. His community had been stunned.

Although the callers were predominantly black, there was a large showing of white friends and acquaintances during the visitation. One white couple flew back to Maryland for Chuck's viewing and service. Another white woman, who came to the viewing in support of Chuck's brother, noted, "There is so much love in this room." Indeed. People sat, meditated, murmured softly to neighbors, and one white woman sobbed so unreservedly that a stranger asked if she was all right. William Reese and Sons Mortuary provided guidance while somber callers continued to flow through the church. Outside, departing visitors transitioned back into the stream of ordinary conversation and pursuits.

★　★　★

At Franklin United Methodist Church for the celebration of life service, recorded music played softly in the white-painted chancel sanctuary as mourners gathered for Chuck's memorial service. St. Matthew's and Franklin UMC Churches' ushers assisted throughout the proceedings. Flowers from the Wednesday viewing were arranged at the side, and a florist delivered more flower baskets, sprays, and cut flowers just before the service began. Surrounded by the flowers sat a brass easel holding photographs from Chuck's life; a second easel held an oil portrait of Chuck, and a folded American flag rested beside his cremated remains.

Joining in the recorded music, Jant Thompson played drums, and then Dale Hoskins replaced the recorded music on the keyboard. Marvin Wiggins added saxophone, and the music captured the undercurrent of emotions suffusing the sanctuary. Accompanied by the combo, a male soloist sang several selections. Occasionally, the congregation clapped or swayed along with the beat of the music.

Friends, acquaintances, and neighbors embraced, shook hands, murmured respectfully, and one wept openly. "You lost a good man," a mourning white lady paused to tell a seated black gentleman acquaintance as she returned from viewing the pictures to take her seat. But there seemed to be palpable strength, comfort, and spiritual joy radiating as people came together to give witness to the passing of this unique, humble man. People still filled the foyer and spilled out onto the sidewalk as they waited to enter.

All stood as the clergy, dressed in black robes and suits, led the family in a processional. Representing a number of churches in the community, the clergy advanced to the chancel, and the family filed into the empty front pews. Those standing along the walls and in the foyer were invited to be seated, but the pews were filled. Ushers worked steadily to seat as many as possible on folding chairs in the aisles and seats and even in the choir loft. Reverend Dr. Eddie Smith, the husband of Chuck's sister, Sandy, officiated. The celebration of life continued with the congregation singing *Hold to God's Unchanging Hand*. Old and New Testament selections were read, prayers lifted, clergy recognized, and soloists heard. The music was powerful in feeling—mournful, yet full of hopefulness.

Darlene Robinson spoke for the class of 1962. As six-year-olds, she and Chuck had started school at Lula G. Scott Elementary in Shady Side in 1956 and graduated from Wiley H. Bates High School in Annapolis. She noted that Chuck was very quiet and shy at first meeting, but that changed to laughter and a twinkle in his eye when you got to know him. Sometimes he had such a serious look on his face that you had to wonder what was on his mind that would make a young child look so serious.

His best buddies at "Lula G." were his cousin Douglas Thompson, Bobby Turner, Blake Holland, and Harold Holland. They especially loved pushing one another on the merry-go-round—something no longer seen on playgrounds. He was a good friend, and his friends looked up to him. In school he was dressed to a tee, with nothing out of place. As a man he became a jack-of-all-trades and a master of many. He was focused in life, knew what he wanted, and was able to get it. The class message was that they thanked God for Everett Lovell Gross's life, they were thankful that he lived, and they were grateful for having their paths cross many years ago. They thanked God for the caring and compassionate young man who will forever remain in their hearts as their friend and classmate.

Connie Nick, Chuck's sister-in-law, brought a chuckle of relief and comforted the audience with her essay, "My Thoughts of Chuck":

> *Just the other day, early in the morning, God looked around his kingdom with all of its magnificent mansions. He noticed some blades of grass that were just a little too long, a hedge that needed a little trimming, and the mulch around the blooming trees and flowers just didn't look as fresh as he wanted it. He thought, "I can't have my kingdom looking like this." So he got out the big book of lawn service. He ran his finger down the page. It stopped at Chuck's Lawn Service. God then thought, "Okay, I need someone that comes highly recommended." He checked Chuck's credentials. He*

read: honest, reliable, trustworthy, a very hard worker, and his clients love him. God thought, "Hmm. He comes highly recommended," and with a slight nod of his head, he called Chuck home.

Chuck was a very generous and kind person. Carla would often say that he was a wimp when a salesperson came to the door or when he saw a TV commercial asking for donations for people in need.

Chuck, there are many things that I will miss about you. I will miss baking you a birthday cake and talking to you and Carla on the speaker-phone. I will miss seeing you tinkering in your yard, but most of all I will miss you. I will always cherish those and other memories of you and will forever hold them dear in my heart. You will be truly missed by all.

Ecclesiastes 3:1 reads: To everything there is a season, a time for every purpose under heaven.

Keeping you in my thoughts,
Connie

Rev. Gregory Nick, Chuck's first cousin on his father's side of the family, delivered the message of hope, bringing energy and laughter with stories and remembrances of Chuck.

After the recessional, people mingled and spoke to friends. One white man said, "I am rethinking my funeral. This was an uplifting celebration of life with the music and participation of the congregation." Another person said, "I want to come to this church for my funeral." Perhaps those attending had found peace and closure in their hearts and were beginning to come to terms with the reality of Chuck's passing.

The hearse and family cars drove to Lakemont Memorial Gardens off Route 214. A green tent covered the gravesite, and immediate family members were seated facing the clergy, a U.S. Army soldier in a Class A uniform, Chuck's remains, and the American flag. An Air

Force sergeant, who had been standing at attention about 30 feet away, positioned his trumpet and played "Taps." As the sounds died away, he marched to the graveside and stood opposite the soldier, and the two military men ceremoniously opened, rotated, and then refolded the flag. Presenting the flag to Chuck's mother, the soldier bent from the waist and spoke softly to her. And then it was time to go. Cars slowly drove away, and a lone cemetery representative remained at the grave.

The community had witnessed the beginning, middle, and ending of Chuck's time on the stage while passing through Shady Side. He never smoked, didn't drink, and never did drugs, including during the chaotic, stressful year of Vietnam. Generous to family and friends, he cared deeply for others and went out of his way to back a person who stumbled. He was known for his conscientiousness and honesty, and his customers left the keys to their homes in his care. "I trusted Chuck with my life," said an older lady who knew he would protect her if necessary.

It didn't matter how you looked to Chuck, but it did matter how you behaved. He was a bridge between the communities and welcome in everyone's home—if he could be convinced to slow down from his busy pace. "He was a hard, responsible worker," said one of his customers.

The United Methodist Women of St. Matthew's UMC had prepared the social hall for the repast, where the family received friends and a meal was served. Rows of decorated tables filled the room, with a head table for the family. The aromas of baked turkey and ham filled the room. Against two walls, tables were densely covered with platters of food. The blessing was given, and people lined up to eat, a first step in returning to the routines and adventures of everyday life.

Dining out, Carla Gross (right) smiles while Chuck Gross points out that he does NOT like to have his picture taken. **Carla Gross Collection**

Chapter 3

Eliza Dennis, Miss Doll Baby

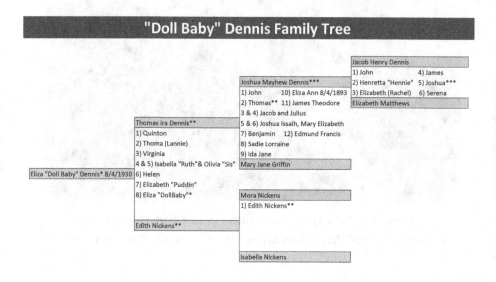

"Doll Baby" Dennis Family Tree

			Jacob Henry Dennis
			1) John 4) James
		Joshua Mayhew Dennis***	2) Henretta "Hennie" 5) Joshua***
		1) John 10) Eliza Ann 8/4/1893	3) Elizabeth (Rachel) 6) Serena
		2) Thomas** 11) James Theodore	Elizabeth Matthews
		3 & 4) Jacob and Julius	
	Thomas Ira Dennis**	5 & 6) Joshua Issaih, Mary Elizabeth	
	1) Quinton	7) Benjamin 12) Edmund Francis	
	2) Thoma (Lannie)	8) Sadie Lorraine	
	3) Virginia	9) Ida Jane	
	4 & 5) Isabella "Ruth"& Olivia "Sis"	Mary Jane Griffin	
Eliza "Doll Baby" Dennis* 8/4/1930	6) Helen		
	7) Elizabeth "Puddin"		
	8) Eliza "DollBaby"*	Mora Nickens	
		1) Edith Nickens**	
	Edith Nickens**		
		Isabella Nickens	

AT THE EDGE OF Miss Eliza's driveway survives a holly tree that her grandfather Joshua Dennis planted over a hundred years ago. A black and white mother cat looks suspiciously at the car as she and her offspring stand by to see which way they should dart. Eliza calls the fatter one, Pot Belly Kitty, but it dashes as quickly as the others under the corner of the house. Company is expected, and Miss Eliza Dennis, who is better known as Miss Doll Baby, answers the knock at the door.

"Probably I am called Doll Baby more times than Eliza. My Uncle Edmond named me Doll Baby when I was first born. He had named my older sister 'Baby Doll,' but when I came along he said the names were too close and renamed her 'Puddin.' I was Doll Baby."

When long-time residents of the village were asked about Miss Eliza, they appeared puzzled, but once they heard "Doll Baby," their response was, "Oh, I've known Doll Baby all my life," or "Oh, is Eliza her real name?"

Older residents seemed hesitant when asked if they knew any stories about Miss Doll Baby's Uncle Julius Dennis or her father, Thomas Dennis. From both European Americans and African Americans, the response was, "I remember Uncle Julius, but I don't remember a Thomas." But Thomas went by his middle name, Ira. Asking Miss Doll Baby about her niece Olivia, Miss Doll Baby paused briefly and then said, "Oh, you mean 'Kicker'!"

Many people have treasured nicknames that are bestowed on them in childhood. Olivia's father named her "Kicker" because she kicked when she was a little child. Everett Gross was "Chuck" before he was even born. Someone referred to him as "Chuck" when his mother was carrying him, and it stuck, although Everett was on the birth certificate. A woman who is called Diane discovered a completely different name on her birth certificate.

But it would be wrong to assume everyone has a nickname. When asked about one person's nickname, Miss Doll Baby explained, "No, he was always called that. He never had a nickname." For the record: Doris Brown is "Nelly," Thelma Holland is "Connie." In the Hicks family, Taliferrio is "Tub," Terri is "Bird," Tyra is "Boo," Todd is "Nookie," and their mother Kathlene is "Pickle"—or Miss Pickle as children were taught to address someone older than themselves. Miss Pickle's Aunt Agnes Matthews Dennis named her "Pickle" because she was tiny like a small pickle. Charlie Thompson's nephews were Owen "Smack" Scott and George "Lindy" Thompson. William was "Piggy," Robert was "Doodie,"

Carroll was "Snooze," and George was "Bootie." Children were taught to always "put a handle" on any older person's name, using Miss, Mister, Cousin, Aunt, or Uncle or even saying the person's full name. To this day younger people in the Shady Side community follow this tradition.

Many African American first names and family names can be seen on road signs when traveling along Shady Side Road: Brown, Ira, Sugar, Nick, and Scott. One of these roads, Ira Lane, leads to where Eliza Dennis was born and where she spent her early childhood.

John Fountain at St. Matthew's United Methodist Church was well known to everyone, but some assumed he had a brother when they saw a 1984 video recording at the Captain Avery Museum about a Swat Team that included boys and girls from Churchton and Shady Side. The title was "An Interview with Phillip Crowner and Raymond Fountain," but as soon as "Mr. Raymond Fountain" spoke in the video, the voice made it clear that it was Mr. John Fountain!

Smiling, Miss Teresa provided the missing detail that John's name is really John Ramon, but people have always called him Raymond. Married 54 years and living on Cedarhurst Road over 45 years, the Fountains raised two children. Miss Teresa, a gifted musician without or with music, is one of the pianists at St. Matthew's United Methodist Church. When someone begins singing a song, she leans into the piano and softly tests different chords and keys and soon matches the notes to accompany the singer.

★   ★   ★

Miss Hattie Taylor Nick, a midwife for many African American women in the Shady Side area, delivered Eliza in the Dennis's home. Born August 4, 1930, Eliza Eva was the youngest child of Thomas Ira and Edith Nickens Dennis. She was named after her father's sister, Eliza Dennis Finney, who was born the same day in 1893, and Eva after her mother's sister. She is descended from one of the earliest African

American families to not only live on the Shady Side peninsula, but also to own land three decades before the Civil War. In all of Anne Arundel County, 52 free blacks had acquired property by 1850. Eliza's great-grandfather Jacob was one of those individuals, and he owned a sizeable farm, not just a house.

Miss Eliza has memories of growing up in the family house, which has been gone for many years. Visiting the Dennis cemetery at the end of Ira Lane during a drive one sunny summer day, she pointed out where the home would have been. "All these woods weren't here. We had a kitchen, dining room, living room, four bedrooms upstairs, and an attic up some more stairs. Some of the kids slept in the attic."

Eliza had seven siblings: Quinton (1915-1994);Virginia (1919-2011); Thomas Mayhew, called "Lannie" (1921-2003); twins Isabella, called "Ruth"(1922-2010) and Olivia, called "Sis"(1922-1980); Helen (1925-); and Elizabeth Margaret, her beloved Puddin' (1929-1993). "My bedroom was the first one with two big beds in it for my sisters: Sis Ruth, Puddin', and me. We went to bed at 8:00, got under the covers, and went to sleep." There were no electric lights, telephone, or inside running water.

"We had a well with a bucket out in the yard. When I was a little child I couldn't work it at first." Of all the chores she had to do, she disliked picking up wood chips and putting them in a basket. These chips were used to start the cooking stove fire. "The older children would bring in the wood, open up the stove top, and put it in. I still remember the sound of the wood fire crackin'. We all had chores to do like doing the dishes. We took turns washing and drying. I would rather wash than dry or wash clothes than iron. I like to wash clothes to this day."

"Daddy had some hound dogs for hunting, and he and the boys would go hunting for rabbits and squirrels. They never killed any deer. He had chickens and hogs." Sounds of roosters crowing and birds singing are pleasant memories of her younger years. "Yes, my dear, it was nice to hear 'em." Miss Doll Baby gathered eggs in her basket, but it never frightened her to reach under the hens, "because they usually hopped off their nests."

Her father left the house at 5:00 in the morning "in the dark" to go oysterin' on the winter mornings. He'd walk out the back over the field toward South Creek. "It was so cold on winter mornings when we would get up. The stove was the only heat, and it was downstairs. We would dress real fast. My mother or older sister fixed breakfast, and we would all sit down to have breakfast together." There were no shifts with siblings coming and going during the meal. Before every meal the family would pray, asking the blessing. "We'd have oatmeal, eggs, sausage or bacon sometimes, and biscuits. Uh-huh, we'd always have biscuits. I love biscuits."

Miss Doll Baby didn't ice skate when she was a child, "but brother Lannie skated with the Nick boys. I'd sometimes slide in the yard. If the river was frozen in the winter, Daddy sat at home because he couldn't work."

The most valuable lessons she learned from her parents were to respect everyone, to speak to everyone, to have manners and say, "Yes, ma'am" and "No ma'am." "My daddy said that 'manners nary cost you a penny.' They never gave us any spankings. They'd just talk to you, but they only spoke one time."

At family dinnertime everyone ate together at the table. "It was fun. We were told to 'stop talking and eat' and 'don't talk with your mouth full.'"

Puddin', a year older than Miss Doll Baby, was very close to her sister, and the two did everything together. Puddin' was told in family meetings to "always watch out for your sister," so when Miss Doll Baby started school in 1936, both girls walked together over the fields to the black elementary school in Churchton. The land was cleared for farming and plenty of paths could be found to get from one property to another. Because of where they lived, they could choose to attend the black Churchton School or the black Shady Side Elementary School. They walked, rain or shine, snow or flood, thick dust or mud, extreme cold or muggy heat. Whether they walked through the fields or along the road depended on the weather conditions. If their shoes or clothes got wet, they learned their lessons in that condition.

Miss Doll Baby's family and other neighbors often walked to and from church, frequently making more than one round trip on a Sunday. Rain, bright sun, heat, cold, inconvenience, or exhaustion did not keep a family home. Children were expected to go and they did. In fact, over time family members might walk to two different Methodist churches in one day: morning services at St. Matthew's in Shady Side and evening gatherings at Franklin Chapel in Churchton. Sunday was the day devoted to praising, appreciating, and honoring God.

Sundays were the most important day of the week, and preparations were made the evening before the family started out on foot. On Saturday, baths were taken in washbasins or tubs and Sunday clothes readied. Mothers and daughters prepared food for Sunday's meals, and fathers and sons completed chores so only maintenance was required for the day of rest. The strength and heart of the black community was the church. In the years after slavery, the church became the most important institution among African Americans other than the family.[1]

Miss Doll Baby's great-grandfather Jacob Dennis was one of five trustees for Franklin Chapel.[2] The 1860 Simon J. Martenet Map of Anne Arundel County labeled a square "African Church" on the site; this information is confirmed in "The Franklin Years." According to official board minutes of the church, which are echoed in a letter by Mrs. Eliza Dennis Finney, the aunt for whom Miss Doll Baby was named, "Franklin Chapel was a building on the left side of the road going to the Churchton Post Office." The building held worshippers of both races at first. The colored had seats in a built-on shed room where they could see and not be seen, could hear but must not be heard. The old church had "three doors, one in the east, one in the west, and one in the south. There was a road at the south end of the church."[3] She may be referring to Offer Road, which is south of Franklin UMC in Churchton.

An early story suggests that Churchton, MD, was actually named for the era of itinerant preachers. When a name was required for a post office, someone suggested Churchtown, because it was always known as the church town—hence Churchton.[4]

By November 1890, Jacob's son Joshua was serving as a trustee when land was purchased for a parsonage 200 yards south of Franklin Chapel.

Edith Nickens Dennis, Miss Doll Baby's mother. **Eliza Dennis Collection**

When Miss Doll Baby was about seven years old, her mother left the family to live in Baltimore with her sister. Soon Miss Doll Baby's family moved to Bennett Crandall's farm so her father and brothers could farm and work the dairy farm for Mr. Bennett. Located on the right of Route 468 going toward Shady Side, after what locals call Dead Man's Curve and before Nick Road comes in on the left, the overgrown lane is still visible today. "We all lived down there from the '40s until Mr. Weems bought the whole place from Mr. Bennett, who sold out in the '60s. All of that were open fields. There were none of the trees you see now. Daddy farmed in the summer and oystered in the winter.

"I would go to see my mother in Baltimore. Sometimes my father took me. Daddy always said, 'Don't ever let me catch you talking about your mother.' We would drive for a half hour to Annapolis and then catch the train from Annapolis to Baltimore. The train trip took about an hour. Daddy's sister, Aunt Lorraine, was not far from Mother and her sister's house.

Doll Baby (left) with her beloved Puddin,' right, visit their Aunt Lorraine with their cousin Ida Dennis, middle, in Baltimore. **Eliza Dennis Collection**

"I saw my mother often. I would go for a week or two weeks to visit. We would go shopping and to church. Mother was a Baptist. Their pastors stay forever and don't change like here [in the United Methodist church]. They can sing, get holy a lot, and preach a lot." Pausing and lowering her voice slightly, Miss Doll Baby said, "Let me tell you something. If my mother were living she would say, 'You're not going in that church without a hat on.' In the summertime it was hot, and she'd say, 'Doll Baby, the sun will cook your head. Put that straw hat on your head.' Mother always sent food back home when we returned to Shady Side. She left us, but she was a good mother."

"Mrs. Marie Moulden was like a second mother to me. Like a book you pick. Her daughter Geraldine and I were like sisters, although she was two years younger. We were raised together, but both are dead now.

"A long time ago during the summer, maybe the '40s or earlier, there used to be a girl's camp on the right side of Columbia Beach Road. A lady from Baltimore ran it until someone else bought it. The campers were all city kids; all were colored children. Their parents paid for their children to come. Some would stay two weeks and some all summer until school started. There was a dining room building, cabins for the campers, a house for the cook, and a house the lady lived in. Bennett's farm was back of the house of the camp. Some but not all of the children were Catholic, and two to three cars would come every Sunday to take the girls to church in Owensville. I worked at the camp some summers. They had planned activities, swings, played games like dodge ball, and went swimming down at Columbia Beach. The kids enjoyed the camp. It was closed around the '60s when Mrs. Imes, the owner of the camp, died."

The property was sold, and the cabins were sold off. One lady bought two cabins and combined them to make a house on Shady Side Road. Over the years they have been incorporated into the brick house just beyond Sugar Lane. The house has been bought, sold, changed, and improved over the years.

"We heard the news on the radio," said Miss Doll Baby. Japan had bombed Pearl Harbor on December 7, 1941. "It was a Sunday morning, and we heard it before church. People were talking that we were going to have a war. I didn't really understand what it all meant because I was still a child. All came back that I knew—William Cleveland, my brother-in-law, the Nick boys—'Tookie,' 'Piggy,' Marshall, and Herman."

★   ★   ★

After graduation, some of Miss Doll Baby's friends left for the city, some married, and some went to college to become teachers, like her sister Puddin'. Miss Doll Baby would have liked to take more typing and become a secretary, but there was no money for her schooling. Instead, she worked as a cook for Bennett Crandall, a bachelor, for more than five years. "It was a big farm with Holstein cows, hogs, and chickens. My brothers Quinton and Lannie worked with all of the animals and helped Mr. Bennett farm. My sister-in-law Rose did day's work," where she worked each weekday for regularly scheduled families. Miss Doll Baby, her father, her brother Lannie, and Rose lived in the farmhouse. Mr. Bennett lived in his own house.

Her father also clammed with Claude Wilde. Vernon Wilde, Claude's son, told a story of how his dad heard that Ira had died, so Vernon and his dad went over to the dairy farm to pay their respects. "When we got there, Ira was sitting at the table in the kitchen! His daughter showed us in that day," the younger Mr. Wilde, now 81, laughed. When asked about the incident, Miss Doll Baby smiled at the memory of the startled men.

Miss Doll Baby took driver's education in high school. "I couldn't drive that car forward for nothing, but I could back the car down that road. Yes, indeedy. My teacher couldn't get over how I could back up but couldn't go straight forward. Oh, my dear." Just remembering this situation brought much laughter from Miss Doll Baby.

Miss Doll Baby, pictured in her 20s,
liked to wear her hair in bangs. **Eliza Dennis Collection**

"I waited to take my driver's test after I was out of school, but it was a couple of years before I took driving up again. I bought a car for $100 at Dodge in Annapolis and practiced on the farm, driving around the fields." Miss Doll Baby kept practicing and working on her driving skills. She had to retake the driving test, because "the parking got me. Finally, my cousin, Frank Gross, said that he'd show me how, and I learned to drive." Asked the accomplishment of which she was most proud, Miss Eliza said, "The day I got my driver's license!"

Miss Eliza also did day's work in the '60s and '70s, when she worked in different homes for a full day each day of the week. She had two Griffith families, some Jacksons, a family in Deale, Mr. Bennett, and

Rev. and Mrs. Hitner, the pastor at St. John's Church. In the beginning people picked her up for work, but later she drove her own car.

"One day Father Hitner, Mrs. Hitner, and I were having lunch at the dining room table, and the parsonage phone rang for Father. When he came back he said, 'I don't believe what I just heard.' He sat down and repeated himself, 'I just can't believe she said such a thing.'" Father Hitner, who had grown up in the North, was appalled at the caller's audacity. He explained that the lady caller wanted to give her deceased husband's clothes to someone who could use them, but "she didn't want them 'to go to some colored person.' And I said, 'Well, she might not like it, but some colored person will get them at the Salvation Army.'"

During high school, Miss Doll Baby worked at the Chesapeake Yacht Club on weekends. First she washed dishes in the kitchen, but she soon became a waitress in the dining room. She enjoyed working at the Yacht Club because of the nice people working with her: Josephine Tongue, Hazel Howard, and Elizabeth Pinkney. "Many are gone, but some club members are still living." For 20 years, until 1969, she worked at the club from the first Sunday in April until the last Sunday in October, when they had an oyster roast that ended the season.

One providential day, Father Hitner said, "Eliza, you're educated; you're a high school graduate. You should be doing more than day's work. You should get another job."

Miss Doll Baby did that very thing. "I went to the employment office on Forrest Drive and filled out an application. As I was leaving, a man that I had seen at the Yacht Club stopped me and asked if I could go to work right now." A request had just come in for a cashier at the hospital: the current employee, a Korean girl, was returning to Korea because her mother had died. Eliza took the job. "I worked there 25 years and 8 months. They had a retirement party for me. I run into people from there yet.

Attending a large Pratt Reunion in Davidsonville, Miss Doll Baby sees Roberta Brown Hopkins, a friend from her working days at the hospital. Note the Pratt family history displays and documents. **Ann Widdifield Collection**

"I would go to Philadelphia on the train to visit Puddin'." Puddin' graduated from college in 1950 and married, and she and her husband lived in Philadelphia, where she taught school. Miss Doll Baby's beloved Puddin' died from cancer in 1993 and is buried at St. Matthew's. Her gravestone is the only one with a cross on it.

While on her way to see her ill son in the hospital in October 1980, Olivia Mae Dennis Scott, Miss Doll Baby's sister, was killed in an automobile accident. "She died in the afternoon and her son died that night." Each year on the Sunday closest to Miss Olivia's birthday, Olivia's son Willie, daughter Olivia ("Kicker"), and Miss Doll Baby speak in remembrance of her life, the loss, and their love for her.

In 2010 Miss Doll Baby's sister "Ruth" died on May 25, and her grandniece Rose Marie (Willie's oldest daughter) died the same week on May 29. Her nephew Thomas (brother Quinton's son) died on July

4. On her 80th birthday, Miss Eliza herself was in the hospital emergency room. "I wasn't able to open my birthday cards until a few days later."

Eliza's father taught her that the Bible says age is nothing to the good Lord. "We didn't come here to stay, and we don't know when we will leave. We came only for a visit." When her father passed away a week before his 100th birthday, some thought that might be the end of Miss Eliza, but she found her way through her saddest loss and the ones that followed. Her father was buried in the Dennis cemetery.

Several family cemeteries are around and near Shady Side. As shown, vaults are often above ground, due to the high water table. This cemetery is at the end of Scott Town Lane. Dennis family members are buried in several other locations. **Ann Widdifield Collection**

Great-Grandparents and Grandparents

In 1882 Jacob Dennis placed his mark on a will that passed his land and possessions to his children. To his four sons—Jacob, Lenard, James, and Joshua—he bequeathed particular fields. In establishing boundaries, he referred to Samuel Parrot's land to the east by the Chesapeake Bay and to the "land to the north by land at present owned by Capt. Salem Avery." Jacob Dennis had purchased some woodland earlier from Capt. Avery and directed that all four sons should have the use of the wood "only for the proper purpose of the land respectively devised to them and none to have the privilege of cutting wood or timber for sale." The sons were to share equally the farm buildings on Lenard's inheritance for the care of the stock and securing the crops until the others could erect their own buildings. He ratified and confirmed that his daughter, Rachel Dennis Crowner, wife of John Crowner, was entitled to the enclosed land on which she then resided. To his four daughters—Jane, wife of Henry Holland; Rachel Crowner; Harriet, wife of William Thomas; and Eliza, wife of Benjamin Smith—Jacob left $100 to each from the money that came from the sale of his personal property minus the debts and estate fees.[5] Jacob Dennis died on July 31, 1888, one year after his neighbor Capt. Salem Avery, who died on July 5, 1887.

Children of Jacob Dennis

As stated in the will, Eliza Dennis married Benjamin Smith. In the census of 1880, Eliza Smith is listed as the head of household, born about 1825, and 55 years old. Her children are Joseph, 16, James, 20, and Pinkney W. Smith, 12. If all the dates associated with her are correct, then she would have been 1 year old when Sarah Norris signed the deed of manumission and 13 when she was actually freed. Often confusing are the estimated dates given for births and different names or spellings used for the same person. It was a common practice for someone to go by a middle name or a nickname rather than the name on the birth certificate. Census takers sometimes missed houses, recorded incomplete or inaccurate names, accepted someone's guessed dates, and could only record the information given by the person, young or old, who was home at the time of his visit.

Joshua Mayhem Dennis, born May 9, 1855, married Mary Jane Griffin on September 12, 1880. Together they raised a large family of eight boys and three girls: John, born in 1883, was followed by Thomas Ira in 1885; Jacob; Isaiah; Julius, and his twin brother who died at birth in 1895; Benjamin, who drowned; Sadie Loraine; Ida Jane; Eliza Ann, born in 1893; James, who lived four months; and Edmund Francis, the last, in 1902. The diseases that seemed to carry off many children were whooping cough, pneumonia, teething, and "spasms."[6]

Joshua Dennis's family's farm would have been similar to his father Jacob's, but tomatoes had become a major crop for Joshua. Son Julius (1895-1996) remembered his father saying, "Let's me raise some 'matoes; I believe 'matoes are goin' up." Tomatoes on the peninsula were known to grow quite well; they sold for 8-10 cents a bushel and were 10 pounds a bushel heavier than those in the highlands. Two tomato canneries were built on the peninsula, and the canned tomatoes were shipped to Baltimore. One canning house was on Chalk Point, and another was off West Shady Side Road. A local man with knowledge of the West Shady Side cannery said an owner of that cannery used to hire new Polish immigrants from Baltimore and was quite severe with the workers.

Baltimore was a major port for the country and was the center for America's canning industry. Even before the Civil War, oysters were shipped to Baltimore for canning and then put on railroads to be shipped all over the country. Thus, farming and oystering made a strong economic base for families like Joshua Dennis and his late nineteenth and twentieth century neighbors.

Olivia Scott Gray Family Tree

Olivia Lorraine Scott Gray*

Wilson Thomas Scott**
1) Thomas Willie Scott
2) Sidney Reginald
3) Olivia Lorraine "Kicker"*
4) Shirley Mae

William Scott
1) Sarah
2) Wilson Thomas**
3) Lilian
4) Vernie

Maggie Shaw***

Unknown
1) Maggie***

Grace (Unknown)

Olivia Mae Dennis**

Thomas Ira Dennis***
1) Olivia **
(Siblings on Ms. Doll Baby's tree)

Joshua Mayhew Dennis****
1) Thomas***
(Siblings on Ms. Doll Baby's tree)

Mary Jane Griffin

Jacob Henry Dennis*****
1. Joshua****
2) Rachel (wife of John Crowner)
(Siblings on Ms. Doll Baby's tree)

Elizabeth Matthews*****

Edith Nickens***

Mora Nickens
1) Edith***

Isabella

CHAPTER 4

SHADY SIDE SCHOOL STORIES

M ISS DOLL BABY EXPLAINED, "When Puddin' started high school in the fall of 1941, Daddy said he didn't want me walking to Churchton by myself, so he sent me to Shady Side because Puddin' caught the bus for Bates High School at Shady Side Elementary." The sisters walked down Shady Side Road about a mile into town, where Puddin' joined high school students catching the bus for Bates. Miss Doll Baby gathered with the children of Shady Side Elementary, the black school, and just up the road white children attended the white Shady Side Elementary School. As children entered school that day, "separate but equal" was the way of life at home, in Shady Side, in Anne Arundel County, in Maryland, and throughout much of the country. In practice "separate but equal" was anything but equal—but it was definitely separate.

Rosenwald Schools

Lining up with their lunches in hand, boys in one line and girls in another, Miss Doll Baby and her classmates in grades one through seven entered a Rosenwald school. Before the Rosenwald schools were built, black children in the 15 Southern states received a limited education, if any. The Shady Side school was one of more than 5,300 schools constructed with help from the Julius Rosenwald Fund. Shady Side Elementary was built in 1926 for $3,500. The school's cost was shared by the local African American community, which contributed 19 percent; Rosenwald donated 16.5 percent; and the state and county provided the balance. Julius Rosenwald was a Jewish man and the head of Sears, Roebuck and Company. After consulting with Booker T. Washington, he agreed to create a fund of $28 million over time for construction of public schools for black students. He was instrumental in opening a door of opportunity and improving the quality of education for rural African American students in the early 1900s. [1]

Tommy Nick (front row second from the right) and his brother, Eddie Nick (fifth left from Tommy) and Helen Crowner (fourth row second from the left) join their schoolmates and teachers, Miss Wiseman and Miss Chew (far right) outside their Rosenwald school, or Shady Side Colored Elementary School. Starting in the first row from Eddie Nick going right are William "Piggy" Nick, James Nick, and Thomas Matthews. Clarence Johnson (front row, third from left) kneels beside Ellis Matthews to his right. Lowell Dennis, who drowns in New

Jersey, is the first child in the second row; the fifth child right from him is Calvin Matthews. Charles Crowner, Jr. (third row, second student from left) is next to Earl Nick (right). The girl next to Earl is Minerva Nick who dies in her teens. Five girls over, sandwiched between two rows, is Eunice Holland who later marries Minerva's brother, Leonard Nick.
Helen Crowner Gorham Collection

Galesville and Churchton also had Rosenwald schools. Galesville has recently restored its school, but the Churchton School, which was located on the Deale-Churchton Road just down from the Churchton post office, is no longer there. It was moved in 1953 to a new location. John Miller, who owned Miller's Garage, moved the two-room Churchton School on rollers to Shady Side, where it was incorporated into the two-room Shady Side School. The move took two days, causing the Churchton School to sit overnight on Dent Road in front of Crandall's Store. It was a bit unsettling for some Churchton children to see their school traveling down the road.

Churchton School was positioned behind Shady Side School during the summer. In the fall the two schools were joined together, and a kitchen and two lavatories were added while school was in session. With these installations, the school finally had inside running water.

The refurbished school was renamed after Lula G. Scott, a respected teacher from Churchton, although she never actually taught in Shady Side. Mrs. Scott came as a single woman from the north to the local community as a novice teacher. She taught at Churchton for many years and married into the Scott family. It was reported that local Shady Side people called her "Aunt Lu." According to a 2002 interview with Alice Battle, teacher and principal in Shady Side for more than 30 years, the decision was made to name the school after Mrs. Scott, who had retired when the Churchton and Shady Side schools were joined. The PTA, under the leadership of president Chesterfield Coates, chose the name, and the board of education concurred.

In 1953 the school staff consisted of the principal and teacher of grades five and six, Miss Alice Holt; the teacher of grades three and four, Mrs. Julia T. Smith; the teacher of grades two and three, Mrs. Olivia Thompson; and the first-grade teacher, Miss Frances Neal.

Joyce Brown Thompson, entering fourth grade, had looked forward to having Alice Holt Battle as her teacher. Instead, when the schools were joined, she got one of the Churchton teachers, Miss Julia Smith. Joyce discovered that she was a "wonderful teacher, wonderful lady." Teachers not only taught academics; they also taught students how to dress, how to sit, and how to stand. In playing the "gossip game," Joyce learned that you cannot repeat what people tell you because it always gets garbled or changed.

Mrs. Alice Holt Battle is pictured on a window hanging as part of the exhibit
"Memories and Mementos" at the Captain Salem Museum in 2011.
Ann Widdifield Collection

Lula G. Scott School was enlarged again during the 1957–58 school year when three additional classrooms, increased restroom facilities, and two offices were added. A special education class was housed in the smallest of the three added classrooms. School staff that year were the principal and fifth- and sixth-grade teacher, Mrs. Alice Battle; Mrs. Julia Smith, who taught fourth grade; Mrs. Yvonne Holland Matthews, third grade; Mrs. Olivia Thompson, second grade; Miss Willamae Pergerson, first grade; and Mrs. Doris Crowner Brown, special education. Galesville children were bused to Shady Side until 1965, when the Carrie Weedon Elementary School was integrated.

★   ★   ★

The school Miss Doll Baby and her friends entered had two doors leading to an entrance hall that served as the children's cloakroom. First-, second-, and third-grade students entered the classroom door on the right, or south side, of the building, and fourth- through sixth-grade students went into the room on the left, north side. These entryways were near the front doors of the building. In the back of each classroom stood a tall, black, round, potbelly stove that the older boys kept supplied with coal from the pile behind the school. Chesterfield Coates, who lived next door to the school, was the custodian and made sure the fire was warm when the children arrived. Each room had a chalkboard, a globe on a stand, and student desks, which were one unit with the desk and chair joined together. The teacher's desk was in the front of the room.

Patty Nick Gross, a Shady Side teacher who taught for 35 years and was still substituting in 2004, said in an interview that students sang "Good Morning," recited the pledge, and prayed the Lord's Prayer. Then an inspector checked the students' fingernails, the backs of their necks, and their ears. Lessons were taught in reading, spelling, writing, penmanship, grammar, and arithmetic.

Miss Doll Baby also remembered the pledge and the "Our Father" prayer. "I liked English literature and grammar the best. Arithmetic was the hardest," she said. "I never wore anything fancy, and we never wore pants to school." Asked which name she wrote on her paper, she replied, "You'd never write your nickname on your paper."

About once a week, students' mothers came to school to make soup on the potbelly stove. Mothers brought vegetables or bean soup, and the wonderful smell of cooking soup would fill the classrooms. Each child kept a cup at school for these delicious events.

Drinking water was located at the end of the entry hall. Delores Nick Harley drew a sketch showing the pump in a small, enclosed area at the back, between the two classrooms. "We were allowed to go out the back door to get drinks at the pump," she recalled. She was in fifth grade when the Churchton School was moved. John Fountain attended Shady Side for grades one through seven—before Delores's time. He remembered keeping drinking cups in a cubbyhole for drinks at the pump.

Children ate their bag lunches at their desks. One child brought sweet potato sandwiches or mayonnaise sandwiches when that was all the family had. Soup day would be especially welcome for such a student. Later, when the cafeteria was added to the school, students still ate at their desks. "Students still brought lunches from home, but the school lunch was inexpensive, maybe 50 cents in my day," said Carmelia Hicks, present director of Early Head Start and Head Start at the Lula G. Scott Community Center. She herself was a student from 1963 to 1969.

Recesses were in the morning and after lunch. As soon as children finished eating, they were dismissed to play outside. The boys always seemed to be playing baseball, caddy, or a game called "500," which required a knife. "Every child brought one to school," said Patricia Gross. "The girls liked hopscotch, jacks, caddy, and dodge ball. If it were a rainy day, then they played inside games like 'Hide in Sight.'" One student remembered checkers, dominoes, jacks, and bingo as favorite inside games. Children took turns being the caller.

"Those were the good old days," remembered Miss Doll Baby, and her eyes lit up when she explained how to play caddy. The player who is "it" pitches a pointed stick into a ring drawn in the dirt. "It" must hit the first stick with a second stick and try to reach the first stick by the number of steps an opponent calls. With skill it can be done, and a successful player had every right to feel accomplished.

An 80-year-old gentleman gave these instructions for preparing equipment for caddy: "Take an old broomstick and cut off six to seven inches, whittle each end until very sharp. Use the rest of the broomstick for the second stick. Draw a large circle in the dirt about 20 feet from a dirt-drawn smaller circle where the 'caddier' will stand to make the pitch. Players get one hit and they're done. The goal is to hit the stick the furthest. Sticks lasted about a month."

In Miss Doll Baby's day, the playground equipment included swings, a merry-go-round, and a slide. If they couldn't find a ball to play with, which was often the case, children improvised by wadding socks up to make a ball. Usually the older boys played baseball in the field behind the playground, and the girls played dodge ball.

"We had Field Days when Shady Side competed against another school like Churchton or Friendship," remembered Helen Crowner Gorham. "Probably people walked to get from Churchton to Shady Side." There was also a Maypole Day celebration on May Day, when students wrapped a maypole. They had flag relays and games and the opportunity to interact and compete with other schools. As to their favorite recess game, Miss Helen and her sister, Miss Daisy, said without hesitation and in chorus: "Dodge ball."

To be excused for "privileges," or to use the toilet, a student raised a hand and, after being acknowledged by the teacher, went out back to use one of two outhouses, or privies. A coal shed sat between the boys' and girls' privies. Although each outhouse was a two-holer, if someone was already in the outhouse, the new arrival waited outside. Toilet paper was available (rather than other more uncomfortable possibilities, such as

Sears and Roebuck catalogs or dried corncobs). The teachers used the same facility as the students.

Punishment was meted out for throwing spitballs, laughing, pulling a chair out from under someone, or talking too much. As punishment, a student might have to miss recess, but serious offenses required a trip to the principal or another teacher for a paddling. The offender had to bend over, touch toes, and receive a whack. Sometimes the adult held the child's fingers and smacked the palms with a thick ruler. If children were punished, teachers did not abuse them, but they could punish without any hesitation. Parents backed the teachers up, and the child probably got a second spanking at home.

One rule that all of the children of that era had to follow was that they were *not* allowed to listen to adult conversations. They were sent outside to play or to another room. Woe to the child who overheard adults and then repeated publicly what was heard. One girl repeated something at school that she overheard while she listened to the adults through the wall of her home. It was about a teacher, and the child announced her discovery at school. Her reward was a speedy dash to the principal, and she held her own ankles while the principal applied the board.

Unfortunately, girls were not always told the facts of life, so when the inevitable happened at puberty, one girl had a terrifying experience. She feared she had fallen down and hurt herself in some strange way. At school, she told her teacher her dilemma and was sent home to get a change of clothes. Once home she was asked, "What are you doing here?" Explaining the frightening problem, the mystery was solved when she was led into the bedroom, given strips torn from an old sheet, handed safety pins for securing the strips, and given the admonishment: "You are a woman now, and you'll be having this once a month." She went back to school.

Marshall Nick, Sr., remembered, "They'd come around, bring the old projectors to the school." When movies were shown, a projectionist, the projector, and a screen had to be delivered. Educational movies were shown, and sometimes westerns were shown in the evening at school. His principal and upper grades teacher was Mary Wiseman, and Miss Lillian Burrell had the lower grades. He attended the two-room school and remembered a cloakroom and pantry that was the teachers' office.

When it was time to get new books, the Lula G. Scott School received the ones that had previously been used by the white Shady Side children down the road. New books meant that the other school was getting new books. "I would see the names of white children already listed in the 'new' book I was given," said a 1960s female graduate. Purnell Crowner (1938-2003) recorded the same memory of receiving books from the white school and noted that segregation was not equal. After school was out, he would race home to do his chores and race back to school to play softball or football.

Tommy Nick told about how he was sent with a note from Miss Wiseman to go to Mrs. Ethel Andrews, principal of the white school, to pick up books. He walked into the school and handed the note to Miss Ethel, who said, "Hello, Tommy. What may I do for you?" In the meantime, the children who knew Tommy were asking, "What are you doing here?"

Graduation was a big day for the seventh-grade students who would be going on to Bates for grades eight through twelve. Traditionally, the girls wore white dresses and the boys wore suits. Miss Doll Baby remembered riding in a car with her twin sisters, Ruth and Isabelle, to buy her white dress and white shoes at G.C. Murphy on Main Street in Annapolis. Her graduation took place in the classroom, and parents came for the celebration, although anyone could come. The graduating class marched into the classroom for the ceremonies. Miss Sarah G. Jones came and represented the county.

*Graduating elementary students from Shady Side, Galesville, Churchton,
Friendship and Lothian schools gathered for pictures in front of Shady Rest
Boarding House, long before it was remodeled. Churchton and Shady Side girls
in the front row are Patricia Nick Gross (second from left) Yvonne Holland
Matthews (sixth from Patty) and Doris Crowner Brown (right of Yvonne).
Directly behind Doris is Virginia Nick Hopkins.*
Doris Crowner Brown Collection

The pictures were taken in 1946, the year sixth and the last year for seventh graders to graduate from elementary school. All of these children are then bused to Bates High School for continued education. Churchton and Shady Side boys in the front row are Oliver Matthews (fourth from left) Bobby Powell (next) and last person (right) is William Matthews. Carroll Matthews is the scout standing between Oliver and Bobby. (First cousins, Carroll and Oliver were great-grandchildren of Lizzy Crowner Matthews Holland.)

Doris Crowner Brown Collection

Miss Jones was responsible for all the "colored" schools in Anne Arundel County for 38 years. In 1926 Miss Jones was promoted from principal of the Churchton Elementary School to supervisor of elementary instruction for the 42 colored schools in the county. She hired all black elementary teachers and visited their schools as frequently as possible. Miss Jones did not have help until 1959, when Everett Pettigrew, principal of Lothian Elementary, was promoted to supervisor and the responsibilities were divided between them. Before retiring in 1964, Miss Jones single-handedly supervised consolidation and standardization of the schools and oversaw the organization of a countywide PTA and its work in purchasing ground for Rosenwald schools. Some of those schools were replaced later with red brick consolidated schools.

"We had very good teachers at Shady Side. We were all eager to learn. I remember Mrs. Oliver and Olivia Thompson. I had Mrs. Yvonne Matthews in third grade, and she says that we were one of her favorite classes," recalled Olivia Scott Gray.

In 1946 or 1948, Miss Mary V. Wiseman was sent to Bates to teach, and Miss Alice Holt took her place. Miss Wiseman had taught at Shady Side for 17 years and was principal for 16 years. Miss Lillian Burrell taught at the school for 15 years. There are people who think that the Shady Side School should have been named for Miss Wiseman instead of Lula G. Scott, because Miss Wiseman taught in Shady Side for so many years and Mrs. Scott never taught there.

All students and teachers, Miss Mary V. Wiseman (left) 4-6, and Miss Burrell (right) 1-3, gather on the front steps of school in 1937. Entrance for grades 1-3 is on the right and grades 4-6 on the left. Matthews' children are Lucille (fourth row second left) Sarah (third row first child) Jean (third row seventh from left) and Alexander (second row seventh from left). Others are George "Bootie" Crowner (front row furthest left), Hughward Crowner (front row furthest right) KD Goss (second row, second from left) and Octif Turner (second row furthest right). **Jean Matthews Johnson Collection**

During segregation every black child who attended high school in Anne Arundel County went to Wiley H. Bates High School in Annapolis. The Wiley H. Bates School consisted of seven classrooms and a gym when it was completed in the fall of 1932. Bates removed Stanton High School students crowded with lower grades in the Stanton building, which was too small for the bursting student population. Anne Arundel County school board policy dictated that parents had to furnish the land for the new building. Costing $58,596, Bates opened its doors to the student body on January 1, 1933, with seven teachers and principal Mr. Frank Butler. Elementary graduates entering Bates had to take a written test. Only those making the required score were allowed to enroll in the school.[2]

John Fountain graduated from Bates and went on to college to become a teacher; he retired as a school principal. Mr. Fountain first taught in Friendship Elementary during segregation. He became a special education teacher and worked with Down syndrome children. He chose to stay at Friendship during integration in 1966 and became principal in 1969. In 1976 he was made principal of Central Special Education School and remained there until 1983, when he retired. When he attended Bates, only trades were taught at school, reflecting society's attitudes and narrow view of how African Americans should be educated, particularly in the South. The theory was that black students needed to learn trades to prepare them for manual labor or work in the industrial world rather than in professional fields.

A bus carried the Bates students from Shady Side, and other buses brought other black students from points farther south, north, and west, each bus passing by white schools to reach the final destination. Students living outside Annapolis were severely restricted in their ability to participate in after-school activities. Cordell Salisbury was an exception: His mother agreed that he could play football in 1956 for the Bates Bulldogs, who dressed in gold and purple. He stayed after school for the required practices, but he had to hitchhike or walk home because there was no after-school transportation. His contemporaries remember seeing him walking along the roads, headed home, sometimes in the dark. Traveling long distances for a high school education was a daily fact of life until 1966, when schools were finally fully integrated.

By the early '60s, students graduated and attended Bates from seventh grade forward. "I was a little afraid of the transition because I had heard stories of bad kids coming from other areas and to 'watch out,'" said Olivia Scott Gray. "But then again, everything worked out fine. We caught the bus at the end of Scotts Town Road as it was coming out of town. It was bus 91. Churchton was bus 79. Richard Thomas Bus

Company from Lothian owned the buses. Family who had previously ridden the bus knew each other. We'd talk about TV, or what we were planning to do socially on the weekend."

Olivia Scott Gray (second row second from left) and Chuck Gross (third row third from the right) stand on the front steps of the remodeled Lula G. Scott School in 1962. Ms. Julia Toliver Smith was their teacher. Others are Wendell Matthews (to Chuck's right), Douglas Thompson, Chuck's first cousin and good friend, (farthest left) and Joanne Crowner Coates, "Bootie" Crowner's daughter, (in front of Douglas, next to Olivia). **Olivia Scott Gray Collection**

During Doll Baby's day, some students from Friendship and Deale were already on the bus when the Shady Side students were picked up. It made a long day for those children, because they were also the last ones to return home.

Miss Doll Baby had a friend who was picked up at Mayo. The girls liked to sit together on the ride to Bates by way of Edgewater, where more students were added. "There was heat on the bus, but we dressed warm," Miss Doll Baby remembered. "We had to stay seated, two kids to a seat. The driver wouldn't take off if someone weren't seated. There was no light at 468 and 214. If there was some sort of problem, the driver threatened 'to stop this bus right now and put you off.'" Students cooperated in most cases. If not, Phillip Brown, principal of Bates, would deal with the troublemaker.

Describing how the buses looked at Bates, Miss Doll Baby exclaimed, "Oh, my dear, there were so many school buses." Every African American student attending high school was arriving at the same general time, so it had to be an organized operation.

"We went to home room, recited the pledge, prayed the Lord's Prayer, and heard announcements." There was one class that was hard to get to on time because of the distance between the two rooms. "Our teacher asked us, 'How come you're always late?' And then she'd say, 'You'll be late for your own funeral.' We had no study hall. I loved the library and Rachel Smith, the librarian. I took typing and shorthand with Miss Bryant, English with Miss Tate, math with Miss Hall, science with Miss Pettigrew, history with Miss Gaither, and PE with Miss Taylor. All of my teachers are dead now. At the end of the day, we went back to our homerooms and were excused by time to go to our buses. Then we took the reverse trip home."

If school were cancelled because of snow, the announcement came over the radio and children stayed home. If students were already at school and the weather became bad, students were sent to their homerooms and dismissed early to catch the buses. Bus windows would be open on hot spring and summer days. "In the summertime we would have storms about every day."

★   ★   ★

A dual system of education for blacks and whites had been maintained since the Supreme Court's 8-1 decision in *Plessy v. Ferguson* in 1896. Black schools had a shorter term, fewer grades in the elementary school, inferior facilities and equipment, no bus transportation, lack of custodial services, and lower teacher salaries. In 1939 conditions improved with the equalization of teachers' pay, but it took years to make small gains. Segregationists were determined to keep the two races apart, so they tried equalizing Negro schools to white schools. From 1950 to 1959, Anne Arundel County spent over $6 million improving Negro school facilities; at one rare point the black children's school buildings were better than the white children's facilities.

Graduating from elementary school in 1960, Clarence Johnson, Jr. smiles proudly as he hugs sister Jean Yvonne on the last day of school. **Jean Matthews Johnson Collection**

Thurgood Marshall, the head legal counsel of the NAACP, led the charge against segregation in the public schools that finally reached the

Supreme Court. With four other cases, *Brown v. Board of Education of Topeka, Kansas,* was argued during 1952 and 1953. On May 17, 1954, the Supreme Court ruled unanimously that "separate and equal" went against guarantees of the Fourteenth Amendment of the Constitution, reversing the *Plessy* decision. Chief Justice Earl Warren wrote the decision. Governors and legislatures in some southern states tried to block the ruling. In Anne Arundel County, the reaction was mixed. Those whites wanting to thwart the Supreme Court ruling attended meetings to strategize resistance to the ruling through public petitions and proclamations. "The West River Proclamation," formally approved by PTAs from Southern High School, Owensville School, and the Anne Arundel County Public Schools, petitioned the state government. The language of the preamble mirrored the preamble to the Declaration of Independence, and the four resolutions implied that all fair-minded citizens were like them in opposition to the ruling. Another group known as the "The Maryland Petition Committee" was adamantly against the Supreme Court's ruling, claiming integration of public schools was an invasion and violation of their individual rights in Maryland.[3]

After the 1954 ruling, some segregated states and the District of Columbia began to desegregate; others waited. Baltimore began its process before the 1955 Supreme Court's implication guidelines were issued. On May 31, 1955, the Supreme Court directed the states to proceed to end segregation with "all deliberate speed." The guidelines allowed for a democratic, voluntary transition, and states were expected to move forward promptly and deliberately and "act in good faith."

Maryland's attorney general's formal opinion (June 22, 1955), followed by the Joint Resolution of the State Board of Education of Maryland and the Board of Trustees of the State Teachers Colleges of Maryland, established that each county and its officials would be responsible for the desegregation of the traditional dual school system into a single system as soon as possible.

The Anne Arundel County Board of Education passed a resolution on May 11, 1955, to immediately appoint a commission of 23 men and women of both racial groups to advise the board concerning desegregation plans for the county's public schools. The Commission to Study Desegregation[4] examined "data concerning population distribution and estimated population growth, school facilities by type and their ethnic growth, and their ethnic populations." As of March 31, 1955, southern Anne Arundel County's school population was 47% white and 53% nonwhite, and the northern county school population was 94.7% white and 5.3% nonwhite. Questionnaires were distributed to county residents "to insure some unified basis for discussion and determining the feelings of the county."[5] Based on the commission's findings, discussions, and six conclusions, the commission submitted 12 recommendations to the board.[6]

The board of education released its plan on May 2, 1956. It stated that 1- beginning in September 1956, the first three grades of the school system would operate on a nonsegregated basis; 2- the program of nonsegregation would expand one or more grades each year; and 3- wherever possible, every child in the first three grades, beginning in September 1956, and in additional grades as the program expanded in succeeding years, would have the choice of (a) attending the nearest school, or (b) attending his present school. [7]

In the meantime Dr. Pullen, the state superintendent of schools, had been making progress reports on the desegregation of schools in Maryland's counties. By August 1956, Baltimore City and every county except Caroline had taken some formal action to implement the Supreme Court's desegregation ruling.

Mrs. Lulu Hardesty, a first-grade teacher in Annapolis, became the first colored teacher to be transferred to an all-white elementary school in 1958; she was followed by principal Everett Pettigrew's promotion to supervisor of elementary colored schools, and Bates High School science teacher Mrs. Thelma Sparks, who was transferred to all-white

Arundel Junior High School in 1959. Additional transfers continued with colored teachers transferring to white schools, but there were some concerns: Experienced, successful colored teachers were being transferred to white schools, but no experienced, successful white teachers were being transferred to the colored schools. A delegation from the Anne Arundel County Federation of PTAs presented their questions to the board in October 1962, and the board responded the next month. Two years later, in the spring of 1965, Rev. Traynham appeared before the board to condemn its practice of delaying segregation of certain colored schools. The board promised to study the complaint, and in the middle of September 1965, it released its report with the subtitle "Ten Years of Progress: May 1954 to 1964."

Three methods of pupil assignment were acceptable to the U.S. Department of Health, Education, and Welfare (HEW) as complying with Title VI of the Civil Rights Act of 1964, and Anne Arundel County chose the third plan for September 1965: a combination of geographic attendance areas and freedom of choice. At that time 41 schools had been desegregated by geographic attendance area, and no other steps were necessary in those schools. The remaining 42 schools had been desegregated on a freedom-of-choice basis; among those were white Shady Side Elementary and Southern High, and all-black Lula G. Scott Elementary and Bates High.

In March 1966 the Office of Education of HEW issued a revised statement of its earlier policy and gave four explicit guidelines for school desegregation.[8] If the county was to receive federal aid, it had to eliminate the dual structure. Anne Arundel's plan was not working: 75% of Negro children still attended all-black schools with almost all Negro teachers. A Citizens Committee report titled *Discrimination in Public Schools in Anne Arundel County* provided statistics, information, and recommendations for an end to the dual system in Anne Arundel County. HEW learned that most Maryland counties were moving too slowly, but Anne Arundel, Calvert, Caroline, Charles, Talbot, and

Worcester were the most delayed. Investigators who studied the six counties concluded that there was nothing to prevent full desegregation of all grades in all schools in Anne Arundel County by the opening of school in September 1966. [9]

Olivia Scott Gray points out a remembrance in one of the Wiley H. Bates High School historical murals. The school is now an active community center. **Ann Widdifield Collection**

Integration

In the fall of 1966, eleven years after the Supreme Court directed states to end segregation, all of Maryland's schools, including Shady Side, were totally integrated. Lula G. Scott School became the intermediate school, with Mrs. Alice Battle as a nonteaching principal, and Shady Side School was the primary school, with Mrs. Nellie Nowell as principal. Kindergarteners from the Shady Side area attended school in the Moreland building in Galesville.

Staff at Lula G. Scott that year was: Mrs. Catherine Wilde (fourth grade), Mrs. Nina Carter (fourth and fifth grades combined), Mrs. Olivia Thompson (fifth grade), Mrs. Julia Smith and Mrs. Ethel Wickman (sixth grade), Mrs. Yvonne Matthews (special education), Beebe Castro (physical education), Mrs. Peggy Reeder (library), Mrs. Beryl Owings (art), Mr. Preston Matthews (custodian), and Mrs. Grace Procter (cafeteria).

Staff at Shady Side "Primary" School was: Mrs. Doris Brown and Mrs. Betty Moreland (first grade), Mrs. Mabel Conway and Mrs. Mildred Krissoff (second grade), Mrs. Doris Redman and Mrs. Frances Brown (third grade), Lucretia Brown (secretary), Beebe Castro (physical education), Mrs. Peggy Reeder (library), Mrs. Beryl Owings (art), Mrs. Irene Strange (cafeteria), and Mr. Edward Dennis (custodian).

People living in Shady Side today say that there were no issues or problems when the schools were integrated. The main reason given over and over: "We already knew each other." No contradiction to this statement was uncovered from former students or teachers.

Ask any middle school teacher what it is like for middle school students of today, and they will tell you it is a huge transition from elementary school to the less structured and more complex junior high level. Students are entering adolescence, and they develop and change mentally, physically, emotionally, and socially. Being included is paramount. Some might argue that this stage and age might have been the most difficult for an integrating student. At the time there were naysayers who predicted that black students could not meet expectations. Therefore, the integrating students, like earlier African Americans who broke color barriers, knew they had to be superlative to show they were able.

When Jean Yvonne Johnson entered middle school after attending segregated Shady Side Elementary School, she felt the isolation. Feeling intimidated and wondering how she would be accepted—and whether she would be accepted—she believed she had to triple her study efforts and work load. Already a serious student, her aim was to get the best grades possible and meet the challenge. During middle school she was shy and didn't join any social clubs or run for offices. But by the time she graduated from Southern High School in 1971, she was in the top ten of her class, a member of the National Honor Society, on the yearbook staff, and served as a secretary in the office of Mr. Thomas Tereshinski, one of Southern's administrators.

As a seventh-grade girl entering middle school at Southern High School, Carla Nick Gross was disappointed not to be going to Bates. All of her older siblings had gone there, and she, the baby, had heard about what it was like and had anticipated her turn to go. Instead, she took a much shorter bus ride to her new school. "I didn't have any fears, but all of the black kids and all of the white kids stuck together. That was in the beginning, and it took some time to get to know each other. By the time graduation came around, you saw mingling and friendships, and it was much better. One thing we couldn't understand, though, was why a white teacher was sent to teach us black history. It didn't make sense, because she had no idea what it was like to live that history. She was a young teacher, and she cried when we told her how we felt."

A small white child who rode the bus to middle school was teased and tormented by the other riders from both races, until a black girl stood up for her, befriended her, and continued to ride to and from school with her—a reminder that the biggest number is one. It takes just one person to change a situation and one to make a difference.

Located on the corner of Snug Harbor and Atwell Roads, the present Shady Side School was ready for students from the primary and intermediate schools to attend in August 1971. Mrs. Alice Battle was the principal, and Mrs. Nellie Nowell was vice principal. At the school's opening, there were 28 teachers on the faculty with one full-time teacher each for physical education, art, and music; two special education teachers; and a media specialist. Eight instructional assistants, three secretaries, and two permanent substitutes also supported the students' educational needs. Cafeteria and custodial staff completed the staff for the operation of the school. Lothian area children in grades four to six were bused to Shady Side Elementary from 1971 to 1978 because of a shortage of available classrooms at the Lothian School for its student population.

Like many schools built during the late '60s and early '70s, Shady Side was built as an open-space school, thought to be the best concept in education. As an open school, walls and partitions were not built between classrooms within a "pod." Quads led off of the centrally located library, which is the heart of the school. This school was quite a contrast to the first schools available for Shady Side children.

Mrs. Doris Brown had been teaching at Shady Side for two years when all of the black teachers in the county were sent letters requesting that they attend a meeting in Annapolis. There they learned that many of them were going to be transferred to balance the black teachers among the county schools. Seven (but not all) of Shady Side's black teachers were moved to other schools. Mrs. Brown traveled to the Severna/Arnold area to reach her school, but she was thrilled three years later to transfer back to Shady Side when an opening for a third-grade teacher made it possible.

It should be noted that the county failed to recruit and hire black teachers to balance the ratio with white teachers. Promotions of principals were also not pursued. Dr. Aris T. Allen, a black man, served on the county board of education from 1955 to 1961. But when he left, Gov. Harry Hughes appointed two white people to the board, thus eliminating any black representation on the board from 1961 to 1970.

Miss Helen Crowner Gorham shared a newspaper article she had saved about Miss Mary V. Wiseman's retirement after 43 years of teaching. Only one other retiring teacher that year had taught longer than Miss Wiseman, but all of Miss Wiseman's years were in Anne Arundel County. After teaching elementary grades in Churchton and Shady Side, she moved to Bates and progressed as a curriculum supervisor, then a principal at Bates Senior High, then a coordinator for a reading program at Bates, and finally a director of the Neighborhood Youth Corps.

Miss Wiseman had strong feelings on how the board of education handled integration. "The plan they used was stupid. You just don't piecemeal anything like that. Many of the problems we're having now could have [been] minimized if they hadn't had the attitude of 'I'll just do enough to get by.' Then the top blew off in the federal government, and they had to send the black teachers out and put the white teachers in. I don't think they knew what to do with me, but then they offered me a job as a director of the county Neighborhood Youth Corps. I knew the state director, so I took it."

According to her obituary, Miss Lilyan L. Burrell died at Johns Hopkins Hospital. She was born in Oxford, North Carolina, and later moved with her family to Media, Pennsylvania. After graduating from the two-year teaching program at the former Cheyney Normal School in 1934, she became a primary teacher at Shady Side School and taught there for 20 years. In 1941 she received her baccalaureate degree in elementary education from Hampton Institute. Attending summer and evening classes, she earned a master's degree in education from the University of Maryland in 1956. Later she became certified in special education. She was among the first group of women starting Girl Scout troops in the county, and she served as a Girl Scout leader for 15 years. A member of the First Baptist Church of Annapolis, she also belonged to Delta Sigma Theta sorority. She was a member of a local group of women who worked through the Crownsville Auxiliary in a therapy program to assist patients at the Crownsville State Hospital.

Columbia Beach School

Many Shady Side residents were unaware that another school existed before the Lula G. Scott School. This school for black children was located on the north side of Columbia Beach Road near the present-day intersection with Bay Breeze Road.

By piecing together individual interviews recorded in 1984, children's books written in 1953 by the fifth and sixth grade students of the segregated schools of Shady Side, and a 1987 report found in the library files of the Capt. Avery Museum Library, one can catch a glimpse of this former school. Fortunately, Anne Arundel County schools assigned a countywide curriculum project for fifth graders during the 1952-53 school year, and the two Shady Side schools produced two books titled *Shady Side, Past and Present.*

According to Carrie Bowles Crowner's 1984 interview, there may have been a school of sorts before the Columbia Beach School. Her first husband, James Crowner, told her "a few colored children may have been taught in a barn owned by the Lerch family."

Sometime during the 1890s, the Anne Arundel Board of Education paid John Crowner's estate "ten dollars" to buy land to build a school for colored children. Mr. Crowner owned a huge square of land between Columbia Beach and Cedarhurst Roads that was bordered by Dennis and Thompson properties. The Board also purchased land from Robert Leatherbury for the white children's school across from the later schools facing Shady Side Road, at the corner of Snug Harbor and Shady Side Roads. These public schools were administered locally by the teacher and trustees appointed by the Anne Arundel County Board of Commissioners. At that time Shady Side and its schools were in District 8; each school was assigned a number by the commission.

Both schools had windows on three sides of the rectangular structures, including the end where the teacher's desk sat. If direct sunlight came in from the windows behind the teacher's desk, students had a challenge looking directly at the teacher. The teacher's desk was on a platform facing the students and the opposite wall with the entrance to the room, giving the teacher a complete view of the proceedings. Bench desks seated two or more students. At the side of the room sat a big round stove heated by burning wood or coal. The wood and coal were kept in a shed on the school property, and the pupils brought it inside. The children swept and cleaned the room at the end of the day to have it ready for the next day. The commissioners purchased textbooks for both schools for reading, arithmetic, history, geography, and science.

The original colored schoolhouse sat on the same spot where Miss Carrie was living at the time of her 1984 interview. While married to James Crowner, she hired someone to clean out the yard where a locust tree had fallen over. During the cleaning project, Miss Carrie found a stone under the tree. Mr. Crowner told Miss Carrie that the stone marked the place where the schoolchildren had to stop if the rag ball were batted into the dirt road. When the "teacher granted permission to recover the ball," a child entered the road to get it. That large rock, still located on the corner yard of Columbia Beach Road and Bay Breeze, is the only reminder of the school's existence. (In 2009 Gerald Taylor, a foster child of the late Carrie Bowles Crowner Matthews from 1949 to 1956, talked about the school described to him by Carrie Bowles.)

Varnell Nick, born in 1906, reported in his 1984 oral history interview that he had attended a corner school on Columbia Beach Road about 77 years earlier. Some of his classmates were Colbert Dennis, Howard and John Scott, Lila Dennis and Edmund Dennis, and Charles, Elizabeth, and James Crowner, who also attended the Columbia Beach School. Some of James Crowner's classmates were Marion Nick, Jerome Nick, Bill Scott, and Ira and Julius Dennis. Josephine Tongue, born November 7, 1907, stated in a 1984 interview that she went to school on Columbia Beach corner with Parker, Angie, and Myrtle Thompson, Julius Dennis, and Thelma and Mary Wells. She remembered that her teacher was Mrs. Jackson and there was also a male teacher. Varnell Nick remembered a teacher named Mr. Lane Mitchell.

In a 1987 interview, Julius Dennis reported that he attended the school in about 1903 and remembered his teacher was Miss Mamie Houston. One teacher separated the children's play areas, with the girls playing on one side of the whitewashed school and boys on the other. At the end of the school day, the girls marched out in a line first, and the boys' line followed. Children were assigned homework and were allowed to take books home.

Sarah Scott Matthews started school in 1907 and recalled that her teachers were Miss Midella, Mr. Lane, and Mrs. Holmes. She remembered that the teacher and pupils kept the fire going in the stove so that the classroom was always warm. There was a blackboard that the teacher used—and students rarely used it. Some pupils had their own slates and slate pencil, but Sarah used pencil and paper for her work. Some of her classmates were Myrtle and Margie Thompson, Seama Dennis, Pearl Wells, Daisy and Gladys Scott, Walter and Joe Matthews, and Talmadge Brown.

Hilda Holland attended the Columbia Beach School briefly, but she switched to the Churchton elementary school nearer her home. Mrs. Lula G. Scott was her teacher and required every pupil to say "Good morning" when entering the school and "Good afternoon" when leaving school for home.

When Columbia Beach School was replaced, a new two-room Rosenwald school was built in the 1920s across from St. Matthew's Church on land purchased from John T. Turner, according to one source. Charles Coates, Sr., reported in a 1984 interview that his father bought an acre from a Mrs. Alton, who also sold property to the school.

Three generations of the Chesterfield Coates family have maintained that eye-catching property across from the fire department. Although Chesterfield's grandson Chuckie and Joanne Coates built a new home behind the original home that was torn down, they have kept alive the tradition of neatness and abundant flowers.

Charles Coates, Sr., said that his father was a "lawn hen." "People said he cut the grass so low that you couldn't see one piece sticking up." Chesterfield Coates was awarded the Good Housekeeping award from the Kiwanis Club for having the best-kept lawn and the best-kept house in Shady Side. Charles, Sr., said that his father used a push lawnmower and then got down on his knees with a pair of scissors to trim. Like grandfather, father, and now son, the tradition of an immaculate lawn continues, but the present Mr. Coates passed on the push lawnmower and scissors and hired a lawn service.

CHAPTER 5

BOARDING HOUSES AND POST OFFICES

S HADY SIDE DID NOT become an official village until 1889, when a post office was established in the community. Early census records and maps show that post offices often changed for "The Great Swamp," as peninsula inhabitants called the area. Sometimes the village was referred to as Sedge Field because of a type of grass that grew in the area. One source said that an area of the swamp where youngsters played baseball every Saturday afternoon was called the Sedgefield.[1]

In 1860 the post office was in Tracey's Landing. In 1870 it was listed as South River Post Office on the census, as it was in the Hopkins Atlas of 1878. A little later the mail from Annapolis ended at Sudley, and a carrier took the mail as far as Churchton. People beyond Churchton had to pick up their own mail, and maybe a neighbor's mail, by horse or boat.

The road leading into Sedgefield could be arduous for the traveler. Often it was muddy and difficult for carriages and wagons to drive on, but that did not stop the population from increasing. Newcomers began purchasing land as larger holdings were broken apart. It has been suggested that early residents were attracted to the Shady Side peninsula because the land was free of underbrush and good for growing wheat.

However, the fertility of the soil gave out and land prices dropped. This gave tenant families an opportunity to buy land of their own. During this period, the Pranns, Matthewses, Scotts, Nicks, Grosses, and Crowners purchased land.[2]

Over a hundred years ago, in the 1880s and 1890s, nearly everyone in the village took in boarders, but none on the scale of the Rural Home. Charlie Hartge's boarding house was further up the West River, not far from where the steamboats docked. Edie Hartge's, Danes (on the Bay) in Idlewilde, Nowells' on Curtis Point, and Sam Parrott's property, named "Shady Side Farm" down on Columbia Beach Road, were also hotel destinations.

"Although her business wasn't like the white boarding houses," said Varnell Nick, "Helen Dennis and her daughter Matiel Dennis Carter ran a boarding house for colored people." Actually, there were two boarding houses for blacks: one facing Parrish Creek on the southwest corner of Atwell Road, and the more well known one on the corner of Shady Rest Road across from the present-day fire department. Both houses are now family homes. When asked about black boarding houses, Woody Avery named these two boarding houses and added that people might also stay "almost like in a home where the rest of the family was."

Charles Coates, Sr., spoke about Rachel Francis, a teacher from Baltimore who had gone to college before he did. She would come down to stay at the Shady Rest Boarding House run by Matiel Carter and husband James Carter, called Jimmy, "who ran a boarding house for Negroes." Their house was not on the Bay, but Matiel's father, Alex Dennis, lived on the water, so he gave their guests boat rides every day. "The people left the boarding house and went down to her father's boat in the '30s, and he took them out for a boat ride including fishing. They just went on boat rides because Parrish Creek was muddy and you couldn't go swimming in the mud."

Alexander Dennis married Helen Chew in Baltimore on September 23, 1888, and Matiel Dennis married James Carter in Annapolis on

August 17,1914, according to marriage certificates belonging to their descendent Irma Dennis Lashley, who visited Shady Side relatives. (Two additional Alexander Dennis records appear in later chapters.)

Miss Matiel held "dances in a room off the back of her house, and people danced the two-step," remembered Varnell Nick. Florine Thompson remembered the dances at the Shady Rest Boarding House. There was no liquor, but there was food, sodas, and music inside and out. "Every year at carnival time there was a Ferris wheel in her front yard."

Charles Coates, Sr., talked about Saturday night dances at the dancing pavilion at the Shady Rest House. "The music was supplied by Aaron Ballard, the Ballard brothers. Aaron Ballard played the piano, John Fountain the guitar, or banjo they called it then, and somebody else played the saxophone. They played from 8 until 12. People would come in and pay 25 cents. I spent many a night over there at the dance, 'cause I loved to dance." Later, Matiel moved down on the wharf and charged $12 a week for room and board.

Charles Coates's wife, Kathleen, spoke about "the large house right here joining our property, and then she moved from here and built up the house down there and moved to that boarding house on the water. She ran a boarding house for 30 or 40 years."

However, there was a problem for all of the boarding houses in the late 1800s, and Sam Parrott wanted to do something about it. He was so busy feeding and entertaining his guests that the four-mile trip on the treacherous road to Churchton to retrieve mail for his guests was a worry worth resolving. The U.S. Post Office Department required proof that there was a true need for mail service to the peninsula, so in 1888 every piece of mail had to be counted daily and carried free for a nine-month trial period. The first local storekeeper Mr. Parrott asked to get the mail for the peninsula turned him down, so Mr. Parrott asked Robert Nowell. Not only did he agree to get the mail daily, but he would also do it for free by sending his son and daughter in a road cart hitched to their horses, Old Bert or Queen. The children carried the mail, and their mail pick-up point was a seven-foot high, three-by-four-foot area in the back of their father's grocery store.

The Post Office Department also requested a name for the post office, so three names were suggested: Parrott, Parrish Creek, and Shady Side. The department chose the place name over a family name and the more limiting name of Parrish Creek. Since the volume of mail justified having a post office, Shady Side—two words—replaced "Sedgefield" or "The Swamp" on maps. (An invisible postal line slices through the West River and South Creek along to slightly north of Dent Road to separate Shady Side from a not so obvious break with Churchton.)

The first Shady Side Post Office was in Nowell's Rural Home, and Miss F. Ethel Nowell's father was the first postmaster. The boarding business grew so much that they soon erected a new building situated on the corner across the road from the hotel and facing Woods Wharf Road. The post office was moved to the store. The hotel faced the store's side, and Snug Harbor Road ran between the two buildings. Since no one wanted to take the examination to be the postmaster, Miss Ethel did so and became the postmaster in 1916. In 1918 Miss Ethel married and continued as postmaster as Mrs. Ethel Andrews. She kept the position until 1946 when she could no longer do the job for eight hours a day and teach school. When the store burned down, the post office was moved for a short period to a house on Snug Harbor Road that is now the Sailmender's shop (established 1985). Next, the post office was housed in the gray building on Shady Side Road across from Hawthorne Street. Finally, the post office that is in operation today opened in the brick building, owned by Mr. Mohan Grover, at the southwest corner of Shady Side Road and West River Roads, where Edy R. Justiniano has been postmaster since 2003.

Standing at the present curve for Woods Wharf and Snug Harbor Roads, one had this view of dirt roads, the Post Office (left part of building) and Nowell's store (right part), and walkers (right) of the store. The Rural Home, later Andrews Hotel (right behind fence), and at the end of the road is the hidden right angle of Snug Harbor Road. Owing's store faces the curve to the right of the pole. **Captain Avery Museum Collection**

Between Miss Ethel and Edy Justiniano, the postmasters were Miss Dorothy Phipps (1946-1972), Wallace Guyot (1973-1992), and James Thomas Smith, beginning in 1993. Where dates do not overlap, an officer-in-charge served until a postmaster was assigned.

Salesmen from Annapolis who came to the peninsula to deliver supplies for the storeowners stayed overnight in someone's home and returned with their carriage or wagon and horse the next day. Robert Nowell and his wife, Anna Kirchner Nowell, ran a general store, which was part of their three-story home built in 1884. They were already accommodating salesmen and overnight strangers, so they agreed to board a lady from Baltimore for her two-week summer vacation. The Nowells' positive response to the woman's request was the beginning of the Rural Home. Additional bedrooms, a dining room, porches, and still more buildings were built until it became "the biggest place in Shady Side," according to Purnell Crowner, quoted in 1991. Flora Ethel Andrews (Miss Ethel, 1888-1997) and her husband, Alexander Willard Andrews, purchased the Rural Home from her parents in 1932 and renamed it the Andrews Hotel.

John (Ramon) Fountain remembered as a boy standing outside Swinburn's drug store and watching people play tennis on the Andrews Hotel courts across the road. "If the ball went in the bushes, I'd get it to throw back, and sometimes they would say to keep it."

Vacationers came to Shady Side to spend their summers, or part of the summer, at the boarding houses that catered to folks wanting to get away from hot city life. Boarders, both black and white, would arrive on the *Emma Giles* soon after public schools were out, and some might stay until it was time for school to begin again. Others would stay by the week. Some husbands and fathers went back and forth on the *Emma Giles* to spend some days with their family. When the *Giles* began coming on Saturdays, another travel day was an option. The word "weekend" wasn't a term that was used until about 1918, according to Miss Ethel in her book *Miss Ethel Remembers*.

In the earliest days, boarders could expect a bedroom for sleeping and privacy, a pitcher and bowl of water with some towels, and, hopefully, a chamber pot for the night. Privies were always available outside. Flies and mosquitoes were a given, so hand fans and mosquito netting were used in bedrooms and dining areas. Oil lamps might be available for the bedroom, although they presented an undesirable maintenance and cleaning task. Candles were another possibility. Water was brought up from a well by a hand pump. Refrigeration was not expected—there was none until 1910. People kept foods that spoiled easily, such as milk or butter, in 50-pound lard cans hanging down in their wells or put them in covered crocks on flat stones in moving cold water. During the frozen winter months, men cut ice from three freshwater ponds in present-day Cedarhurst (they are now gone due to drainage). The chunks, which were never used for drinking or cooking, were kept in a deep hole lined with wood or logs, and the ice was covered in sawdust to preserve it. It could also be kept in an icehouse designed similarly for such a purpose.

In 1888, when the Rural Home opened, one could expect to pay $3 a person weekly for a room, three hearty meals a day, and all activities. These activities could include parlor games, piano playing and singing, reading, socializing with other guests, walking along dusty roads, dancing, attending parties at other large boarding houses, swimming, and daily boating opportunities. Sea nettles, or jellyfish, were present, but guests who were stung could either rub a handful of sand on the sting and keep going or call it a day and wait for the sting to subside. After World War I, guests were paying $7 a week, and in 1932, the renamed Andrews Hotel charged $9 per week. Sold in 1967, the hotel was then charging $40 a week.

Leaving the Andrews Hotel, bathers approach a wooded path leading to Parrish Creek for a boat ride to a swimming point. **Glen Trott Collection**

The larger boarding houses needed plenty of extra help besides the immediate family members to prepare and serve the many meals, keep the household running, and transport and entertain the guests. This provided summer jobs for people in the local community, and these jobs were filled mostly by black women. At the Andrews Hotel, Grace Hicks worked as a cook with Miss Missouri Scott and Carrie Nick in the kitchen, and Fanny Davis, Eugenia Nick Gross, Susie Gross, Ethel Scott Gross, Christolyne Scott, Thelma and Jean Matthews, Pauline Gross, and Moa Scott worked as waitresses. Jimmy Nick, his son Tommy Nick, and George Thompson also worked summers at the hotel.

Tommy Nick, dressed in his overalls for work in 1936, stands outside the Andrews Hotel. Written on the back of the picture was "Tommy Nick-helper par-excellent." He and the Andrew's son, Derwill, remained good friends into their late 80s. Jimmy Nick killed, plucked, and cleaned 50 chickens for the famous Sunday dinners. He then cranked a three-gallon freezer to make ice cream. Miss Ethel recorded that Sellman Scott helped relieve them of the worst problem they had in operating the hotel: disposing of garbage. He arrived daily with his horse and wagon to haul it away. **Captain Avery Museum Collection**

In *Miss Ethel Remembers*, Miss Ethel wrote about Carrie Wells Nick, who worked year round at the Andrews Hotel. It was not unusual to have a hundred guests needing to be fed, and Carrie Nick, starting in 1930, spent 40 years working at the hotel: "no matter how difficult the task or the amount of time required to accomplish it, [never] did I see her frown or hear an angry word. Never."

As a child, Carrie went to work with her mother, Martha Scott Wells Briscoe, when she worked at the hotel for Miss Ethel's mother, Anna Kirchner Nowell. Carrie watched and learned from her mother. Many years later, Carrie took her youngest granddaughter, Carla (Nick Gross), to work so Carla could play with Miss Ethel's granddaughter, Jackie (Andrews Grace).

Throughout the year, Jackie and her parents, Derwill and Anita Andrews, often drove down from their Annapolis home to visit. The Andrews Hotel was home for her Andrews grandparents and Aunt Glorious and Uncle Howard Shenton until the Shentons moved to their new West Shady Side Road home in 1958.

Miss Carrie worked year round for the Andrewses. In the off-season months, she was their housekeeper, which included ironing and cooking for the Andrews and Shenton families. Miss Ethel wrote: "Dear, dear Carrie Nick. She was a part of our family for 40 years, and we just could not have made it without her. Glorious declares her the greatest person she has ever known and the best friend she ever had."

Miss Carrie Nick in her apron near the Andrews Hotel in August of 1957,
"The greatest person I have ever known and the best friend I ever had,"
reported Glorious Andrews Shenton. **Miss Carla Nick Gross Collection**

Jackie said that Carrie was like a grandmother to her. Her own nana was busy running the business end, so Jackie would turn to Carrie. "I absolutely loved Carrie Nick. She would ask me, 'Are you hungry, Baby?' and then fix me my own pancakes in the big cast iron skillet in the big kitchen. She was the head cook and an absolutely brilliant woman. Today, she would be the head chef in a wonderful restaurant somewhere."

Miss Carrie's and Miss Ethel's granddaughters were about five when they first started playing together. "The hotel was a wonderful place to play because you could explore all of the rooms. The best room was Nana and G-Dad's dressing room, because there were all of these old clothes and Nana's wonderful hats—they never threw anything away. We'd get under the clothes to hide and tell stories." Depending on the time of the year, if there weren't any guests, the girls played hide-and-go-seek in the guest rooms. "We'd play on the swings, the woodpile, or take the kittens that were always around and play in the barn. In the barn G-Dad, A. W. Andrews, dried mud from the river or Parrish Creek to make his Alive-O fertilizer." He started the Maryland Bay Soil and Fertilizer Company around the 1950s. The dried pulverized mud took on a smoky, silky texture that didn't smell as bad as when it was wet. "He put it in cans with a white label with red lettering and tried to market it, but it didn't ever take off well. I used it on my garden in Annapolis." Backyard Boats now owns the barn, which is used for boats and sits back from Woods Wharf Road across from the boatyard. Some parts of the barn were covered with metal plates like the plates older watermen used to protect their boats from the ice.

As a youngster, Jackie Andrews Grace liked to leave the hotel and walk the trodden dirt path through some trees to cross over Woods Wharf Road and go crabbing with her crab string and chicken neck off the pier behind the Sheckells' property. She was too young to know anything about the measurement laws that governed crabbing, so she wound up catching some undersized crabs on her line. Back with her catch, Jackie asked Carrie to steam the small crabs to eat. Carrie teased, "Ah, chile, your Uncle Howard is gonna put you in jail." Jackie's Uncle Howard was a marine police officer for the Department of Natural Resources. Jackie laughed when she told this story. "I was scared to death because I'd heard people say he'd arrest his own mother. Well, of course, he didn't have a mother, but he would if she did something against the law. He upheld the law and had a reputation for being fair." (Howard was just a young child when his mother died. His father remarried, but the new wife would not accept the children, so Howard was brought to Shady Side at age 10 to live and work with a local family.)

"Guests came down from Baltimore, Washington, or wherever for a week, two weeks, or more. Sunday was the big dinner with chicken and crab cakes." After the meal the women washed the dishes in the big, deep sinks that were in the back of the house in a long narrow room off of the kitchen and facing the field. It could get unmercifully hot working over the steaming water. Fortunately, there were windows above the sinks. The women would sing as they washed, dried, and stacked the dishes on the counter on the opposite side of the narrow room. "I imagine I was underfoot at times, but they were always so warm, patient, and loving to me," said Jackie Grace.

Miss Carrie made delicious apple pies, and her crab cakes were reputed to be the best anywhere. Carla told about her grandmother preparing and baking custard in individual custard dishes and making bread pudding in large pans to then spoon in smaller serving dishes. She made her own bread dough for sticky buns, then rolled the dough out in a big rectangle and smeared it with about a quarter inch of soft butter, sprinkling it with brown sugar, and rolling up the dough from the long end first; then she would cut them in sections and put them on big pans to bake. The swirls would caramelize and were so good. For a treat Carrie made fried bread for Jackie by pulling off some dough and frying it in lard and then putting butter on it. "There is nothing better in the whole world. I can still smell and taste it," recalled Jackie. Sweet potato pies were another specialty, according to Carrie's granddaughter Connie, and "the best lemon meringue pie." "And baked beans from scratch," Connie's sister Delores chimed in.

Although many people remember seeing Carrie walking to work, Carla's oldest sister, Delores Nick Harley, remembered riding in the Andrews's car to go with her grandmother to work at the hotel about 10 years before Carla started going. Jackie Grace remembered her grandfather driving Miss Carrie home. "I played when I was five or six, but when I was older I helped with food preparation, did some serving, but I never cooked," remembered Delores. "I earned my first money working at the Andrews Hotel." The kitchen was screened in when Delores was there but enclosed with windows later.

Connie Nick, seven years older than Carla, remembered helping her grandmother Carrie make up the bedrooms: "That's how I learned how to fold up the sheets and tuck them in at the end. I learned that from my grandmother." The sisters said that it was a treat to go with their grandmother, but none of them went at the same time because they were spaced out in age. They each had a time and season of their own being at the hotel with Grandma Carrie.

Jean Matthews Johnson recalled the days when she worked in the hotel dining room. As a 14- or 15-year-old, she and her friend Pauline walked to the hotel and asked if they could have a job. They were hired on the spot to be waitresses. The girls walked from either Scott Town or West River Road early enough to serve breakfast at 8 o'clock. Many times they walked home from work in the dark, but they never walked alone because they traded off spending the night in each other's homes. "We were buddies all the way through high school."

Tables were set for parties of two, twelve, or twenty-four. "She wasn't kin but we all called her Cousin Carrie, and we loved her. We would cut up and tease her all the time. The 'hired girls' usually waited on the smaller tables, and Cousin Carrie waited on the big tables. When her group would come in, she would want to give her group the best of everything, so she would take the best of something and hide it in the oven. We'd see her put it in there, so when she'd leave we'd go get it and serve it to our people. She'd come back to the oven and say, 'Oh, where's my food?' and we'd be back in the room cracking up because we'd already served it!" At this point in the telling Jean was chuckling and said, "That was the funniest part. We'd watch where she would hide her pies and things and we'd serve those, too."

"Miss Carrie was the head cook," Jean continued, "but she had a lot of help from Little Grace, Miss Mary, Miss Missouri, and even the men and things: Mr. Jimmy and Tom Peek. Missouri Scott Davis worked as a helper with the cooking. I liked waiting on tables, and we really had a nice time, Pauline, Christolyne, and I."

Jean's mother, Sarah Matthews, had worked as a chambermaid at the Andrews Hotel and at Weems Boarding House, helping her father wait on tables when she was young. Her father also worked on the farm during the summer.

After breakfast was over, the waitresses would clean up, wash and dry the dishes, and then it would be time to serve lunch. After lunch the routine was repeated and again at dinnertime. The workers might eat something in between, but they never sat down to indulge. Many returning guests chose to sit at the same waitresses' tables, and the atmosphere was always very friendly. Tips of $4 or $5 would be given at the end when people checked out of the hotel.

Sometimes the waitresses would have enough time to go clean Miss Ethel's brother John Nowell's rooms across from the hotel or do some other cleaning. "There was always something going on." Hattie Nick, who was also a midwife, worked at the hotel as one of the maids. When the hotel was overloaded, guests were given rooms above the post office. Supposedly there were 13 bedrooms over the post office, and the first telephone was installed there.

There were two groups of boarders taking boats from Parrish Creek to enjoy recreation on the river. Asked if the white hotel people waved to blacks when both were on Parrish Creek, the black person's answer was: "No, in segregated times whites did not socialize with black people. Whites would not bother with blacks. Even when a black person worked for a white person, the black person was paid and sent home with only minimum conversation."

★   ★   ★

Sailing vessels carried goods to and from the West River because the road was difficult to travel in the 1830s, and the water was the quickest way to reach the peninsula. Because Baltimore had become a major industrial city, especially for canning and then shipping goods by railroad, local oyster packinghouses wanted to send hogsheads of shucked oysters and picked crabmeat to market. Refrigeration hadn't been invented yet, so speedy delivery to the canning factories was imperative to prevent spoilage. Moving locally grown produce or animals to market was prohibitively expensive. Mass transit was unknown and cars years away, so people did not travel great distances. Steamboats were the perfect answer for these needs. A steamboat, the *Maryland,* was the first to arrive in the West River in 1832. The Maryland Steamboat Company increased the *Maryland's* trips to the West River and provided passengers with a more reliable way to travel. She also made a stop in the Rhode River.

The most beloved steamboat was the beautiful *Emma Giles,* which traveled the Rhode and West Rivers every Monday, Wednesday, and Friday beginning in 1891; she made five trips a week in the 1930s but stopped service in 1932. Owned by the Tolchester Company, she was a side-wheeler with a carving of a beehive on her paddle boxes. Everyone—black, white, adult, child, and dog—wanted to be at the piers to watch the loading and unloading of the *Emma Giles,* to see for themselves who and what were arriving and then, perhaps less interesting, what people and things were carried away. One item that arrived by steamboat can be seen at the Captain Avery Museum. It is a lady's desk that was purchased at the Larkin Furniture Company in Baltimore with Larkin Stamps (reminiscent of the more familiar "green stamps"). A shipping label is on the back of the desk. There is no verification that it came on the *Emma Giles,* but it is remembered as so.

The beloved and popular steamboat, "The Emma Giles," prepares to depart from the Galesville pier. **Captain Avery Museum Collection.**

The sounds of steam and whistle, the churning water, the size of the steamer, the bustle and excited calls to one another, and the energy of the workers unloading or loading never failed to entertain. Charles Coates, Sr., said that he and a friend walked two hours from Shady Side to Galesville port, "which was four and a half miles," and two hours back to see the *Emma Giles.* "We weren't in any hurry. We left, had plenty of time to go, and we had plenty of time to come back." Today's plane travel doesn't touch the wonder and splendor of the *Emma Giles.* It should be noted that black travelers had to stay on the boat's decks and were not allowed inside to more desirable areas.

Josephine Tongue recalled riding on the *Emma Giles* to Baltimore with her mother. She remembered thinking as a child how wonderful it was to be in the middle of the water. One of her aunts would come down from Philadelphia on the *Emma Giles,* and they met her at the wharf in Shady Side. The oldest person she remembered was "Mr. Wattie Prann, who lived down near Idlewilde."

Sarah Scott Matthews and other family members took the *Emma Giles* to Baltimore. She remembered leaving in the morning and arriving in the afternoon.

Other smaller powered boats made trips between Shady Side and Annapolis, including the *Mary M.*, the *West River*, the *Ercliffe*, the *Severn*, the *James Benson*, and the *Shady Side*. One boat owner reported that he transported 275 people on one Saturday.[3] However, as private automobiles became more common in the 1930s, the boats ceased to run.

"I think Mr. Wagner, who lived in Washington, bought the first car in Shady Side. After that it wasn't too long before [there were] different cars . . . . I don't remember who," Mr. Nick recalled. Several people remembered that Mr. Jim Crowner was one of the earliest car owners.

"Squeeze Brown and Earl Gross were young children down in the "bogs" at the turn for the Brown's home. They were playing near the dirt road, which had plenty of dust, when they looked up and saw something coming down the road. It was blowing a horn—a sound they recognized—but all they saw was a horseless carriage. It frightened them, so they ran in the house. This was the first car they had seen in the Shady Side area, and it was quite a sight!

In the 1920s, a Shady Side civic group, organized by Mr. and Mrs. Alexander Andrews (Miss Ethel), began holding summer carnivals in the woods next to Centenary Church (where the fire department now is). The objective was to raise money for hard surfacing the muddy, impossible roads. The county matched the $5,000 cleared by the carnival, and the county began hard-surfacing Shady Side Road.[4] Viable roads in turn encouraged vacationers and spurred the development of new residential areas in Shady Side. Before the Bay Bridge was built, Shady Side was a practical family summer destination, because the long wait and a ferry ride to the Eastern Shore could be avoided. But with the bridge, the Eastern Shore was an easier possibility, and that brought about the decline of the boarding house trade.

CHAPTER 6

NICK FAMILIES

Delores Nick Harley, Connie Nick, and Carla Nick Gross, granddaughters of Carrie Nick, shared memories of their grandparents, Jerome and Carrie Nick, one Sunday afternoon in 2009 after church at Carla's Shady Side home. Carrie Wells Nick (1893-1988), a cook and housekeeper, and her husband, Jerome (1888-1967), a carpenter, farmer, and waterman, lived in the triangle between the curve of Shady Side Road and Bay Breeze Road that connects to Columbia Beach Road.

Carrie and Jerome Nick sit in the kitchen of their home. His granddaughters remarked that their grandfather Nick always wore dark glasses.
Connie Nick Collection

Most people in Shady Side, black and white, knew about Miss Carrie Nick through her renown as the head cook at the Andrews Hotel. Ethel Andrews referred to her in her book and left no doubt that Miss Carrie was respected and beloved by the Andrews family. She also did not hesitate to give credit to Miss Carrie and the people who worked at the hotel for making the hotel experience desirable for vacationers. Miss Carrie's fried chicken, crab cakes, coleslaw, rolls, and desserts were huge attractions.

Because of Ethel Andrews's book and Virginia Fitz's book, a desire arose to know more about black citizens of the Shady Side community in the earlier years. One question was: How were people like Miss Carrie living their lives when they were not visible working for white people—or "out of sight, out of mind" of the white inhabitants?

Miss Carrie's son, Leonard Nick (1914-1987), was the first and only surviving child of Jerome and Carrie Wells Nick. Their younger daughter, Minerva, died as a teenager. Leonard married Eunice Violet Holland, daughter of George and Gladys Gross Holland, of Shady Side. They gave the senior Nicks four grandsons and four granddaughters, and the grandparents actively participated in their lives. Three of their six surviving grandchildren reside in Shady Side.

Delores said that she spent every weekend with her grandmother Carrie when she was little. When she was about five, her grandmother bought her a white fur coat with a little matching muff. She always shopped on Church Circle in Annapolis and bought the top of the line. "She wanted me to get my ears pierced, and they're still not pierced," said Delores. "She had an old treadle machine and made petticoats for us," added Connie. She made Delores a brown and gold checked dress suit when Delores was about 30. "She was an industrious person because she worked every day and still made things for us at home." If their parents went someplace, the children stayed with either set of their grandparents. Grandma Carrie bought a bicycle for Delores, and it was handed down to Connie.

Carla remembered that her grandmother had a way of opening things, and on one particular occasion she opened a box of pepper or salt and tore the top. "She had me go over to Swinburn's to buy a new box because she didn't want to put a torn box in Miss Ethel's kitchen. She took the torn one home."

All three granddaughters remembered when some hot grease spilled onto Miss Carrie's ankles, probably when she was frying chicken at the hotel, they imagined, and she tried to doctor it herself. She wrapped rags around her ankles, kept her working schedule, and wound up with an infection. "She was a tough lady. She worked until she was 80. She worked for a woman who moved, and Miss Carrie rode up to Annapolis with Mr. Frank Tongue to work for the woman on Fridays. She walked to work for people in Shady Side."

Carla remembered that during the winter when the snow came, she and her siblings bundled up and walked to grandmother Carrie's house, "And when we'd hit the door she'd go, 'OO! OO! You all liking that snow!'"

For several years, the Kiwanis Club had an annual function where oyster dinners were sold, and Connie, as a teenager, went with her grandma Carrie to fry oyster puffs. Miss Carrie made the batter for dipping a whole oyster. Using a spoon, Connie dropped the coated oyster into hot grease and lifted it out once it was browned, ready for serving. "Her batter was a little heavier than the McCormick's I use today, the quick way," said Carla.

"Our grandmother was one of the first black people in town to have electricity and a TV," reported Connie, "so we would go to her house to watch the westerns like Gene Autry and Roy Rogers." By the time Carla came along, their parents had a TV. "Grandma Carrie didn't have a phone until I moved in, and she didn't want one, but then she thought it was better than sliced bread," laughed Connie.

There were often daytrip bus excursions that the local black community would take during the year, including to the York,

Pennsylvania Fair, to Frederick, and to Atlantic City. Miss Carrie loved to go on those trips, and she took Carla with her to the York Fair.

"Our granddaddy was laid back, and he always wore dark glasses, even in the house. He did oystering in the winter and crabbing and farming in the summer. He was a local lay preacher down at St. Matthew's. He wasn't ordained, but he would preach from the pulpit. They always had a big Bible on a stand at home. They had a friend, Mr. Pinkney, and the Pinkneys would always come to the house on a weekly basis, and they'd get their religion on. Grandmother Carrie was communion steward for 20 years or so at St. Matthew's," said Connie.

"I helped Granddaddy plant tobacco when I was a pre-teen," said Delores. "I was young enough to consider it fun at that time. He'd plow the fields, and then I would come along behind and drop the plants in the holes that he had made, and I'd pull the dirt up around the tobacco plant. He had a horse, but I don't remember if he used it or the tractor then. He'd plant the tobacco from the point of the triangle up to the house and then plant on the other side of the house. After he cured it, he sold the tobacco."

"We'd go crabbing down at the end of West River Road," continued Delores. Being the second oldest grandchild, she had the opportunity to do more things with her granddaddy. "We'd use a trot line." Carla, the youngest interjected, "Not me. I'd just play with the crabs in the driveway and play with them 'til their legs fell off or they died, . . . but we wouldn't eat those." Carla, like her sisters, knew how to handle crabs as a little girl, so she never got pinched or wore rubber gloves. "If we drop one, we know how to put our foot down on it to pick it up. You put your foot on the back of the shell and grab it from behind on that back fin and he can't get to you. You just chuck 'em in the pot."

Leonard followed in his father's footsteps of oystering in the winter, carpentry in the summer, but he did no farming other than his large garden. The last 20 years of his life, Leonard built homes in Shady Side. He built the foyer addition at St. Matthew's church. Two of his homes, owned by John Fountain and Daisy Thompson, sit side by side on Cedarhurst Road. He also built Jean Matthews's house on Shady Side Road. Asked if she still had anything that her father made, Delores thoughtfully replied, "Well, he built my house [in Lothian] for me." His sons, Ernest Nick and Nelson Nick, followed their father in the carpentry tradition, and both still live in Shady Side with their spouses.

Just arriving from church, Leonard Nick smiles for the camera. A carpenter and builder, he built several homes that are in Shady Side. His sons, Nelson and Ernest Nick, followed him into the carpentry business and they still reside in Shady Side. **Connie Nick Collection**

"Our oldest brother, Ernest, moved in with Grandma Carrie when he was in the sixth grade and loved it. When he got married, they lived with her for a while and [then] moved out. Later another brother married and lived with her for about three years, and then I [Connie] lived with her from 1969 until she got sick and had to go into a nursing home."

Every two weeks, Leonard drove to Annapolis to get his mother for home visits until she died at age 95, shortly after surgery to amputate her leg. He, her grandchildren, and her great-grandchildren faithfully visited her at the nursing home. "For her ninetieth birthday we took her a birthday cake with trick candles that wouldn't blow out. She kept blowing, and we kept laughing," Carla smiled.

Looking Back

Jerome Nick (1888-1967), father of Leonard, was the oldest son of William "Bill" (1860-19-?) and Hattie Taylor Nick (1864-19-?). Married on April 25, 1886, they had ten children, eight of whom, six boys and two girls, survived into adulthood. Jerome's brothers were Marion (1892-1978); William G. or "Uncle Flump" (1896-1970); Glover or "Uncle Calley" (1900-1982); and Varnell (1906-1987), who was interviewed for the Captain Avery Museum library.

Discussing her great-uncles, Delores Harley remembered them as watermen, farmers, and craftsmen, but she did not recall much about her great-aunts. She thought that they probably left town in their mid—to late teens to find work in Baltimore, Philadelphia, or New Jersey, where the women then settled. Very few came back except to visit. The women who stayed tended to marry local men.

Nick men served in the United States military over many generations. Jerome's name appeared on the 1917-18 World War I registries, and he was drafted into the Army in 1942 to serve in World War II.

Before the present main road entering Shady Side was cut, the original road ran along Nick's Road, curved right on Scott Town Road, continued on Columbia Beach Road, and curved left on Bay Breeze, back to the main road. Marion Nick, brother of Jerome, and fourth child and second son of William "Bill" and Hattie Nick, owned the property where today's road is; part of his property was cut off with the making of the road. It is not known if he received any compensation for the loss of land, as property owners did when the county widened Shady Side Road around 2005. Jerome Nick's property was on the east end of Nick Road, where family members still reside.

A waterman, Marion married Irenia Gross Nick (b. 1895) in 1914. Their children were: Alverta or "Bert" (b. 1915), Elnathan or "Brother" (1916-1998), John H. (1918-1987), Earl or "Billy" (1919-1988), James or "Tookie" (1922-1984), William G. or "Piggy" (1925-2008), Marshall (1926), Mary (1928-2009), Herman or "Uncle Green" (b. 1930), Virginia (b. 1932), and Rosetta (b. 1934). Five of their seven sons were drafted and served in the military during World War II: one was in the Navy and the others were in the Army. Elnathan and John, the older sons, were not called. Marshall served stateside in the quartermaster service for two years until the war ended. He was sent to Korea for his last year.

As Marion Nick's children, they were allowed to go out and play, going house to house. There were no telephones to call the children home, so parents just hollered outside, and the children came. "If someone saw you doing something that you wasn't supposed to do, you'd get a double one because they would correct you also," said Marshall Nick. His family lived in the upper part of Columbia Beach Road. The families closest to them were the Brooks and Matthews families.

"My father was very much interested in transportation for others and always had a concern for other people," said Marshall. This fact was also reported in Philip Brown's book, *A Century of "Separate but Equal" Education in Anne Arundel County*. It described Marion's idea of providing school transportation to Wiley H. Bates High School in Annapolis. In 1933 Marion made a bus out of a car and a truck and started carrying passengers to school. Charles G. Coates, who rode the bus for his first three years at Bates for 50 cents a day, called it a "Chevy bus." The bus had no heat. In the meantime, white children rode to Lothian for school in Mr. Seagar's bus, paid for by the county, while the parents of black children paid out of their pockets for their children's transportation—sometimes with food or produce or maybe not at all. The Depression years made money scarce.

Once the county provided buses for blacks to attend high school in 1937, they rode in the older buses that had carried the white students. Marion Nick then drove the bus provided by the county and wound up having his future daughter-in-law and her sisters among his riders. Several former Bates students told stories of how some other bus drivers made kids get off the bus for bad behavior and left them at the side of the road. The student who had crossed the line was on his or her own to hitch a ride to school or back home.

Transportation for others was Marion Nick's business. If someone needed to get to Annapolis, Baltimore, or some other location for a doctor's appointment or to the hospital, he drove him in his car. One of his early cars in the 1930s had a snap-on curtain top. He made trips to town on Saturdays, and customers called to reserve a seat on the bus.

Marion Nick was a strong Christian and a spiritual man for as long as his granddaughter June Smith could remember. "He was always talking about the Bible, and that was the last thing I wanted to talk about then." When she went to his house in the evening, he would be sitting in his chair with the Bible beside him on a table. He asked her, "Do you know what I was reading? Well, just let me tell you this, . . ." and he would start reading to her. Or he might ask if she had heard about John and proceed to tell her all the people who were connected to this John, and by the time he had finished, she did know someone who knew John. "He was always sharing the Bible. In his later years he drove to Annapolis to stand on a corner and discuss The Word." When he could no longer drive himself, he would catch a ride with someone, so he could continue this practice. "My father called him Old Man and said that if Old Man didn't stop worrying people to death somebody was going to knock him in the head one day if he wasn't careful. Times were beginning to get rough."

Marion Nick, failing in health, continued traveling to Annapolis as long as the family would let him. He lived to be 86. Proverbs 22: 6 states, "Train up a child in the way he should go and when he is old he will not depart from it." Third and fourth generations of the Nick family are examples of his teachings.

Henry and Rhoda Nick's Sons in Shady Side

According to the searches made by June Nick Smith, the earliest known Nicks living in the area were Henry, born in 1820, a farmer, and Rhoda Nick, born in 1822, a housewife. They were parents of ten children, six boys and four girls. Two brothers—John, born between 1840-1850, and William, born around 1860-1862—were the ancestors of the two Nick family lines residing in Shady Side today.

John Nick and his first wife, Mary, lived in Sudley. His children were William (b. 1883), Eugie (b. 1883), Eva (b. 1884), Herman (b. 1889), Annie (b. 1890), Emma (b. 1892), Louisa (b. 1893), and Votus (b. 1894). When Mary died, John married Rachel Brown of the Churchton-Shady Side area. According to research recorded by great-granddaughter Carmelia Nick Hicks, by 1923 all of the offspring had moved to Baltimore except for daughter Annie. At some point John purchased land from the Averys. John Nick's house had a white picket fence and stood behind St. Matthews' present-day graveyard. He gave land for this graveyard as well as a second parcel including the Nick burial ground with seven graves. The site was located beside Shady Side Road in front of Centenary United Methodist Church and was leveled in 1960.

Annie's son, James, and his wife, Marian, lived with John Nick in his home after Rachel died. John's living children agreed that if James and Marian stayed with John, the home would become their property. When John fell down some stairs and fatally broke his neck, James and Marian Nick moved to their own home on Shady Rest Road. Another family rented John's house until that family outgrew the house and moved.

Because of a family member's ill-timed unwillingness to sign the proper papers, the property fell behind in taxes and was lost to the family.

James Edward Nick started oystering at age 11 and left the water in 1956 when he entered the bricklaying trade. He lived in Shady Side but worked in Virginia and Washington, DC, as a bricklayer from 1956 to 1993. Carmelia Nick Hicks is his daughter, and Tommy Nick is his brother.

William (1862-abt.1945) and Hattie (Hettie) Taylor Nick (1864-abt.1959) were parents of Jerome, Marion, and the other nine siblings. Many people today remembered Hattie as one of the two midwives in the community, because she probably was present when a grandparent or great-grandparent came into the world.

Great-granddaughter June, about five years of age, stayed overnight with her great-grandmother Hattie after Great-Grandpa Bill died. The house caught fire, and Great-Grandmother Hattie told June to open the door and let the smoke out. Fortunately, June ran next door to get her granddaddy Marion, who successfully got his mother out of the house before it burned down. From that point on, Miss Hattie stayed with Marion until she moved to Philadelphia to live with a daughter during the winter. As long as she was able, she returned to Shady Side every summer to stay with her son.

Grandpa Bill was a farmer and worked the water in the *Virginia B* with his sons Jerome and Varnell. June Smith's only memory of her great-grandfather Nick was of him sitting in the garden and that he had one leg.

In the St. Matthews' historical notes, it reports that "Bill" was one of the builders of the original church, which was a frame building. William Nick, Joseph Matthews, John T. Gross, Edward Dennis, and James Boyd were trustees of St. Matthew's Episcopal Church on October 22, 1887, when the first parcel of land was deeded. Land was purchased from James and Mary Jane Thompson. John and Rachel Brown Nick once owned the original church property, according to a second source that appears in the church's historical data.

Marion Nick's last boat was *Hooks,* and son Marshall's last boat was *Mary Ellen.* Often a man named his boat after a wife or daughter, but *Mary Ellen* was not named for Marshall's wife, Magdeline Brown Nick. He bought the boat from someone else, and since that was how it was registered, the name was not changed. (It was not because changing the name would bring bad luck, as some people thought.)

Marshall Nick, Sr., worked on the water, hand tonging during oyster season until he was about 18. "That was the only means anyone in this area had to make a living. Just about everybody almost had his own boat. In the spring people worked at construction or gardens and around their homes." For a time Marshall worked at pile driving but decided, "I had to skip and wanted to try for myself." His grandfather and father were builders, so when Marshall wound up doing concrete work on a construction job, he had found his calling. He loved the work. From there he started his own business and put his heart into it. He always tried to please the customer and put his best into every job. His policy worked because many people reported that Marshall Nick was the person to see when it came to concrete. For a few years in the 1950s or 1960s, he also worked as a maintenance man and caretaker of "Our Place" before the owners sold it to the Shady Side Rural Heritage Society.

★   ★   ★

The Leonard and Eunice Nick family had to drive to Grandma Gladys Gross Holland and Papa "Boojack" (George) Holland's house because they lived "way down in Shady Side." They traveled from Nick Road to Shady Side Road, taking a right turn on Snug Harbor and a left on Atwell Road, passing the land for the present-day elementary school; they followed a narrow road to reach their grandparents' property on the water. Their Holland grandparents raised seven children there. The older Nick granddaughters remembered going into the water up to their knees and seeing their feet—the water was still clear in the early 1950s. Every Fourth of July the Hollands would have a party, and all of their family, including many Baltimore relatives, would come—maybe a couple hundred people would show up. "There was all kinds of food. I can remember my Papa Boojack, a waterman, would catch a big snapping turtle and keep it in some water until the Fourth of July, and Uncle Bill would make the turtle soup." The three sisters, Delores, Connie, and Carla, have quilts made by their Grandma Gladys. Connie thinks hers was made when her grandmother was in her eighties. Carla helped her grandmother by pumping water in the water buckets and going to the store.

Delores, Connie and Carla Nick's grandparents George and Gladys Holland lived on the West River off Atwell Road. **Carla Nick Gross Collection**

Carla had always admired her grandmother's wedding ring, and she asked if she could have it one day. Her grandmother's answer: "Okay, Carla, it's yours." After her grandmother died the ring disappeared, so Carla assumed that someone else had the ring. Carla's mother, Eunice, had a dream about her mother telling her that the ring was in the bureau. Several times they returned to the house to check and it wasn't there. Ten years passed, the property was sold, and Carla's grandmother's house was emptied. Family members chose pieces they wanted and sold other pieces to Beebe Castro, a teacher and recreation and parks department supervisor turned antique dealer. Beebe called Carla's mother later, saying, "You'll never guess what I found!" Eunice said, "You found my mother's ring!" Indeed, as Beebe was cleaning and spraying the hutch outside her house, the ring bounced out of a drawer and rolled across her driveway. Beebe recounts the story: "The ring bounced ping, ping, ping across the driveway." Carla prizes the story and the ring that is engraved "HH to GH Feb. 23, 1914." He couldn't afford to give her a ring when they married, but Grandmother Holland received the wedding ring about five years after the marriage.

After Gladys Holland died her husband George later married Elizabeth Crowner Matthews, widow of Joseph Matthews.

CHAPTER 7

WATERMEN AND WATER STORIES

IN THE EARLY DAYS, on cold winter mornings, most Shady Side men, black and white, left home in the dark, walking to the water's edge to go oystering. Almost all Shady Side men worked on the water at some point in their lives. Through the generations the watermen knew each other, the names and sounds of their boat motors, and the personalities of each boat, motor, and man. Each day was a new adventure on the water because it had its behavior, too, depending on the wind and weather. Beneath the water, attached, defenseless, hinged oysters opened and closed their shells to extract food while they functioned as a filter for the bay waters. Against this setting, lives rose and fell like the tides, and stories of "here today and gone tomorrow" unfolded as four generations of watermen followed the water to claim the oysters that contained a tidbit of taste and sensation for the discerning palate.

Oyster season traditionally runs from September to April, the months containing an "r." For generations, wives and children went to the county wharf or stood along Parrish Creek to greet watermen returning from the first day out. Now opening day comes and goes without anyone giving it much thought.

Men on the Water

Once when he was out on the water, Varnell Nick (1906-1987) became lost in the fog, when there "was lots of wind and the engine stopped. Although I was shaky in the *Susie Q,* named for my wife, I trusted in the Lord." Varnell worked for himself and with his father, William "Bill" Nick, on the water.

Joyce Brown Thompson, daughter of Martha Simms and Clark "Squeeze" Brown, remembered her father getting his hand tongs ready for oystering. When he returned home, it was her job to turn his gloves. (Interview in 2002) Oyster gloves were big, black, rubber gloves with a cloth lining. Once they were turned inside out, "all of this cruddy old water and mud from the oysters" would come out. She put the gloves beside the wood stove to dry for the next morning. Squeeze Brown told his daughter, "There's nothing more beautiful than being out on the water when the sun rises."

Commenting on the adventure and the love of being on the water, Doug Hinton, grandson of waterman Captain Crandall Trott and great-grandson of Captain Dick Trott, said, "I guess I felt like: I was doing something that most people couldn't or wouldn't do. Maybe I felt a little macho, I'm not sure, but I felt proud 'cause I knew my grandfather and my great-grandfather did it. I truly enjoyed it. When I'd get home, I was so tired I just ached all over, but it was a good feeling, a good tired. I slept good."

On the water it didn't matter what race one was. If someone broke down, he was helped. The only man who was discriminated against was one who wouldn't do his fair share of work. Usually three or four watermen worked together on a boat. If someone didn't own a boat, he worked on an owner's boat. The oyster catch was divided: a third for the captain, a third for the boat, and a third for the others. For instance, John and Sarah Matthews's oldest sons, Thomas and Ellis, worked for someone else for years. Once the day's catch was sold, they were immediately paid a third in cash, so Thomas and Ellis each received a half of a third. If a captain failed to pay at the going rate, then the worker suffered a loss of income. Obviously, an unfair captain would be the last choice for employment, but watermen would take such a job if no other one was available. "You did what you had to do," said a knowledgeable waterman.

Today, someone who is addressed as captain of a boat is licensed through the state and has to demonstrate the necessary boating skills and knowledge of safety issues. Until quite recently, a waterman who owned his workboat was addressed as "Captain," especially if he was white. It was a tradition and a title of respect. Less often "Cap'n" was used to address a black boat owner, and rarely did a white person address a black person as "Mister." For example, Julius Dennis was called "Uncle Julius" by both his relatives and others, black and white. Black and white children were taught never to call a black or white person by his or her first name because it was disrespectful. Children, black or white, never addressed adults by first names only.

All watermen, black and white, had a special story or comment about Raymond Fountain, known as "Cap'n Tuck," from Galesville. "He was a legend in this area. If you knew Tuck, you loved him. He was a super guy. Tuck Fountain would give you hell. He would tease ya'. If he thought he could get a rise out of you, he'd just tease you more. He was a hard worker, a good-hearted person, and a fun person to be around because he always had something funny to say. He was a strong man—strong as two bulls," reported Doug Hinton. T. C. Magnotti, past president of the Shady Side Rural Heritage Society, recalled the day of her husband's viewing at Hardesty's Funeral Home in Galesville: "I hope you say something about Tuck. He was the first person to come to the funeral home. I thought the world of him."

A story was retold about Captain Rodney Gross and J.R., his son, too. "They went out oysterin', patent tonging, and got out on the oyster bar. Before you start to work your patent tongs, you have to throw weights off the side, and the weights are tied by ropes to a pulley that are connected to the hoses that keep the hoses out of the way so you won't catch 'em in your tongs. Captain Rodney was up in the cabin, and J.R. was out walking up on the bow and the washboard to get the weights overboard. He fell overboard. He was yelling, 'Help! Help! Help me.' And Captain Rodney was in the cabin with the radio on, and he thought someone was screaming over the radio. He says, 'Those boys ought not play jokes like that. That's not funny.' And his son was overboard, drowning! He finally realized what was happening and got him out. That's the story that was told to me, so I assume it was true," explained Doug Hinton. When J.R. Gross was reminded of the story, he confirmed the event as he stood on *Miss Cindy* at Miss Lucille Brown's pier on Parrish Creek.

Being on the water was dangerous work, and surprisingly some watermen couldn't swim. "It really didn't matter if you could swim or not," reported a former waterman. "In the wintertime you could be an Olympic swimmer, and if you fell over and someone wasn't there to help you, you'd die. First, the water was so cold, and second, a waterman usually had on hip boots that would fill up and take him down. Saturated clothes weighed about a hundred pounds and took you down. In the summertime chances were better to stay afloat for a while."

As a teenager, Doug Hinton was duck hunting at his duck blind on an island located a stone's throw from Wagner's Point, or Cedar Point, on the West River. (In the early 1950s the island, where Doug's great-uncle Pack Trott had a working maritime railway, totally disappeared.) Doug saw a boat that looked like the *Edna Florence,* the boat at the Captain Avery Museum. Two men were on the boat's decks and using their tongs to break the ice to move through the frozen river. One man fell off and went under the ice. The man's hip boots took him down right before the teenager's eyes. The second man couldn't get to him in time.

Oystering in the ice was extremely dangerous, because ice could cut through a wooden boat like a razor. To prevent this, watermen used copper sheeting from printing presses to cover the boats for protection. Printing plates were useless once the printing was completed. "You could read sentences and see pictures. Some were stainless steel." As the watermen worked their way out of a frozen West River, they used an ice saw or pick to break through the ice and then push that broken ice down and under the intact ice to the side of the break, inching the boat along. Once the boat was free of the ice, work could begin. Returning home could be a second grueling chore if the pathway had refrozen.

Bill Lescallett, a waterman from 1956 to 1972, reported that before the metal was added to the boats, some watermen used rope to hang 1"x 12"x 12' boards over the sides of the boat to protect their boats from ice. He also said that the Edmund Hallock family had an old Coast Guard cutter or landing barge they used to open up a channel to the Bay from Parrish Creek.

Because of this constant ice threat, many men kept their boats in Annapolis or Eastport during the worst part of winter. An icebreaker kept the Annapolis port open for the daily ferry. At the end of an oystering day, the watermen washed, refueled, and oiled their boats before heading home to Shady Side.

At the end of the oystering season, some watermen tied a rope on their boat, let the rope sink, and left the boat there until oyster season rolled around again. Using a railway or carriage put in the water to pull up the boat, the owner added a motor and started the new season.

A Community's Heartbreaking Loss

The Shady Side community experienced a tragic loss on the West River on April 7, 1929. Three Scott brothers, Prescott, Carter, and John, drowned during a dark storm that came up quickly while they worked on the water. They were in their late teens and early twenties, and John was the only married brother. "It was a terrible day," said those who were young at the time but are still living today. Miss Doll Baby Dennis was born a year later, but she remembers how her father recalled the fatal day. "Looking at the clouds and wind, my father told a neighbor, 'Somebody is going to get drown today.' Then, that night we got the bad news that the three Scott boys had drown."

Miss Daisy Crowner Thompson, 88, and her sister Miss Helen Crowner Gorham, 89, discussed the tragedy. "The father [Sellman Scott] came over and asked Mama if she would go and sit with his wife [Gussie Scott] because the boys had gotten drown. It was a terrible time. The mother never got over it," Miss Daisy added. "I was six years old."

Buddy Holland's father Blake told him about how awful it was and how they had to go out and find the bodies. "They knew about where the boat capsized, so they were dragging for them. They used a rope tied to a grappling anchor, like you throw over to hold your boat in place, but you drag the anchor and drag and drag. You keep dragging and hope it catches on their clothes. Several men would be crisscrossing wherever you think it was. Bodies will always come to the surface, but that happens quite a bit later, so it was important to get the bodies before the elements got to them. Dad said, 'Their father was screaming and crying, and you could hear him a mile away when they found his boys.' They were probably going out of South Creek but capsized on the Bay opposite Idlewilde. Those boats were so small; nothing like what you see today."

Gussie and Sellman Scott's youngest son, Milbert, was too young to go with his brothers, so his life was spared. The three brothers' bodies were laid out in the front room of their parents' home back in woods off Cedarhurst Road and Shady Side Roads, behind their daughter and son-in-law's house on the corner.

At 105 years old, Titus Blunt was the oldest person living in the Churchton-Shady Side area until his death in July 2010. A year earlier, he had talked about going out from Deale that April day in 1929, but he headed home when he and those with him saw the clouds in the distance. "It looked like a bad storm was coming, and we got in before it broke."

Mr. Titus Blunt, 105, lived with his daughter Diane Blunt in Churchton.
He was oysterin' on the water in April 1929 but came in ahead of the storm to
Deale. Most Churchton men went out from Deale.
Ann Widdifield Collection

In taped interviews in the 1980s, Sarah Matthews (Miss "Sweetie")
and Varnell Nick also recalled the drowning of the brothers. (These
audiotapes and transcripts are housed at the Flora Ethel Andrews
Memorial Library at the Captain Avery Museum.)

The clearest picture of that fateful day comes from an interview
with Julius Dennis on his 97th birthday in 1992. Doris Crowner Brown
introduced his granddaughter, Deborah Mackall who helped during
the interview. Doris had a strong connection to the story, because her
mother was a sister to the three brothers, Doris's uncles.

Julius Dennis was oystering with Ira on a day that was "so mild" that "nobody paid much attention to it. All at once . . . Oh, look up northwest." There was a storm, black and blue, coming. "I begin to hear thunder and said, 'Ira, you hear anything?' He says, 'No, you want to go back?' That time my back was turned the wrong way, and I said, 'All right,' and Ira give me some slack. And Ira? I turned around and said, 'Oh, my Lord, no! Get, get, get. Come and wait back here.' He got down and came in the cabin saying, 'I can't see, can't see.' It was raining and blowing and everything, yes, sir. I say [to Ira], 'Give it to me quick,' and I took her. I was steering with two lines on the rudder. Got her around on the side. Then I taken her and I just kept her steady, like 'at. I kept her bow to where I saw the north wind struck. That was between Cedarhurst and Capt. George Brockton's shore. I run like that for a little while and she finally lightened up. I saw Cedarhurst and said, 'Well, I'm all right now. You can take her.' And I mean to tell you, it blowed.

"We went down to Captain's [Gustav's] store. I saw Cousin Sellman Scott out there on the road, and he come into the store: 'Son, son, son, you see our John?' I said, 'No, I was down the Bay and they was up the Bay.' It was then he heard their boat had sunk. I couldn't do nothin'. I said [to the others], 'Well, better come on home.'

"Next morning I gets up and Ira and me goes down the shore and 'stead of foolin' around I say, 'Come on. Let's get ready and see what we can do.' So I got my boat and cut down there on the river and saw a boat coming from out there off Kootz [off Idlewilde today]. I said, 'That boat's so long getting here, wonder what's wrong?' I come to find out he had towed John Scott's and them boat. He left the rig, didn't bother with it. They thought that maybe if they got the boat, one or two of them'd might be in the boat. But there was nobody in the boat. They towed the boat on up to Rhodes River right against a high bank, and boys jumped in and started bailing the boat. But there wasn't nobody in there.

"Right that evening they got two [bodies]. I believe it was Pres and Carter. Next day they went back and got John."

Varnell Nick said that he wasn't out on the water the day the men drowned. "John, Carter, and Preston were my buddies. They got caught out in the storm, and their boat sank on them."

Other families have lost relatives on the water, but no other family had to face the Scott family's loss of three sons in one day.

Julius Dennis on the Water

Julius Dennis told of a storm equally frightening for him as the 1929 storm. "Ira and I started out one morning and reached the Kootz when Ira said, 'Takin' water over the bow. Mighty lot of boats turnin' back.' I said, 'Oh, they just don't want to work,' just like 'at. I didn't realize it was so bad. We kept going. Soon after we got out, it breezed up; the wind shook up. So rough. About then Ira threw the anchor overboard as I called, 'Good Lord, down quick!' Shucks, I come up about two feet at least and yelled, 'Get off the washboard!'"

The two men spent a miserable day sitting in the boat with their hands crossed over their chests, backs laid against the cabin. Looking out from the cabin, they watched the waves: "Seas comin' that, Good Lord, looked like mountains. It didn't look like we was gonna get back.

"That evening the wind calmed right down, settled down." The men made ready to go, but "the anchor was hard, gone sleep, so I told Ira to just pull it up and make fast. I heard her when she jumped, broke up, and Ira pulled her up on the deck. I started on up the river, the creek there. The Lord was with us. See, you don't try to be smart about the Lord's work. The Lord knew I got to make a livin', no foolishness. I go out there to make a livin'. (otherwise) I'd starve to death. Next morning, to tell you the truth, I said, 'We was blessed.' Ira went home to his family, and I went home to mine."

Before going home they went to the oyster house, because they had taken a couple of licks and brought some oysters in to sell. Julius was asked where he had been. When he explained, "Down the Bay," someone marveled and wondered how in the world they were able to stay out there. "Man say, 'He fixed for it. Had to have a good grab line, a good anchor, a good engine, and a good boat.'" When the boat was swamped the anchor held, and the waterman lived to tell his story.

Once when Julius was working in front of Thomas Point Lighthouse, he saw a man come out on its porch and wave a big white sheet at him. He thought, correctly, that the man wanted him. Julius went to the bay side of the lighthouse where the ladder came down and tied his boat fast. The lighthouse keeper called, "Captain, come up here." When Julius reached the house he saw sheets, pillowcases, everything was "as bloody as could be"—from a nosebleed. Julius asked the man for a bunch of keys, which the man found and handed to Julius, who looped a string around them and tied them down the man's back. "I always hear my mother say they was good to stop a nosebleed. My half-brother, my Lord, nose bleed like somebody stuck a hose down it. So I hung the keys down the light keeper's back and the bleedin' done stop."

Then the lighthouse keeper asked Julius to do him a favor and take a telegram to Fishing Creek, a place where "I ain't never been, but I could find it." Julius was told he didn't have to come back to the lighthouse, because the lighthouse keeper just needed to get his message to land. Julius did as he was told: look for a long wall once he got to the creek. Once there, he saw the "little ole office." A man came down, and Julius gave him the telegram. "The man got on it right away. Wasn't no time, here she come, down eastern side, a boat and he started blown'. I think he was lettin' the lighthouse man know he was coming." Rescue was on the way. The man gave Julius half a shoulder of pork, eggs, bananas, and oranges, because he didn't have any money to thank him. This was all right with Julius, who was glad to help. "So anyhow I went on, never even got his name or his number or nothin'."

Waterman Julius Dennis is pictured in his 97th year. Explaining his work experience he said, "Then I took up oystering, went on the water oystering; and, oh my, I stay out there and worked and worked. That's my living . . . Following the water." **Doris Crowner Brown Collection**

How many Shady Side rescues and Good Samaritan stories have gone untold? Bruce Cornwall, professional mariner and Marine Superintendent for the University of Maryland Center for Environmental Science, Research Operations, discovered one such story. (Bruce can also trace his roots to the original Parrish settlers.) During research, he found the name of Matiel Dennis Carter's father, Alexander Dennis, in a wreck report.* Listed as master—and most likely captain—of the schooner *Watchman,* Alex Dennis and his crew aided the schooner *Thomas Nelson,* which had capsized near Tolly's Point, off Bay Ridge, near Annapolis not far from Thomas Point Lighthouse. Captained by William E. Avery, the *Thomas Nelson* with two crew members had

---

* National Archives and Records Administration, Philadelphia, PA, Records Group 36, Records of the Bureau of Marine Inspection and Navigation, (Custom House of Annapolis, MD, *Wreck Reports*: 1875-1912)

delivered its cargo in Baltimore and was sailing home to West River on a Friday evening, September 12, 1890. A sudden squall capsized the vessel. Alex Dennis was in the vicinity of the accident and was able to save Captain William Avery and one crew member. The wreck report confirmed that "George Garrett, colored, was lost," and "assistance was rendered" by Alex Dennis. No description was given about the race of any other men in the report.

Watermen helped each other no matter who they were or how they looked, no questions asked. Blacks and whites worked together in all seasons, weather, and situations. The objective was to do the job and work together to bring in the oysters. Like the military, each man has the back of the other. This was the place where men were equal and free to be who they were and to appreciate the value of the other in an unpredictable environment.

On land Shady Side and Galesville have a longer, stronger history of positive community cooperation than in the Deale area, according to comments made by black and white citizens of all three communities.

Storms

To this day storms spring up on the Bay surprisingly quickly. Today's weather forecasters try to keep the public informed in a timely manner, but earlier generations did not have this technology available and had to rely on their ability to read the signs in the sky. One waterman said that a nor'easter took a day to come, a day to stay, and a day to leave.

The watermen had to react immediately if cloud formations looked dangerous, and they needed to seek a safe haven on shore. If they were at home, they followed family traditions as to what should be done if the storm hit at night. There was always the fear that the house might be struck by lightning. Kathleen Thompson Hicks remembered her mother getting her up at night to go downstairs and sit quietly until the storm had passed. Even now booming thunder with crackly crashing lightning and violent winds disturb her.

Jackie Andrews Grace remembered her grandmother Ethel was deathly afraid of thunderstorms. Other grandmothers held the same fear. There was a carnival at the community center or Kiwanis Club every summer for many years, and one year a terrible storm occurred during carnival week. Jackie was spending the night and sleeping on the third floor at her friend's grandparents' house, Marguerite and Packard Trott's home on West Shady Side Road. The house had lightning rods, but Jackie remembered being awakened three times to go downstairs until the storms were over.

Families on Linton Road would rush from their houses to gather at the grandparents' house when a storm was approaching. Someone teased that if lightning hit the house, the whole family would be wiped out. After one of the daughters grew up, married, and moved to a different part of Shady Side, neighbors would know a serious storm was coming because she would be seen leaving for her mother's house.

In one Matthews family, the children were told to lie down on the floor until the storm had blown over. A Gross family member said that they would say nothing and sit still and quiet until the storm passed. The reason usually given was: "God was doing his work" and everyone should wait. "If you think about it, these were old wooden houses, and if they were struck by lightning you're better off down on the floor. Some upper class families who had money had lightning rods, but our families didn't."

One story circulated that someone had opened the front door during a storm, and a ball of lightning barreled down the hall and out the open back door. Another person said that she was taught to raise a window opposite the way the storm was blowing to keep the house from blowing up. This might be a wise rule if a tornado were coming with its characteristic low pressure. The open window would allow the higher air pressure on the inside of the house to escape and stabilize the air on the inside of the house.

Florine Thompson related that her family did not talk on the phone, watch TV, or eat during a storm. Once the storm passed, life went on as usual. "Our elders were quiet. They would put down the shades and would not stand in the view of a window. Forks, spoons, and anything made from glass were thought to draw lightning. If my elders were already in bed, they stayed in bed."

The Charles Crowner children were taught to be quiet, turn off everything, and sit quietly. As children, they had to sit on the steps inside the farmhouse until the storm passed. "Say nothing; do nothing." If the storm came at night, then they could stay in their beds.

In July 2010, the *Capital* reported that a Churchton house was struck by lightning and burned, so storms remain a modern destructive possibility that demand precautions. A fireman guessing as to how many lightning strikes on homes he had responded to during the summer finally said, "A lot." An insurance adviser said that he wished he could require all policyholders to install lightning protection, but people object to the extra cost. Compared to automobile crashes for both property and injury, lightning is at the bottom of statistics.

Port Norris, "Jersey"

For perhaps 25 years or more, groups of Shady Side watermen drove to Port Norris, New Jersey, or "Jersey," to work on large oyster boats dredging for oysters on the Delaware River. Waterman dropped the "New" from the state when referring to their destination. At the end of the local oyster season, starting May 1 until the end of June, these men would work 10-hour days on board a ship that cranked up at 3:30 a.m. Monday and in most cases did not return to shore again until Friday evening. Some men stayed in New Jersey the entire time, while others tried to make the trip home every other weekend. Buddy Holland,

DeWayne Salisbury, and James Nick always tried to get home. They are among the last living Shady Side residents who worked and experienced the adventure. Buddy's comment: "Let me say: I'm glad it's over."

Besides packing suitcases with work clothes, some men like Buddy also had to supply their own bedding and towels for their accommodations on board ship: a bunk bed with an extremely thin mattress and a bucket for washing. DeWayne Salisbury, who went as a teenager, had to take only clothes because his boat supplied raincoats, boots, bedding, and towels. Starting Sunday night, he stayed out on the water for a week culling oysters. When the men and teenagers had a boatload, the oysters were sold. On Friday evenings the workers would take a bath on the boat and then head for home. DeWayne's group came home every weekend for five weeks "when we were young and crazy."

A group left Shady Side with four or five guys to a car. There was no Chesapeake Bay Bridge until 1957, so a car waited for the first ferry at Sandy Point to reach the Eastern Shore to take Route 50 to Route 13 into Delaware. Travelers waited in long lines, sweating in hot cars with the windows down and the hood up to keep themselves and the engine as cool as possible. From Pennsville, Delaware, a second ferry had to be taken to reach New Jersey. To avoid one ferry, some traveled on Route 40 through Baltimore to Route 13 to reach New Castle, Delaware. The second ferry still had to be used to reach New Jersey. If a group traveled home for the weekend, the men had from Friday evening until the 3:30 a.m. Monday engine crank to make the trip's circuit. Many hoped to get things washed while at home, but mostly they wanted to connect with their families.

Charlie Thompson and Earl Gross were two of the three men who formed up crews of watermen for the New Jersey work. No one remembers how Shady Side men originally started working for the dredgers. The earlier ships were sailing vessels, but they were motorized when Buddy, aged 14 or 15, went with his father, Blake, the first time in 1947 or '48. They were fed three meals a day beginning with breakfast from 5:00 to 5:30 a.m. Buddy's crew under Earl Gross worked on Captain Walter Henderson's boat. There were sixteen men including the cook on his ship. Smaller boats carried eight to ten men and usually returned to shore each evening, allowing those men some recreational time.

The men mainly worked on their knees, culling 3,000 bushels of oysters a day! The dredge brought up the seed oysters from public oystering grounds until 3:30 in the afternoon. That work stopped, the boat was cleaned up, and then they'd run the boat to private grounds, where the men shoveled the seed oysters onto those grounds. There the oysters could grow to regulation size for harvesting later. It took three years for the oysters to become market size. The owner of the private grounds might dredge oysters to sell from October to December, but Shady Side men did not participate in that operation.

Some men may have worked on boats that went out on the Atlantic Ocean to bring in round, hard-shell clams, which were different from the soft-shell ones from the rivers. Oysters will not grow below 32' to 35', so no oysters were caught beyond the Delaware Bay in the Atlantic Ocean.

Looking at a map, one sees that Port Norris is northeast of Shady Side, so people might logically say they were going "up to New Jersey," but this was not the expression. Instead, it was "down to the Shell Pile." Shell Pile was actually the name of a shantytown close to where Shady Side men boarded the workboats. Good money was to be made, but it was dangerous, tedious, harsh work in all kinds of weather. Comfort didn't enter into any part of the experience. Lowell Dennis, son of Oregon Dennis, was one of several men who drowned while working in New Jersey. He fell overboard and just disappeared because he was weighed down by his work clothes.

Charlie Thompson worked as a chef for the same owner and family all the years he went to New Jersey. Captain Bill Lee and his family showed their appreciation by remembering Charlie with a check at Christmas time, even after his work ended. When his sons, Josh and Calvin, were fourteen and fifteen, they went with him during one eight-week season and each made $60 a week. The three made enough to pay off the mortgage on the family's new home.

Gerald Thompson (left) Charles Thompson and James Edward "Tap" Holland wait on a boat "down" at Port Norris, New Jersey.
Darlene Thompson Washington Collection

Western Shore and Eastern Shore Views of the Bay

The oyster business was booming in 1947 and continued to do well into the 1970s. Anne Arundel County had the greatest number of watermen on the Western Shore. In the Shady Side, Churchton, Galesville, and Deale areas, men, both black and white, oystered. During oyster season watermen were working from before sunup to sundown. Oyster season originally ran from September 15 to April 15, until the 1980s when the dates were changed. In the off season, most of the watermen on the Western Shore turned to farming, carpentry, bricklaying, cement finishing, painting, or construction jobs in Shady Side or in the cities.

On the Eastern Shore men usually had only one line of work: the water or farming. They worked nearly 24 hours a day. The economy revolved around the success of the watermen, who worked twelve months a year, oystering, crabbing, clamming, and fishing. Their politicians watched out for them, including Governor Tawes, who was originally from Crisfield. On the Western Shore, most counties did not have men making their living on the water, as did Anne Arundel County and a smaller group from Calvert County.

For reasons unknown, the abundance of oysters would vary from year to year. Some years they were greater in number on the Eastern Shore and the next year better on the western side. When it was a bad season, some Anne Arundel County watermen did other work.

Sometimes the skipjacks came over in the night from the Eastern Shore (Tilghman Island) to dredge on the West River oyster bars. Around 2 or 3 in the morning they would come in to dredge while the watermen on the Western Shore were sleeping. Anne Arundel did not have any of these dredge boats, which were sailing vessels. "We always had good oysters because we didn't dredge the oysters with the skipjacks," said a Western Shore waterman. "Buy-boats came to the West River from Virginia and the Eastern Shore to purchase our oysters."

It was illegal to use a motor on the skipjacks, but they carried a little motorized boat, called the push boat, on the stern of the skipjack. When there wasn't any wind, they would use the motorized boat to push the skipjack. Howard Shenton was a maritime police officer and watched out for infractions. Mr. Shenton told a story about boarding a skipjack and finding a motor in a bed, covered up to look like a sleeping man. Watermen held Howard Shenton in high regard because, although he was hard, he was fair. "He would arrest his own daughter if necessary," several laughingly reported. "He was an honest, fair guy. Some marine police would come on board to check the length of crabs but intentionally step on and crush the crab's edges so that the measurement would be short of the limit. Howard Shenton was never like that."

In the 1960s the Anne Arundel County Waterman's Association, both black and white members numbering about 300, fought a plan to open the Bay statewide for licensing but to no avail. The law was changed to allow watermen to go to *any county* where they chose to fish. Many people, including Howard Shenton (in a 1984 video), believed that this new law was the final blow to the oyster industry. Up until that time a waterman could only be licensed in his own county and that was where he worked.

Oysters: The Objective

Oysters have been living on the bottom of the Chesapeake Bay and up and down the east coast of North America and beyond for centuries. Oysters are bivalves, and the two-hinged shells seal tightly together unless they are eating and filtering water. They are shades of gray and white and appear to be miniature moonscapes of pocked craters and irregular patterns, depending on where they attach and grow.

Becoming an oyster seems "iffy": It depends on a chance union of gametes spawned by male and female oysters that unite in the water and become larva. About seven hours later the larva has developed cilia that allow it to swim, and it even has the beginnings of a shell. The larva swims about for two or three weeks until it is ready to set up housekeeping on the bottom of the Bay, preferably on other oysters. Once the developing oyster larva attaches its foot to a suitable spot, it is called spat. If the salinity is high enough (10-28 parts per thousand), the oyster will grow about an inch a year. Oysters can survive on firm mud bottoms, hard sand, or shell bottoms. The shape of the shell reflects the type of bottom environment. The softer the bottom, the more elongated and narrow the oyster; the harder the bottom, the rounder the oyster. Since oysters spawn in the early warmer summer months, at that point they are thin and watery and their taste is compromised. By fall, or the middle of September, oyster meat rebounds in taste due to cooler water, and the "r months rule" applies through April. [1]

Oysters were abundant during the times of the Woodland Indian tribes and European settlements along the Chesapeake Bay, and oyster reefs were reported to cause navigational problems for early shipping vessels. It was reported that Bay oysters were four times larger than those in England and had to be cut in two to be eaten.

Oysters are a most effective water filtration system; one adult oyster can pump and strain two gallons of water in an hour. The oyster population in the 1880s filtered the volume of the whole Bay every four days. Now it takes over a year—thirteen months plus—to do the same job. In the past hundred years, the harvests have declined to 1 percent of what they were at the end of the nineteenth century.

The American Oyster or Eastern Oyster of the Chesapeake Bay can live on oyster bars in brackish waters in the more northerly part of the Bay or in the saltier regions of the southern part of the Bay. In the colder regions of the Bay, they make their beds in deeper waters because of the freezing temperatures. They can be found in water depths from 8 feet and 25 to 32 feet, meaning they were not readily visible to the watermen. Buyers preferred the round shaped oysters and paid 10 cents more a bushel for round oysters than for the long, skinny ones that catch on stones. Watermen often referred to those as "snack" oysters. The culler divided the two oyster shapes into separate baskets as the oysters were dropped on his culling board.

Purnell Crowner (left) and his brother-in-law Leon Brown, wearing a yellow rubber suit, culls oysters near Holland Point. Hands protected by rubber gloves, he tosses oysters (left) that are within limits. Mr. Leon works the patent tongs, but the men traded off jobs. **Miss Doris Crowner Brown Collection**

In a 2004 interview, Marshall Nick, Sr., named some of the oyster bars near Shady Side: the Kootz off Idlewilde, Wild Ground, Thomas Point, Hackett's, and Three Sisters. Bill Lescallett, a waterman until 1972, added Parker's Rock and Holland Point by Herrington Harbor South Marina. The state of Maryland has mapped all of the oyster bars and also has maps showing where leased plots, or leased bottoms, are located.

Oysters were bought and sold by the bushel. During the early 1900s, two bushels were going for 25 cents. Varnell Nick said that his father oystered on a sailboat and spent 50 years on the water. Varnell himself started oystering when he was twelve and spent twenty to thirty years on the water. The youngest son of William and Hattie Nick, he and his four brothers culled oysters with their father. They were getting 20 to 25 cents for a bushel of oysters that they sold to buy-boat captains and oyster houses such as Woodfield's and Benny's Oyster Houses in Galesville, and to Gustav Heinrich, Henry Bast, or Mike Hartge at Cedar Point in Shady Side. They sold to the "best market," meaning where they would get the best price for their oysters.

Anchored and ready for the return of the watermen, boats will carry the oystermen toward the best bars for "taking a lick" with hand tongs. The ubiquitous oyster shell pile and the small boats are links to a waterman's livelihood. **Captain Avery Museum Collection**

At one time there were 75 tong boats going in and out of the Bay.[2] Hand tongs were used to bring up the oysters. Churchton waterman Titus Blunt reported hand tongs of 18 feet, 20 feet, and 30 feet. "Some were longer than the boat." Mr. Blunt referred to a man in Shady Side who made the best tongs. He may have been thinking of James Atwell, whose tongs were famous all over the eastern seaboard.[3] Or he may have been referring to Kenneth Rogers Nieman, nephew of James Atwell, from whom he learned his trade. Kenneth Neiman was skilled in "hanging the heads" so that the critical hinged raking parts met correctly. "He had racks of tongs piled up in the back," said Bill LesCallett, who learned the technique from his father-in-law, Kenneth Nieman. "He made all lengths of tongs and even had regular customers from the Eastern Shore" and the Delaware Bay area.[4] They came by boat to Parrish Creek to buy their tongs, which required two men to carry on board. To reach the deepest oysters, Kenneth Nieman's father "was on his knees tonging with 28' shafts," said Bill LesCallett. The upper body strength of tongers was phenomenal.

Drop tongs, which had a cable running down the middle and attached to an engine similar to a lawn mower, replaced hand tongs as the oyster-harvesting tool of choice. It required two men to open the tongs once the oysters were brought up onto the boat. Patent tongs were hydraulic and worked automatically so two men were no longer required to open the shafts.

★ ★ ★

Baltimore became a big canning center in the 1840s. Once they were canned, oysters could be kept for long periods of time. With the steady supply of oysters, the canning factories' production, and the expanding railroads, the demand for oysters could be met far beyond the Bay. During the Civil War, canned oysters were sent to Union troops. Once the Union Pacific and the Central Pacific met at Promontory, Utah, in May 1869, canned oysters were regularly shipped to the west and points in between. Canned oysters traveled to Pittsburgh, Chicago, and St. Louis and were eaten in mining camps during the Gold Rush.

While working on the water, watermen sold their oysters for cash to buy-boat captains. The captains, the middlemen, delivered oysters to sell to packinghouses at Baltimore docks. This meant the catch was fresh, and it made it possible for the watermen to continue working without having to go into port to sell their oysters. Oyster harvests on the Chesapeake Bay peaked in 1884-1885, when 15 million bushels of oysters were harvested on the Bay.

When Baltimore buyers received the oysters, they wanted bushels filled and rounded at the top rather than leveled out straight across, to manipulate the amount paid for the catch. Since measuring the catch was not precise, the buy-boat captain, in this case, would come up short.

Local watermen also sold their catches to oyster houses along the West River. The biggest operation was Woodfield's, but watermen also sold to the Bennett Oyster Company in Galesville. Woodfield's was always in competition with the buy-boats and trucks, but it was also a place where watermen could consistently sell their oysters.

Outside Heinrich's Store on South Creek, a rowboat's bow points to a workboat. These boats are fragile as compared to the sturdy workboats of today. Some watermen arrived by rowboats to Heinrich's where they kept their dredge boats. **Captain Avery Museum Collection**

Shady Side had Leatherbury's Oyster House on Parrish Creek and Gustav Heinrich's Oyster House and store at the end of West River Road on South Creek. Originally, Gustav Heinrich's father was a sailboat buy-boat captain running oysters, or other "stuff like canned goods and tomatoes," from West River to Baltimore. He started his oyster house in 1914 and continued running it until 1950.

In the 1930s one oysterman decided if he couldn't get at least 30 cents for a bushel, he would put his oysters on his leased ground at the bottom of the West River. There his oysters remained until the price went up to 55 or 65 cents a bushel, and then he brought them up to sell.

In a 1984 interview, Gustav Heinrich, born in August 1908, said that his father's oysters brought "anywhere to 35 cents a bushel up." When his father quit in 1950, it was $1.50 to $2.00 a bushel. He said that there were plenty of oysters until 1948, and "they dropped off completely. I don't know what happened unless it was silt in the Bay."

Fifth graders from Lula G. Scott School, writing in "Discovering Our Community" in 1952-53, found that "most of the tong boats are owned by colored. Some of the colored families who own their tong boats are Mr. Melvin Brown, Mr. Elnathan Nick, Mr. Dewey Brown, Mr. Charles Thompson and Mr. Benjamin Brown." The Wildes and Crandalls, white families, were listed as still oyster tonging. They also reported that, whereas 75 tong boats used to leave the Shady Side area, there were then about twenty.[5]

Former watermen living today say that the early 1970s ushered in the final demise of oystering for a living. Hurricane Agnes in 1972 was a rare June hurricane and arrived as a damaging, ravaging tropical storm in the mid-Atlantic. Bill Lescallett said that the health department closed down the Bay for all seafood, a moratorium that lasted about two years. That is when he left the water completely.

In the 1950s, after the oysters were sold and the next day's preparations completed, the watermen tied up their boats in Parrish

Creek by Leatherbury's Oyster House next to Woods Wharf. Almost all of the boats were on the west side of the creek, and none were across the creek on the east side. Today, the scene is completely different, with workboats sparse and all types of recreational boats present.

One local waterman estimated that about 75 percent of African American Shady Side men owned their own boats as far back as oystering days in sailboats, before motors were available. Family names mentioned as probable owners at that time were Gross, Holland, Matthews, Thompson, and Dennis. "By the time of J.R. Gross's era, 85 percent of the watermen had quit."

In September or October, there might be four or five buy-boats running up their flags to buy oysters as watermen returned to the West River with their catch. Another buyer was Cephas Carter, who transported oysters by truck from Leatherbury's, adjacent to the County Wharf in Shady Side, to Warsaw, Virginia. Mondays through Fridays and sometimes Saturdays, a truck, sometimes two, was filled with a hundred bushels of oysters to make the trip to Virginia shucking houses. Leatherbury's and other shucking houses had closed down. Inside Leatherbury's building, Cephas Carter paid the watermen, but local guys and the waterman himself worked together to load Cephas's truck.

As a teenager in the late 1960s, Ron Holland and Courtney "Lightning" Blake worked on land as the waterman worked from his boat. Like bringing water up from a well, the three men used a boom, pulley, rope, and a bucket to hoist the waterman's oysters. Catching the bucket at the end of the slack rope, the waterman filled the bucket with oysters, swept his gloved hand across the top to level the contents, and called out, "One." As each full bucket rose, the waterman called out its number: "two, three, four," until the fifth bucket ascended and he shouted, "Mark me tally." He then placed an oyster on the side of his boat to represent five buckets of oysters. Ron remembered that Rodney Gross, Sr., always called out, "Mark me one. Mark me two. Mark me three. Mark me four. Mark me tally," as he offloaded his oysters.

The bucket was attached to a rope over a pulley and Lightning would "Pull, pull, pull, pull, pull," on the rope to bring up the full bucket and swing it over to Ron. Ron grabbed the bucket and walked a few steps over to dump the contents into a hopper. The hopper was at the base of a conveyor that carried the oysters up into the truck. As the oysters piled up, the driver eased forward so that the truck continued to fill from the front to the back.

During the process of loading the oysters on those cold winter days, Ron quickly became coated in mud and the refuse that accompanied the oysters: amphipods, clamworms, and white-fingered mud crabs. At the end of each day, Ron's clothes were a laundering nightmare. As soon as the truck was loaded and all workers paid, including Ron, the truck headed for Warsaw. Ron caught a ride on the truck and was dropped off at Cedarhurst Road, from where he walked home. He gave his $15, $10, or $12 ("It was never the same.") to his mother, and she gave him a few dollars back.

This routine of winter work and mud coating continued until one evening "Tootie" Wilde showed up with an unexpected gift for Ron. It was a rain suit! Also called "all skins," Tootie had bought Ron a pair of bib overalls with a coat that changed Ron's cold, muddy, wet experiences forever. The appreciative young man "thanked him a thousand times."

Crabbing

To ready a trotline for crabbing, the crabber baited the line with chicken, eels, menhaden, or even bull lips. The baited line was then wound around in a circle at the bottom of a big tub. The important thing was to have the line ready so the crabber could pick up the circle to carry to his boat, where the weights were stored overnight. The line was attached to a floating bottle or buoy, which was attached to a weight and dropped over the side of the boat. The crabber unwound the line to its end, where a second weight was attached and dropped in the water.

After a period of waiting, the crabber, with crab net in hand, worked his line by scooping crabs, always too greedy to let go of their food, off the line and into a basket. Crabs let go of the line when they break through the waterline. If the crab was undersized, he was tossed back into the water. The waterman had to be licensed to crab in a particular area if the crabs were to be sold.

A crabber whose father and grandfather had been crabbers from Parrish Creek offered up two crabbing tips. One: You can tell if a storm is coming because the birds fly lower. Two: Crabs bite better right after a storm. He claimed it had worked for him.

Some watermen didn't sell their crabs but brought them home for friends, relatives, or the family's dinner. One daughter said that she was always making crab cakes because her dad had brought home another two pounds of crabmeat. She would freeze the crab cakes and prepare them for dinner in the winter. Gustav Heinrich said that people around the community would pay 25 cents a dozen in the early days. When they were selling best, he'd get about $2.00 a bushel.

Many older residents told about walking along the shore and seeing crabs for the picking. Getting in the eelgrass, they could find peelers to put aside until they shed to become soft crabs.

When Clark "Squeeze" Brown retired, he kept his little rowboat down at James and Rachel Crowner Wicks's home at the end of West River Road. During the crabbing season, if anyone in his family went looking for him, they knew to go to the Wickses, and "You could see him way out there," his daughter Joyce Brown Thompson recalled.

One rainy January morning at City Dock in Annapolis, J.R. Gross watched his oyster boat, *The Puddin,* burn to the waterline. He was in his 20s at the time and had owned his 42' wooden boat, built in 1954, for three years. He had lit the kerosene heater in the cabin and then pulled on his yellow slicker. The heater exploded and threw him against the side of the cabin. Luckily he wasn't burned, but his shoulder was slightly injured. Since the boat still floated, his father told him it could be rebuilt, so this was J.R.'s goal. Tony Scrivener at Parrish Creek Marina gave J.R. space at his yard on Parrish Creek, and two of his cousins worked on *The Puddin* to get her back in shape.

Calvin "Pee Wee" Matthews and J.R. Gross were the most widely known and recognized black watermen working in the Shady Side area in the 21st century. J.R.'s great-grandfather had hand-tonged for oysters in the early 1900s.

J.R. kept his working boat, *Miss Cindy,* on Parrish Creek, where generations of Grosses have had historical connections to the West River. Distantly related to J.R., Kendall "K.D." Gross and his son, Beville Gross, own and operate a successful pile driving and marine construction business out of Parrish Creek. At the end of a summer's workday, friends Bev and J.R. could be seen talking on *Miss Cindy* at Miss Lucille Matthews Brown's pier on Parrish Creek.

When J.R. was six years old, his father, James Rodney, Sr., took him clamming, and J.R. picked clams off the conveyor. By the time J.R. was thirteen, he could operate 500-pound hydraulic oystering tongs. Working with his father during high school summers, J.R. joined his dad full time after graduation. Except for a short stint building piers and working as a mechanic at Jiffy Lube, J.R. worked on the water year round at all hours of the day depending on what was in season and what the rules allowed. He agreed with the saying, "A bad day on the water is better than any good day on land." He found satisfaction in the quality of life working on the water and valued the independence of being able to go out and conquer nature when catching oysters, fish, or crabs.

Brainstorming in a Franklin United Methodist Church's men's group on fund-raising ideas for the church, J.R. recalled the Blessing of the Fleet in 1955, when a group of South County watermen echoed the centuries-old European practice. They agreed that repeating the tradition on Parrish Creek was a great idea. When J.R. approached Adam Hewison of Discovery Village, he heartily endorsed the idea, and the project moved forward. A committee of watermen, church members, and volunteers formed, and they all worked together to resurrect the Blessing of the Fleet on Parrish Creek.

The Blessing of the Fleet took place in August 2002. Parrish Creek has been called the busiest waterman's creek on the Western shore. [Go to www.discoveryvillage.net to see pictures of the festival in 2002 and of Captain J.R., his stepson Eric, and *Miss Cindy*.]

The community was stunned and deeply saddened when J.R., James Rodney Gross, Jr., died on July 9, 2011, at age 43 after a lengthy illness. In addition to his daily work, he was on county boards, advisory committees, and watermen's associations. He captained three boats: *The Puddin'*, *Miss Cindy*, and *Southern Belle*.

Following the water was a hard way to make a living. In fact it was a rare waterman who did make his living entirely on the rivers and Bay. If the season was a good one, then he and his wife could purchase needed items that had been kept on hold for the family.

During the Depression, Shady Side fared better than big cities because of the family gardens, domestic animals, small woodland animals, and river and Bay resources. Relatives and neighbors were always helping one another fill in the gaps, but nothing was predictable, and the unexpected was a common fact of life.

Waterman often had several jobs and thought in terms of how much the family could bring in over a year's time. If the oyster harvest was weak, it was a greater scramble to fill the gap with other work. In the summer, watermen farmed, did carpentry, took out fishing parties, built or worked on boats, worked at construction, or took on odd jobs in the community.

Varnell Nick took other jobs during his lifetime: shucking oysters at Gustav Heinrich's, working on boats in New Jersey, and working in Baltimore at fertilizer factories. He and five or six other county youth paid room and board at his sister's of $10 to $12 a week. His sister washed and ironed for him for $5 a week. He also worked at Thomas Lumber Company for twenty years and for Woodfield's Fish Market for about the same length of time.

When not oystering, DeWayne Salisbury worked in construction, pouring concrete underground to build the subway in Washington, D.C. Every summer for forty years he got up at 4:30 a.m. to carpool with other men who also worked for the same construction company. When he arrived home, he went to work at his school janitorial job.

As late as 1974, the Bay supplied half the national oyster harvest. Oysters remained the state's most valuable cash crop until 1983 when crabbing surpassed it. Parasitic diseases MSX and Dermo nearly wiped out the Bay's oyster beds in 1987. Due to the lack of rain that year, higher salinity levels helped spread the disease. By 1988 the annual oyster harvest fell to 359,000 bushels, the lowest in more than a century. The oyster harvest dropped to 1 percent of the 1900 levels.

Pollution from sewer plant discharges, animal waste, and fertilizers have also contaminated the Bay. Runoff containing nitrogen and phosphorus fertilized algae that robbed plants and fish of light and oxygen. Development, overfishing, pollution, and disease changed the output of the Bay. The Chesapeake Bay Foundation, West/Rhode River Keepers, and those concerned with the Bay and its rivers have worked tirelessly to educate the public and to reverse the damage.

Increased regulation, restricted catches, and shorter seasons have hurt the watermen. Waterfront property can only be used commercially until the end of a waterman's career. He cannot transfer the zoning exceptions to anyone, including his children. Part-time watermen and sport fishermen now compete for any catch. Meanwhile, more people are getting licenses, but fewer people depend on those licenses for their livelihood. Idled watermen's tools of the trade can often be seen among yard decorations, at the side of an old building, or abandoned in an out-of-the-way plot of ground.

African Americans Varnell Nick, Julius Dennis, the Scott brothers, the Grosses, the Matthewses, the Hollands, the Salisburys, the Thompsons, and many more Shady Side men, black and white, left a waterman's legacy in Shady Side as they lived productive, challenging lives in a waterman's community.

CHAPTER 8

CHUCK GROSS

Chantal Gross Banks Family Tree

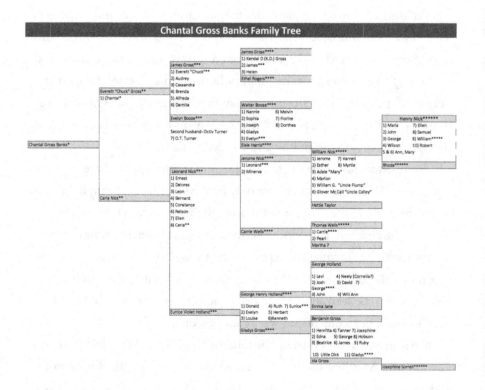

C HUCK GROSS WAS LOVED by all who knew him. He was a good man who cared about and watched out for others. Formally named Everett Lovell Gross, he was always called Chuck—even before he was born.

The only son of James and Evelyn Gross, Chuck was delivered by Dr. Aris T. Allen on January 6, 1950. He began life in the white frame home on Shady Side Road where his mother still lives. Four sisters soon followed. The expanding family was no different from other families in the area until a tragedy struck when Chuck was eight years old and his last sister was on her way.

In 1958 and 1959, the Naval Academy was undertaking another land reclamation project, using landfill to create the Farragut playing field near Bancroft Hall along the Severn River at Spa Creek. In 1958 Chuck's father was working the dredger, a giant pipe that funneled racing mud and dredge through it. James lost his footing, slipped, and fell from the piling; he drowned before anyone could rescue him.

Chuck remembered someone coming to the Lula G. Scott School to take him home: "They told me Dad had died. Being [I was] young, it wasn't really that bad. I'm a kid, but, I cried, but it wasn't like if I had been 16 or 17. It wasn't that devastating, but it's worse now, believe it or not, than what it was when I was eight." Eyes lifted in a remembrance, Chuck took a deep breath and exhaled, "But I was blessed, because, well, Mom had five kids at the time. My grandmother, Ethel Gross, just took me in. Like, I didn't miss a beat after that because she was like a mother *and* a father to me. I didn't want for anything. Not that we were rich, but I never wanted for anything." Carla, his wife, softly interjected, "She spoiled him somewhat." Chuck agreed, "She did. She did. She loved her son, and I was the next thing to it."

Chuck had a strong memory of riding with his grandmother and his father to buy a new car about a month before his father drowned. His grandmother liked to have a fine car with some zip, so she purchased a

1958 Ford Fairlane. "I was sitting in the back seat, and dad was driving with my grandmother in front."

Chuck also remembered seeing his father laid out in the living room of his family home. Years later, when Chuck himself worked as an adult on a barge in South Creek, another pile driver told him that he had been on the very barge from which Chuck's father had slipped to his death.

Chuck grew up in the house he later owned, on the corner of Columbia Beach Road and Route 468, "on the main drag there," from the time he was eight until he went to Vietnam. He and his grandparents lived in the back of the house, and his uncle and family of six lived in the front. Chuck slept on a twin bed in an upstairs bedroom with his grandparents. There was one tiny window, and the room was unbearably hot in the summer. There were two separate kitchens in the house, with a wall and door between. Chuck's Aunt Rosalie Gross embraced him like her own child and bought him clothes when she was buying for her son, "Boy," whose real name was Kendal. Miss Rosalie mothered Chuck as well. "If Kendal wore something, and she hadn't brought me something, then I wore it the next day," Chuck recalled. The two cousins were devoted to each other.

"Grandma had the seafood place there. Everybody knew Ethel. The local watermen would bring in their seafood. Maybe in the eighties, if business was good, she might get crabs from Virginia. She was a great person; she was a businessperson and she was educated," Chuck said emphatically.

"My grandfather James, called Jim, was not educated at all, but he knew how to make money." Jim had a junk car business, and Chuck would often go with him to Baltimore to sell parts of cars—for example, maybe a bunch of fenders. "He was a go-getter and self-employed." People liked his grandfather, who frequently loaned money to others, but Chuck doubted that he always received repayment. "I looked up to him." This grandfather was the man who taught Chuck the importance of responsibility and the work ethic. The lesson stuck, because Chuck certainly was a worker, as anyone in Shady Side will attest. He knew how to get things done efficiently, effectively, and energetically.

"I started driving on Shady Side Road when I was 13, and I drove every one of the junk cars that would run. There was never any police on the road when I was that age. I couldn't wait to get my driver's license. As soon as I turned 16, my grandmother took me up to get it. I went to pick Carla up that very same day. Didn't I, honey? My senior year I was the only black dude with a car, a nice car."

Chuck's grandfather was also a waterman. "I remember when I was a little boy, and I used to go oysterin' with him. He'd only run the boat, and he had two guys, one on each side working the rigs. I would get seasick [clapping his hands together] all the time. He said, 'You know what, Chuck; I'm going to stop this. The next time we go out, we're going to take a couple of lemons, and when you feel your stomach want to turn on you, you suck on that lemon.' He used to take ropes and tie me on the stern of that boat, and I would just suck on that lemon and *it worked*, believe it or not."

Other watermen experienced seasickness in their early forays on the water. They spoke about getting terribly sick—and then one day it was over. "That's the thing, now. I used to get seasick all the time, but then, all of a sudden, it just stopped."

Chuck worked on the water and made a living from it for a time. In the summer he worked as a pile driver, building piers and bulkheads, and in the winters he oystered. He owned several bay boats. Carla and Chuck told about a frightening incident in the 1970s, the night before oyster season opened. Chuck's grandparents put together his first boat, with everything hydraulic. Excited, he decided to go down to Parrish Creek to his Uncle K.D.'s to check it all out once more. "It was raining and I said, 'Honey, I'm going to run down to the shore and check my boat out.' Right? Everything was perfect earlier that day, but I just wanted to make sure I was ready for that first day. Went down and had a gas leak in the bilge. I hit the key and it started. All of a sudden I pick the engine top off to just look down, and it exploded. It blew the cabin, the floors, it knocked me on the stern; I couldn't see."

Luckily the fire department heard the explosion. In fact, everyone in Shady Side must have heard the explosion—including the guys playing basketball in the brick school building—because they all came running.

And it was also lucky that Bev Gross, Chuck's cousin, was home. "He ran out and got me off the boat. All my eyebrows, hair, everything was gone." Carla agreed, "Um hum, scorched it." Chuck continued, "They just packed my face full with ice. I was just burning."

Chuck had a very bad experience on the water. Back from Vietnam in December (about 1973 or 1974), he and some other watermen sailed across the Bay to the Eastern Shore because a new oyster bar had been opened up and they could dredge for oysters and make some money. A 45-mile-per-hour northwest wind had been predicted, which is pretty much straight across the Bay, but they expected to have enough time to get over and back.

"All of us go, I'm in my boat, I pretty much have my limit, and my bilge pump wouldn't stop running. I took up a piece of the floor and looked and the whole bottom is full of water. I say, 'Oh my God, what am I going to do?' So I turned toward shore and came past a couple of guys and said 'I'm going down.' They knew because they couldn't see the copper line or the paint on the bottom of my boat."

Chuck decided to try to hit bottom so he wouldn't sink, and he gave the engine all the gas he could. "Lucky enough," he said, he hit bottom. But all of a sudden everything went down, and Chuck jumped on the top of his mast and held on. "I was freezing, freezing cold, my fingers were numb, and I was soaked. Nobody could get to me, so they called the Coast Guard and Department of Natural Resources, who came across the Bay in a Boston Whaler."

The wind picked up. It was so cold and so rough that Chuck could see whole bottoms of nearby boats with the props spinning out of the water. He felt the *wham* of the whaler as it came up beside watermen's boats to pass. "They got me, gave me clothes, and brought me back. It's lucky that none of us drowned that day. I quit oysterin' for about two years after that," he laughed, "but I went back."

Chuck, the waterman, and his boat wrap up a good day on the water.
Chantal Gross Banks Collection.

Carla and Chuck's romance reached back to their middle and high school years. Their two grandmothers lived in the triangle of Columbia Beach, Shady Side, and Bay Breeze Roads. Ethel Gross ran her seafood house from her home on the corner of Shady Side and Columbia Beach Roads, and Carrie Nick, head cook at the Andrews Hotel, was at the other corner of Shady Side and Bay Breeze Roads. Carla was a close school friend of Chuck's sister Sandy, so Carla knew Sandy's brother. Carla said, "He was cute, a sharp dresser, and he had wheels." Chuck interjected, "I was persistent. Her father knew my father, and he knew I was a hard-working man, and he liked me a lot. [Chuck was 16 and Carla 13.] They would let me come up and sit at their house. Maybe I would take Carla out for some ice cream or movies at State Circle on West Street in Annapolis."

Chuck graduated from Bates High School in 1969, and Carla graduated from Southern High School. They married before he went to Vietnam. Letters kept him going during that terrible time. "Unless we were out in the field and the chopper couldn't drop the mail bag, there wasn't a day that I didn't get a letter from Carla or my grandmother."

While serving in Vietnam, Chuck Gross had a family picture composed with Carla and Chantal. **Chantal Gross Banks Collection**

Inducted in 1969, he was discharged from the service in 1970. He received the National Defense Service Medal, a Vietnam Service Medal with two bronze service stars, a Combat Infantryman Badge, a Republic of Vietnam Campaign Medal, and an Air Medal. For those who served in the Vietnam War, returning home was an experience unlike that of

144

the veterans of any other war Americans fought. They did not receive a welcome or appreciation of any sort. Instead, many were ostracized, insulted, and humiliated. Because it was an extremely unpopular and controversial war, the men who served often bore the brunt of the anti-war feelings. Chuck was pained by these sentiments.

Chuck started Chuck's Lawn Service driving Hechinger riding mowers in the late 1970s. Jerry Yochelson and "Our Place," now the Captain Avery Museum, were his first customers. Chantal, his only daughter, worked with her dad when she was in middle and high school, but she didn't get paid. He added new accounts, and his customer base grew steadily each year. His lawn business was thriving, and there were constant additional requests for delivery of rocks, hauling, and specialty yard work. Chuck and Carla's home and yard were never neglected in spite of the demands on his time. Their yard and home reflected his construction and gardening abilities, as he continued to expand his creative ideas.

In addition to the lawn service, he ran a limousine service for a few years, and he worked as a crane operator for eight years during the winter months. His boss said that Chuck got twice as much done as any other other person working for him. O.T. Turner, Chuck's brother, reported that truck drivers loved for Chuck to be working the crane because he never spilled, so they never had to wash their tractor-trailers. Several seasonal families hired him to take care of their property when they were away from Shady Side, and they knew all would be secure with Chuck at the helm.

For reasons that no one will ever know, can only guess and still be wrong, Chuck separated himself from Shady Side. It was a devastating, shocking blow to his family and friends and the community.

The obituary read: *Everett Lovell Gross, 60, died April 9 at the crossroads of Churchton and Shady Side. He was born January 6, 1950, in Annapolis. He was a resident of Shady Side his entire life, and he completed 12 years of schooling. He owned Chuck's Lawn Service, and he served in the Vietnam War as a Specialist 4th Class. He loved fishing and giving his fish back to his family and the community.*

CHAPTER 9

STORES AND BUSINESSES

S TORES AND BUSINESSES IN Shady Side in 2011 seem limited, but they
serve the immediate needs of the local population, who do their
major shopping outside the community. Like the ebb and flow of the
West River and the Chesapeake Bay, Shady Side has witnessed businesses
that burned down and were rebuilt, businesses that were converted to
homes, and one that resurfaced as the post office; some buildings even
became material for other businesses. Almost all of these businesses were
white-owned.

Several restaurants have occupied the space on the corner of Shady
Side and Cedarhurst Roads. Meeting with varying degrees of success have
been the Blue Heron, Ritchie's, Richard's, the Moose Club, and Aida's
Country Store. When it was Aida's Country Store, African Americans
could not go inside to eat because of an enforced segregation law. They
could go to a side window to buy food but could not go inside the
building to sit, be served, and eat. Ironically, the James Crowner family
lived on the corner lot until Aida Hogg and her husband bought the
land from them to build a restaurant—a restaurant where the African
American Crowner family could not eat

A postcard shows Aida's Country Kitchen in Shady Side. Cedarhurst Road (right) and a glimpse of the Crowner house that was moved from the corner are in the background. The back of the card states: Home Cooked Food, Beer and Wine, Dancing. Orchestra Sat. Nites. Tel: West River 4421.
Jean Matthews Johnson Collection

Leatherbury's

On the corner opposite the restaurant on Cedarhurst and Shady Side Roads, Erwood "Woody" Avery and Edward Leatherbury built a store in 1938 that was known as "Woody's Store." Woody ran it for period of time, then Edward Leatherbury ran it for a few months, and then he sold it to Luther Leatherbury.

Erwood Avery went into the septic tank business. Cornelius Dennis drove a truck for Mr. Avery and worked for and with him for over forty years. Public sewers were brought into Shady Side during the 1970s, although there are properties still using septic tanks today.

When the original Leatherbury store burned down, Mr. Leatherbury rebuilt and opened the new store in July 1944. Doris Crowner Brown remembered the fire and the heat radiating from the windows. Another person remembered kids going through the ashes looking for coins and meeting with some success.

Mr. Leatherbury carried a supply of items you would expect to find in a rural store, and many African Americans did business with him. One lady told about Mr. Leatherbury's wife inviting her to dry her children's clothes inside the store on a rainy day after business hours.

Luther Leatherbury tends his store at the corner of Shady Side and Cedarhurst Roads. This is the original store that burned down. **Captain Avery Museum Collection**

Delores and Connie Nick told about the penny candy at Leatherbury's— you could get so much for a nickel! For a quarter, you could get chips, cupcakes, and a pack of gum. If empty bottles were turned in, the redeemer made 2 cents for each empty, so glass bottles could reap a candy gold mine. Their mother, Eunice Nick, usually sent the girls off on Connie's bike to the store a couple of times a week. Delores remembered that she would give the list to the storekeeper, who used a hook to reach up high to get goods.

"The winter trade is largely colored and the rest of the year there is mostly transient business. According to information supplied by Leatherbury's Store, business increases about fifty percent in the summer with the transient trade." [1]

When Ron Holland was young, Luther Leatherbury hired him to pick up trash and sweep the store in the summer months. The best part of the job was cleaning behind the slot machine; if there were any stray nickels on the floor, he got to keep them.

Leatherbury's sold the store to a realtor in 1969, and Richard Van Dyke opened a grocery store and sold appliances in 1970. Several remembered a pinball parlor being in the building for a short time, someone else selling steamed crabs briefly, and another man having a business that failed when the bank repossessed the property. Since 1975 the owner of Foamount, now called Unique Mounting Services, has been running a successful business where posters are mounted on foam and shipped all over the country.

Heinrich's or Gustav's

Many senior community members remember Gustav Heinrich's store, oyster house, and home on the West River. It was located at the end of West River Road, sometimes called Kooster Lane, because "We didn't have a name for the road then." Gustav, born in August 1908, never married, and his sister Anna, born in 1911, said that they lived on South Creek with their parents. (The siblings were interviewed separately in August and September of 1984.)

Their father, Augustin Heinrich, came to Shady Side from Germany in 1890 with his mother when he was fourteen years old. Later, Augustin married Agnes Wilde. The couple, Grandmother Heinrich, and five children, including Gustav and Anna Agnes, moved from Cedar Point, or Wagner's Point, in 1913 and built a small store with block walls and rough lumber about 30' long. (Gustav said in 1984 that Ms. Sommerville owned the property that his family left in 1913 to move "up West River.") There was no real ceiling in the store, only open joists. Gustav worked in the store for his father from the beginning but started actual clerking in 1920. From then until it closed in 1950, Gustav spent most of his days at the store. He believed he didn't have the time to play as much as his younger siblings did; however, if the store closed in the winter, he would happily skate on the river.

Tongers brought their oysters to the pier and unloaded them, and ten to fifteen oyster shuckers shucked them in the oyster house. After the oysters were shucked and washed, they were put in big barrels with ice until they were transferred and packed into gallon cans and carried to Washington or Baltimore by Augustin Heinrich. The watermen probably got "like 25 cents a bushel."

"The oystermen bought a lot of meat and canned goods. Where we was, was mostly colored fellas lived up that creek [South Creek] .... Dent Smith had a family and Ed Smith, his brother, owned land near Avery .... Gross, Scott, plenty of Scotts up there, Matthews and all them kind. Henry Scott owned some homes ... he died in '24. A colored fellow had a log canoe sailboat and oystered for Hal Owings around 1922. He oystered for Hal Owings and died around 1950. Will Smith lived across the river, come over in a rowboat, and sit in the store and talk for a while. Lived up at the head of the creek. Nobody close by, so he'd come over to the store once in a while." Gustav remembered Sellman Scott's three sons drowning in the 1929 "awful storm. They found them the next day."

"Oyster boats started out at 6 o'clock in the morning, according to the weather" and the season. "We'd close anywhere around 8 or 9 o'clock. Always be somebody either going or coming." The store carried boat supplies such as pumps, boots, and rain gear. Beer, bacon, some pork, and pig's feet could be purchased. Gustav's nephew, Norman, remembered seeing Uncle Gustav cutting chunks of cheese from a "great big old thing of cheese, which would sit on the chopping block"; the cheese was sold by the slice at 10 cents a slab. The cheese came in a round wooden container, and the lid of the box was kept to cover the cheese. "Uncle Gustav grabbed the big old knife, removed the lid, hacked off a hunk of cheese, wiped off the knife, and left it beside the cheese. It probably never got washed." Four to five gingersnaps or a bag of candy with six pieces cost a penny. There was a big jar or keg of pickles that cost about five cents a pickle. "I know he would have cans of peanuts, and he sold them to the children by the handful for a nickel. I remember that very well," said Charles Coates.

Welcome to Gustav Heinrich's Oyster House and store on South Creek that flows into the West River. The cat will accept any handouts.
Captain Avery Museum Collection

Varnell Nick remembered men gathering in Gustav's store to talk and tell jokes about what someone did. They bragged about how many oysters they caught or tried to determine who the best oysterman was. Varnell Nick said that Wilbert Hall was the best tonger, because he brought up 75 to 100 bushels tonging all alone. He also told that he liked to go into the woods and watch Mr. Dennis's oxen pull his two-wheeled cart. "He talked to them and trained them what to do like horses with reins." Varnell recalled, "Mr. Weems hired a man to bring his threshing machine to thresh the wheat on his West River Road farm. Mr. Bob Pike's threshing machine come down the road blowing its whistle and going 'Putt, putt.' Everyone helped one another on the farms." The farmer paid a certain amount per bushel for each bushel threshed. Measuring by the bushel seemed to be the way of setting prices, whether for oysters or wheat.

Gustav's father had a big field of oyster shells and sold them to the county by the bushel for building the base of West Shady Side Road. "They measured one truck load and then the others would go out and sell them the same way." The state planted purchased oyster shells in the Bay for the oyster spat to catch on.

According to Gustav the first state road of gravel came into Shady Side around 1930. It was a big year, because the oyster house burned down and the family had to rebuild it. The fire started during the day and burned into the night. "We had a crowd there." There was no fire department yet. "Wasn't no way to get to it; just let it burn. We called West Annapolis, but when they [one truck[got there it was gone." The oyster house was in operation from 1930 to 1950 and the store "up until 1957." Eight years after the oyster house fire, the store burned and was rebuilt in 1941.

A coal stove heated the store, and the store carried any kind of groceries that the Heinrichs could get. Molasses was sold from a barrel with a spigot, and crackers, sugar, and cases of nails arrived in barrels. Canned goods were half as plentiful as they are in more modern times.

Gustav reported three or four steamboats were running up and down the Bay and bringing in supplies. He went down to the wharf to pick up the freight. The *Emma Giles* he described as a "right good sized steamer" that carried up to maybe "1,200 passengers; I think that's right. In 1927 they quit." Anna loved to go down to meet the boat with the other children when the groceries came in. First it was with horse and wagon and later by truck. "We would go out on the pier and watch the people from Baltimore get off and boats or carriages picked them up for the boarding houses." Another person reported that people traveled down Steamboat Road to pick up whatever had come in for them.

In her 1984 interview, Gustav's sister Anna Heinrich Hazzard told about living "right on the South Creek. We ice-skated on South Creek with others who lived in the area. There were a couple of the colored girls, the Crowners: Rachel, Anita, and Ben, and they always skated in the same area as us. I don't remember about the skating in crowds because we didn't have the children in our area." Varnell Nick recalled skating at night, and adults built a fire on the ice at night. "Some folks would bring hot soup and we had a good time."

Anna Heinrich's father's boat was named *Commodore,* and he ran oysters to Baltimore before he had the oyster business. Beside the oyster house he had a large pier, and all the oystermen from up in South Creek came to buy gasoline at Heinrich's gasoline tanks. She thought a gallon of gas cost 25 cents.

Anna and her siblings walked two-and-a-half miles to school but took a lot of short cuts: to the Weems's house picking up friends, over a little bridge, through the woods avoiding Lerch's cows, over steps topping a wooden fence behind St. Matthew's, and on to school. (The Crowner children may have followed the same route, but their destination was a different school.) Her son Norman told about a little lane that "came to our neighbor's Kate Crowner, a black lady that lived right next to us. And then I'd cut through her yard" to get to his grandmother's house.

Kate Crowner or a family member could take a rowboat from her house on the water and row around to Gustav's. They could also walk down her road past Benjamin Dennis's present home on the corner where the road hits West River Road and wraps around to Gustav's. Kate Crowner's daughter Rachel married James Wicks, and the land passed to the couple. The James A. Crowners named their third daughter for Kate: Katherine Crowner.

Squeeze Brown kept his workboat at Heinrich's, and his young daughter Joyce loved to buy "ice cream that you dip, hard candy, and it was always fun there. When they were working on the boat you could get ice cream from the store." She described the wooden floors, shelves lined with food, and the long-handled arm with a grip to reach the high items.

All traces of Gustav's store have been erased, but Miss Doll Baby Dennis or Miss Florine Thompson can point out the very spot where Heinrich's stood. Today, a new home is on the land and is just yards away from the home of Miss Doll Baby's cousin Benjamin Dennis, son of Julius Dennis.

A Movie Theater

If you traveled from today's Churchton traffic light along Shady Side Road, there was a movie theater on the left side of the road just before Deep Cove. But the image of a marquee with lights and a ticket booth would be completely wrong. The theater was in a building that once looked like a schoolhouse and had served as a unity hall, a church, a residence, and a hang out for a motorcycle group. It stood forlornly empty with an outside door hanging open until it was finally renovated into a charming gray cottage. During the time of the unity hall, black children and families attended movies on announced nights of the week. A man from Baltimore brought a projector and the movies to be seen. The building had no electricity, so the projectionist also brought a generator, which hooked up to the projector. The audience sat on wooden benches with no backs or sat on the wooden floor and watched the movie projected on a sheet. Joyce Brown Thompson remembered seeing "Charlie Chan" and a "Dracula" or scary type show. Walking home, her father would put her on his shoulders if she got really tired.

Virginia Nick Hopkins laughed at the memory of the theater and recalled that her cousin Patty Nick Gross would row the two of them "in a boat from Patty's house over to the other side of South Creek and walk from there." After the movie, Patty rowed them back home. Lucille Matthews Brown remembered seeing westerns without sound and having to make up your own words to the action.

The closest and only other option for blacks to see films, outside of those brought to the Lula G. Scott Elementary School, was to make a trip to the Star Theater in Annapolis. However, Charles Coates, Sr., and at least one other friend watched a movie in a place for whites. "They had a moving picture parlor way down in Shady Side right across from the store" (now Shady Side Market), "so we would go upstairs and look out, peep out the window. We could see it anyway, without paying for it." He was referring to William C. Nowell's theater in the Keith Wilde Building in the late 1920s. [2]

★   ★   ★

It is safe to say that Shady Side had a sawmill. Gustav Heinrich recalled that until the 1930s Mr. Price's sawmill was beyond the intersection before where Swamp Circle Road meets Route 468. Varnell Nick remembered that when he was between ten and twelve years old, he liked to go to a sawmill in Cedarhurst and watch the wood go through. It was probably Glen Trott's grandfather who owned the sawmill that Varnell remembered. Another source said that a sawmill owned by Robert F. Nowell and Robert Murray Leatherbury sat on the corner of Snug Harbor and Woods Wharf Roads where a private home has been for many years. [3]

In his interview, Gustav Heinrich also mentioned a lumberyard on West River Road that Will Thomas started around 1922 or 1923. Around 1950 "he moved up on the corner where it is now . . . Ms. Smith's house." W. M. Thomas and Fernando Weems formed the company in 1921 when it was located on Weems Creek between the Weems's farm and Mr. Thomas's home. In 1927 Mr. Thomas bought out Mr. Weems, and Mr. Thomas sold the company in 1952. By 1968 the company was owned by the Smith brothers, who expanded the business and added a hardware store.[4] Jack Smith bought out his brother, and the company at the corner of Routes 468 and 258 offered job opportunities to local employees until he sold the property in 2001. In 2011 the large corner lot has an empty house with attached building and a vacant lumberyard.

The Shady Side Beverage Company

In the 1920s the Shady Side Beverage Company was located near the brick entryway at the T of Snug Harbor Road and Shady Side Road, just down the road from Hopkins and across the road from the white Shady Side Elementary School. Owned by Robert Murray Leatherbury, it produced glass bottles and a "very sweet" soda pop. Varnell Nick remembered buying and popping the top off bottles to drink ginger ale or sarsaparilla flavors that "had some strength to it—very strong." The Leatherburys also had a bakery and ice cream parlor at this location for a period of time. Gustav Heinrich remembered buying soft drinks at Leatherbury's Shady Side Beverage Company but did not recall the ice cream parlor and bakeshop as clearly.

This is part of a salvaged bottle from the Shady Side Beverage Company. K. V. Gessford Plumbing in Shady Side found the bottle years ago.
Noel Widdifield Collection

The bakery was relocated to Churchton, and lumber from the original Shady Side bakery was used in the new bakery. In her 1984 interview, Josephine Tongue said that Tillie or another Leatherbury used to run this bakeshop. Now, in 2011, the Heavenly Grill is located on the spot on Route 258.

Swinburn's

Swinburn's store seemed to be mentioned frequently by many local residents as a popular store. Located at the first 90-degree turn curving left on Snug Harbor Road, the store was built in 1903. Some people laughed and reported that drivers could almost drive through the store because it was so close to the road. Owned by the Owings family and George Hopkins, the store was bought by William Swinburn in 1937. Marshall Nick and his friends would cut through the bushes from school and go to Hopkins before it was Swinburn's. In 1976, Edward Brevnik became the proprietor at Eddie's Store.[5] The building stood on the east side of the Kiwanis Community Center, but it fell into decay and was destroyed. Now a modern white two-story house faces what would have been the side of the store.

Other Businesses and Professionals

Although earlier buildings have disappeared or have been absorbed into other businesses, some original structures still exist today. For example, William H. White from Kent Island lived on the peninsula for a few years and built the "Brick House" in present Cedarhurst. Later, Capt. Salem Walter Avery, son of Capt. Salem and Lucretia Weedon Avery, married Mary Ann Crandall in 1893. They settled in the Brick House as bride and groom. Today the Brick House is a restaurant in the back and a lovely refurbished private home in the front.

Herb Crandall's store sat on the corner of the junction of Shady Side and Dent Roads. The road was named for Dr. Dent, who lived further down the road. Several families recalled going to the store, and someone from the Marion Nick family said that they mostly went to his store to buy eggs or flour.

Dr. George Dent came to practice in the Shady Side area in 1893, following Dr. Washington H. Bennett, who practiced in Shady Side from 1874 to 1899. Both doctors traveled by horse and buggy to call on patients. Patients could also come to Dr. Dent's home, which he rented until he could buy it from U. G. Owings. Because the nearest drugstore was in Annapolis, Dr. Dent kept a ready supply of medicines at home; however, if an unusual medication were required he would write a prescription for the druggist. The surest and quickest way to Annapolis was by water.

An older two-story house still standing on the corner of Scott Town Lane at the point of Nick Road was once a country store belonging to John Crandall, father of Bennett Crandall, for a few years around 1930.

However, it has been a home for most of its existence. Buddy Holland had his shop in the garage near the house, and his brother built his boats in the larger dilapidated building behind the garage.

Missouri Matthews, a black woman often called Aunt Missouri, owned a business located in the field by St. Paul's and across from the present Methodist church. Everyone dealt at the store. [6]

Josephine Tongue mentioned "an ice cream parlor on a corner" before another building was built in its place. Richard "Dick" Scott, called "Uncle Dick," ran it for a short time. "He didn't make the ice cream; someone brought it in. He got sick and closed the store."

First run by Lynn Siegert, Shady Side Market has been in its present location since about 1926. The store's past owners were Max Ambach, Murray Selsky, Alan Wilde briefly, Ellis Smith, and Bill and Ruth Paulus. Bill and Betty Catterton have been the owners since 1978, and the family continues to operate the store today on Snug Harbor Road.

Renno's Market was built on former Weems farmland. R. E. Renno purchased and remodeled the former store known as Floyd and Daisy Crompton's Supermarket, which sold vegetables and meat. Mr. Renno turned it into a modern market around 1949. When DeWayne Salisbury was in high school, he worked there stocking and delivering sales fliers on his bicycle. The Krissoff family bought the market in 1954 and kept the Renno name. They remodeled the store again in 1958, and they later acquired the first liquor license in the Shady Side area and ran Renno's for 20 years. Raymond Fountain and Cordell Salisbury worked there in addition to the Krissoffs' three sons. The Krissoffs referred to Raymond and Cordell as "adopted sons." [7] Mohan Grover bought the market in 1974 and continues to provide for the Shady Side community. Because of his many civic contributions and leadership, he is known as the unofficial mayor of Shady Side.

CHAPTER 10

CROWNER FAMILIES

Gayle Thompson Family Tree

Ira Thompson				
1) Ira S.				
2) Beverly				
3) Daisy Gayle*				
4) Celeste				

Gayle Thompson*

		John H. Crowner	
		1) James Crowner	
Charles Henry Crowner***		2) Charles H.***	
Ida's Children	Serena's children	3) Elizabeth	Jacob Dennis
I) John H.	1) Blanche Johnson	Rachel Dennis****	1) Rachel****
2) Robert	2) Calvin Johnson		(Siblings on Ms. Doll Baby's Tree)
Daisy Crowner**	3) James A.	3) Evelyn	Elizabeth Matthews
	4) Laura	7) Charles Francis	
	5) Merthan	8) Helen	John Offer
	6) Viola	9) Daisy**	1) Serena***
	Serena Offer*** 3rd Wife		
	Ida Thompson-dies 1st Wife		
	Ella Swan- no children 2nd Wife		Darcus Shaw

HE OLDEST MEMBER OF St. Matthew's UMC, Helen Crowner Gorham, turned 89 on October 31, 2010—Halloween. The family ministry of the church honored her with a bouquet of fall flowers and a dinner reception after the service. She just hoped the reception wouldn't interfere with her plans to watch the afternoon Redskins game on television.

To know Helen Crowner Gorham and her baby sister, Daisy Crowner Thompson (born September 5, 1923), is to love them. Affectionately known as the "Golden Girls" because of their humor, outlook, and joy in life, they are meticulous in their dress and always stylish. Their hats and dresses fashionably complement each other, and if there is not a smile on their faces, one is coming soon. A Sunday morning church visitor can find them sitting on the right hand side of the church, about three rows from the front, with an end space left for Miss Daisy's daughter, Gayle, to join them. Farther down the same row usually sit Doll Baby Dennis and Virginia Nick Hopkins.

As a reference point: Miss Helen's and Miss Daisy's grandmother, Rachel Dennis Crowner, was a sister to Miss Doll Baby Dennis's grandfather, Joshua Dennis. Both Rachel and Joshua Dennis and their brothers inherited land from Jacob Dennis, their father. Capt. Salem Avery's farm—Swamp Farm—was located in the central part of the peninsula and was bounded on the south by John Crowner's land and on the east by that of Jacob Dennis in 1876. [1]

Miss Helen talked about her father: "Papa had hogs, cows, horses, chickens, ducks, and all kinds of gardens. He raised crops and had an orchard with fruit trees such as apples, peaches, and pears. Papa was a horse lover." In addition to farming, he collected trash, sold papers, cut and sold wood in the Cedarhurst area, and worked with his brother Jim fishing and hunting ducks. "Mama used to can tomatoes and other foods," and she kept the household running smoothly.

The Crowner family farmhouse was made from wood that came from the Johnstown flood of May 31, 1889. (The 1889 flood killed 2,209 people and was the greatest single day of civilian loss of life in the United States before September 11, 2001. The Red Cross, founded in 1881, arrived in June 1889 to offer disaster relief under the direction of Clara Barton. This was the first major peacetime response for the Red Cross.)

The wood was salvaged from the Bay, where lumber and debris had been carried down the Susquehanna River, which empties into the Chesapeake Bay. Charles Crowner, like many others in the Shady Side community, recovered the wood to build new structures. Charles's wood was brought by boat to the Cedarhurst shore, transferred to a wagon, and then hauled to where the Charles Crowner home was built. Miss Daisy's house is across the road from where her family home originally stood, but the home place was demolished in 1981, and someone else now owns the property.

Life in Charles and Serena Crowner's family was centered on church, school, and family. Being at church on Sunday was a must, and the family was usually there all day for activities. Charles sang and his brothers Jim and Johnny were musicians. As Charles's own children reached adulthood, they, too, served on committees and sang in the choirs. The following generations are continuing in the examples set by Charles and Serena.

Serena wanted her children to play with each other rather than go from house to house to play like some of the children got to do on Columbia Beach Road. Holiday celebrations were rotated between the sisters' houses, and holiday picnics were rotated during the year. Birthdays were always celebrated because Charles, who loved his own birthday celebrations, had set the tradition. "Papa loved his birthday. He could laugh more than anyone else, and he was a kissing bug," said Miss Helen.

In 1947 Miss Helen sits on her father's lap while her mother watches from the right. Directly behind them a car heads toward Cedarhurst.
Miss Helen Crowner Gorham Collection

Charles owned a car but never learned to drive, so he would have to find a chauffeur to take the car and the family out and about.

Like all of the students of Shady Side, Helen Crowner Gorham and Daisy Crowner Thompson attended elementary school in Shady Side up to the seventh grade. Higher education was a dead end unless a county child could live with someone in Annapolis and go to Stanton High School, which became available in 1917. Wiley H. Bates High School in Annapolis was built in 1932 for the colored children of Anne Arundel County, but there was no public transportation for any of Anne Arundel County's black students to reach the school.

Two communities were the first to come up with a way to get their children to school. One community was Skidmore, about eight miles from Annapolis, and the other was Shady Side. Marion Nick (1892-1978) came up with a plan for the Shady Side area and started his school bus service in 1933. He was already driving local people to various places and was always interested in helping people get to their destinations, so it was a natural fit. While he was in town and the students were in school, he would run errands for Shady Side people.

By the time Helen and Daisy were ready for secondary school at Bates, Marion Nick had the vehicle to get them there. So that Charles Crowner could afford the monthly $5 per person fee to send both daughters to school, his youngest son Charles went to work to help cover the expense. The Depression had been in full force since 1929, so money was an issue for all families. Tommy Nick said that Mr. Andrews gave him $1.25 every Sunday so he could ride to school.

The bus was a character unto itself and provided a daily adventure for the riders. Mr. Tommy said it was an old bus; someone else said it was part truck and part bus; another person said it was a homemade bus made from an old truck that Mr. Marion fitted out for the passengers; others laughed and said, "It was something else!" But Miss Helen simply said, "You should have seen that bus!"

Whatever the description, it enabled the parents to get their children to Annapolis for a higher education. Rows of padded double seats did *not* face the front of the bus, and Mr. Nick did *not* drive from the left side of the bus or operate the door on his right. Instead, he sat somewhat in the middle of the bus and shifted gears with his feet. Lowell Dennis sat to his left, perhaps on a box, and Tommy Nick sat to Marion Nick's right, by the door. Whenever the bus stopped to pick up students, Tommy opened the door, got out of the bus to allow the children to get on, and then jumped back inside, returning to his front seat. The other seats were three parallel wooden benches the length of the bus. Two benches were against the sides of the bus, and one bench, without a back to it, was in the middle, parallel to the other benches. Children put their legs wherever they could. If it rained, Tommy would pull on a string to move the windshield wipers one way, and Lowell pulled on his string to move the wipers the opposite direction. The bus had a reputation for having flat tires, breaking down, being hot, or being cold because it had no heat, and it was "late getting in and late getting back." Yet, there wasn't a mishap every day, and a dozen or so children had transportation. As the bus chugged past walking Annapolis students, the walkers would call out, "Hey, is that Shady inside?" City "children used to laugh at our bus."

"Bates was a great school. They wanted you to get it. Everybody dressed right. Teachers looked like teachers," Miss Helen added.

Finally, in 1938, the year before Miss Helen and Mr. Tommy graduated, the county provided four buses for all the county colored students to reach Bates. One of the drivers hired was Marion Nick—with a real school bus.

★   ★   ★

Camp meetings and going to church brought different outcomes for the two sisters and their brother, Charles. Some black churches sent out notices announcing and inviting other black congregations to

164

attend their camp meeting, which was being held on a specific date. The meeting was an all-day affair—but not overnight—where food was sold in the church's yard and there was plenty of fellowship. The invited churches brought their choirs, and they performed and entertained the attendees. Charles said that if he ever got grown, he'd never go to church. Miss Helen said, "And he lived to 92 and never went to church except for funerals."

Not so for Miss Daisy. She was 13 when she first met her future husband in church at Franklin Church during a camp meeting. She was a Shady Side student, and Ira Thompson attended school in Churchton, so their paths had not crossed. They courted, but he went into the service in 1942. "That post office in Shady Side . . . I walked there every day. I wrote him a letter every day, and I looked for a letter from him. I'd put my letter in the mailbox and see if I got any mail. If I had one, I'd be happy; and if I didn't, I'd go home." When Daisy received a letter, she would wait to read it at home, and then she would answer Ira. The next day she retraced her steps, taking her letter to the post office once more.

A neighbor who was working at the Naval Academy told Miss Helen that they were hiring people because the men were going to war and wondered if she was interested. "So I went down there to Bancroft Hall and signed up. I talked Daisy into going, too, but Mama didn't want her to go." Their mother wanted her daughters to always be at home with her, but finally she was convinced that her daughters could go as long as their older sister, Evelyn, kept a close eye on them and they followed her instruction.

Daisy and Helen lived in Annapolis with Evelyn at 89 Washington Street across from the Stanton Center. During World War II, they worked at the Naval Academy commissary cutting cakes and pies for the midshipmen. They walked from their sister's house to the Academy, where they were expected to be by 5:00 a.m. "But it was a lot of fun," they both agreed, "because we was young and had just come out of the country and didn't know nothin' about the city, and I tell you . . . ." Miss Helen's voice trailed off in memories. After serving breakfast, the workers could take a break in a room with benches or they could leave until lunchtime. After clean up and another break, they returned to serve dinner and worked until the four pantries were in order for the next day. Then the sisters walked home to Evelyn's house.

"I was there when the first black midshipman was there. The last time I saw a picture of him he was in a wheelchair. They named a building after him." (This was a reference to Wesley A. Brown, who was the first African American to graduate from the Naval Academy, on June 3, 1949. The Wesley Brown Field House is named for him. Other blacks attended the Academy after the Civil War, but none graduated until Ensign Brown, according to Jim Cheevers, senior curator and associate director at the Naval Academy Museum.)

When Ira Thompson had furlough in 1945, he arrived in Annapolis by train. Miss Daisy related the story of Ira's return: "I was sitting on the porch. I was expecting him, but I didn't know when. I saw him on the pavement of the steps with his foot on the porch." Asked if she ran to him, she smiled sweetly: "Noooo, not really. I was glad he was home and all that. Of course, I left Annapolis and came on back home because he was here. He was home for one month. We were married on July 30, 1945, and he got out of the service in October."

After the sisters left Annapolis and work at the Academy, they took jobs at the YWCA, which is now West River Camp. Miss Helen's mother-in-law was in charge of food preparation at the camp.

Helen met her future husband in a completely different setting than her sister. "Oh, I met my husband at Frank Blunt's bar down in Churchton. I was living in Annapolis, and I came in and saw this strange fella, and you know I'm curious, so I tried to find out who he was. He was home on furlough visiting his parents, Lucille and Lawrence Thompson of Churchton. Carrie Crowner [not Carrie Bowles Crowner] introduced me to him, and I invited him to dinner. That was it. That was a couple months before I got married. I didn't do a whole lot of court'n like Daisy did. See, I fell in love a dozen times. She just fell in love once. I was 25. I was the last one in the family to get married, and everyone was wanting to know, 'When are you going to get married?' So, I thought I'd better go ahead and get married."

The Crowner sisters were not allowed to go to Blunt's Beer Joint when they were in high school, but Miss Helen and Miss Daisy reported that they used to "steal away" and go under the pretense that they were going to a friend's house. "We had no business doing that," said one sister, but from the laughter that followed in telling the story, it was clear there were no strong regrets. They caught a ride with someone and went to Blunt's to dance and meet their boyfriends. Miss Helen filled in some details, saying, "They had a jukebox, and it cost a nickel for a song. We never drank anything because we were under age. Three of us were dating Thompson boys. See, the others got away, but Daisy was the only one to catch one."

Helen and William Gorham married November 27, 1946, at the church parsonage just down from Franklin UMC on Route 256. Daisy and Ira stood up with them and were witnesses. There was no such thing as going away after the wedding. "We didn't do anything. My husband was home on furlough from the service. He said, 'Why don't we get married?' because he was going on back in the service, so I thought I'd better catch him before he go."

Instead of reenlisting, William took a job as a supervisor at the experimental station, later called the David Taylor Research and Development Center, near the Naval Academy. Miss Daisy's Ira also worked at the David Taylor Research and Development Center, and the brothers-in-law drove to work together each day. William worked at the Center for 33 years until he retired. While Helen was an active member at St. Matthew's UMC, he was faithful to his Catholic upbringing and went to Our Lady of Sorrows in Owings. Their happy days together ended when he died in 1987. They were married 41 years. "I still have his love letters and pull them out to read every once in a while," Miss Helen said. "I save everything."

The Gorhams didn't have any children of their own, so they instead became involved with helping other children. For 31 years, Miss Helen provided childcare for three families with babies and children who grew into successful adults and for others for a shorter period of time. They still keep in touch with her. One couple came down for Miss Helen's birthday recognition at church and talked about what a difference she had made in their daughter's life.

Miss Helen has seen many changes during her lifetime in Shady Side: All children are now bused to schools, rules and expectations for children are more relaxed than in her day, she gets her mail delivered to her home rather than having to go to the post office, she must lock her doors, trash is picked up twice a week, and in her day there was never a food problem because everything was available on her parent's farm.

While they were a young family, Helen's older stepsiblings' mother died. Henry, Robert, James, Laura, and Viola were grown and gone by the time Helen's parents were married. Their father, Charles, gave all of his children land, and Laura's house was next door to Helen's. While working in Washington, DC, at National Geographic, from where she retired, Laura met and married John Mays, who worked at the White House. Laura kept her house next door to Helen's, and she and her husband came from the city for vacations. Because they didn't own a car, people from Washington drove them to Shady Side. Helen also visited them, and said, "He couldn't do enough for you" in seeing to her comfort. "He was the host with the most," she explained.

Once, when Mr. Mays was sick, Eleanor Roosevelt came to visit him at his home on Irving Street. After Mr. Mays died and Laura became unable to care for herself, "I took her here," said Miss Helen. Before Laura died, she gave Miss Helen a unique remembrance: two $1 bills autographed by President Harry Truman. On the back of the newspaper clipping below was written: "Went to the White House in 1909" and the date "1952."

From Helen Crowner Gorham Collection

Truman Honors Two Doormen On White House Staff 41 Years

Two colored doormen who went to work at the White House 41 years ago today and have been serving Presidents ever since were given autographed $1 bills by President Truman today.

The men honored are John Mays, 78, who doubles as the President's barber as well as serving as doorman, and Samuel C. Jackson, 74, now working at the President's office.

Mr. Truman called the two men into his office this morning to give them their mementos. He told them he hoped each would live to serve as many Presidents in the future as they have in the past.

Mr. Mays told reporters that he and Mr. Jackson met at the east entrance to the White House at 7 a.m. 41 years ago today, both looking for a job as White House doormen. They both were given jobs and stationed at the door at 11:20 a.m. that day, just as retiring President Theodore Roosevelt and incoming President William Howard Taft left for the Capitol for Mr. Taft's inauguration.

Expressing the pleasure of both men at Mr. Truman's recognition of their long service, Mr. Mays said, "We are little wheels in a great, great mill—the greatest mill in the world, the home of the President of the United States and his family."

Mr. Mays said he had been doubling as barber to Presidents ever since President Wilson.

From Helen Crowner Gorham Collection

★ ★ ★

In Kenneth Walsh's book, *Family of Freedom,* he discusses the role that blacks have played while working at the White House and their interactions with the presidents and their families. Such jobs were extremely prestigious in the African American community and could help middle-class black families both socially and economically. [2]

"Mr. Mays and Mr. Jackson both came up from South Carolina," said Miss Helen. Her comment is echoed in Isabel Wilkerson's *The Warmth of Other Suns, The Epic Story of America's Great Migration,* which talks about the black people who migrated to Washington for better opportunities. They "had no personal recollection of slavery, were free but not free because of the severe limitations of Jim Crow, and they resisted the subservience of their slave parents and grandparents. Gone was the contrived intimacy in which slavery might connect the two races. Whites appeared more hostile to blacks than even during their slaveholding ancestors had been. Their generation needed a way out."[3] Leaving the South was like "getting unstuck from a magnet." [4]

★ ★ ★

"That love stuff—that's my favorite subject," said Miss Helen when she and Miss Daisy were asked how they met their spouses. Although Miss Daisy never had an interest in spending time with someone else, Miss Helen courted for 22 years with a gentleman friend who was a classmate throughout her elementary and high school years. Mr. Tommy Nick, a widower, and Miss Helen, a widow, reconnected at a Bates Alumni dance. Daisy had convinced Helen she should go to the event if only for a little while. Chatting with Helen, Tommy, a Glen Burnie resident, asked if he could "steal away" and come visit her in

Shady Side. She told him he didn't need to "steal away, but come on down." However, first he had to gently break up with someone he was already seeing. He and Miss Helen saw each other until he became ill at 89 and could no longer drive, but they continued talking on the telephone.

Penned in her beautiful cursive, Miss Helen wrote: "John T. Nick was born in Shady Side, MD. Most of us know him as 'Tommy.' Tommy attended Shady Side Elementary School and graduated from Wiley H. Bates High School in the class of '39. He was employed at the Experimental Station for two years before being drafted into the U.S. Army. While there he served in five countries: Italy, Manila [the Philippines], Guam, Germany, and Korea. While in Germany he graduated from the NCO Academy. Mr. Nick retired from service after serving 26 years. He went to work at Fort Meade as a civilian where he worked for 18 years in the Transportation Motor Pool. Mr. Nick had 46 years of Federal Service, which ended July 31, 1993. Tommy is a faithful member of St. Marks United Methodist Church, where he served on the Ushers Board. He is a member of the NAACP, lifetime member of Bates Alumni, and a lifetime member of Chapter 9 Retired Enlisted Association of Baltimore, MD. His hobbies are watching TV, working puzzles, and dancing. Tommy is very neat and everything must be in its proper place. He has received many awards and certificates from his job. John was married to the late Arthea Greer for 39 years. He has two children, John T. Nick, Jr., and Lillie Mae Smith. Tommy is a gentle, kind and lovable person."

Tommy Nick and Miss Helen Crowner Gorham, whom Mr. Tommy called "Kelly" from the time of their early school years together, visit in Miss Helen's home. **Ann Widdifield Collection**

Daisy and Ira Thompson had four children, and today her daughter Gayle and grandson Jeremiah live with her. The two sisters live diagonally across from each other on either side of Cedarhurst Road. Miss Daisy's house is where the farm's pigpen used to be, and Miss Helen lives where the cornfield once grew.

Miss Daisy Thompson, her daughter Gayle, and Miss Helen Gorham in 2010. **Ann Widdifield Collection**

The Sisters' Parents

Charles H. Crowner (February 22, 1866–April 21, 1954) and Serena Offer Johnson Crowner (January 1, 1886–June 13, 1964), his third wife, were the parents of Miss Helen and Miss Daisy. Charles married Ida Thompson in November 1887; she died after eleven years of marriage and six children, one of whom died at birth. He was briefly married to a woman named Ella, but the marriage didn't last, nor did they have children. When Charles and Serena married, both brought children to the union. Charles brought his five and Serena her three, and they had their own two girls, Helen and Daisy, and a son, Charles Francis, who died in 1986.

Helen Crowner Gorham pictured with her older brother Charles Crowner in the 1920s. **Miss Helen Crowner Gorham Collection**

Charles H. Crowner was a full-time farmer, rather than a farmer and a waterman during the winter. His farm was on Cedarhurst Road and extended north of Cedarhurst Road from the Brent's down to Lake Street and south of Cedarhurst Road from the Moulden's down to Shady Court, adjacent to the Dennis property. When the sisters were growing up, three families lived on Cedarhurst Road: their family, the Sellman Scotts, and the James A. Crowners, Charles's son by his first wife, Ida.

★　★　★

In February 1993 James's daughter, Doris Crowner Brown, presented a program on the Crowner family for the Shady Side Rural Heritage Society's luncheon series. A retired elementary teacher and active member in St. Matthew's United Methodist Church, she researched her family in the Maryland archives and in family bibles and talked to older family members. Her work and that of a niece revealed what could be found as far back as her great-grandfather, John W. Crowner, who was born around 1835 in "The Swamp." He married Rachel Dennis (born 1839) on February 3, 1858, two years before the outbreak of the Civil War. Beginning with the birth of Jacob in 1859, John and Rachel had 12 children, but at least four children died before adulthood. Jacob, their first son, died at age six, and Ellen, their last daughter, born in 1880, lived only two months. Twins, Rachel and Henry, lived only a year. Surviving into adulthood were sons Solomon, Alexander, John W., and Hezekiah, daughter Charlotte, and the three children who remained in Shady Side: Charles H. (born 1866), James E. (born 1874), and Mary Elizabeth (born 1872). Rachel Crowner died in 1895 at age 56.

Several Shady Side families can trace their ancestry back to Rachel and John Crowner. Rachel is buried in a small Dennis cemetery close to Columbia Beach Road. **Ann Widdifield Collection**

John W. Crowner purchased 67 acres of land in 1896 for $20 an acre. In addition he bought a dwelling, three farm buildings, a canoe, a buggy, a road cart, a carriage, and animals: four horses, two oxen, three cows, six sheep, and eight hogs for $2,632. The Crowner land was between Columbia Beach and Cedarhurst Roads, east of Bay Ridge and Shady Side Roads, and reached to Lake Street. When John W. Crowner died, the land passed to his sons Charles H. and James E. Crowner.

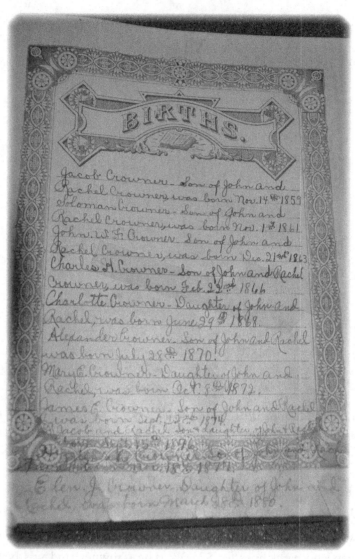

Rachel and John Crowner's children are recorded in the Crowner family bible.
Miss Daisy Crowner Thompson Collection

Rachel and John Crowner's sons and daughters married into the Scott, Thompson, Offer, Smith, Matthews, Holland, Swan, and Bowles families.

The seventh child and second daughter, Mary Elizabeth, called "Aunt Lizzie," was born October 8, 1872. She married Joseph Matthews, and they had 15 children. Their home was on waterfront property along the West River next to the Rogerses and Atwells to the north and the Henna Matthews family to the south. Lizzie cooked, quilted, sewed, and sometimes took in laundry for the Andrews family. To help defray some of the church expenses, she and other church members served dinners from the Matthews's home. Her husband, Joe, was a waterman and raised hogs, ducks, and chickens. After Joe died, Lizzie married George Holland, the grandfather of Delores, Connie, and Carla Nick. They had no children together.

James Crowner and Carrie Bowles

James E. Crowner (September 22, 1874–December 23, 1950) married Frances Swan, who died in 1936. They had no children together. Their home was located on Bay Breeze Road on the west corner of the Crowner property. Like many Shady Side men, James was a waterman and farmer, but he had other interests as well. He owned his own boat and fished with a pound net. As a farmer, he raised and slaughtered hogs; had turkeys, geese, and chickens; and had a garden that he shared with family and friends. He sang in the St. Matthew's choir, played the piano, fished for pleasure, hunted, and took out duck parties. He also ran a boarding house for people who wanted to go out duck hunting. He was the caretaker of land on Columbia Beach Road that was owned by an admiral from the Naval Academy. Occasionally, the admiral and his family stayed at the Crowner's home during the summer.

In the 1930s, Uncle Jim bought a Model T Ford, becoming one of the first owners in the area of a horseless carriage. Laughing, a relative recalled, "Aunt Frances drove in the ditch more than on the road."

James E. Crowner.
Doris Brown Collection

A young Virginia woman from Fork Union later crossed the widower's path, and the incident started a plot worthy of a novel. When Carrie Belle Bowles (April 21, 1909 - October 4, 2000) arrived in the Galesville-Churchton-Shady Side area, she was well educated and a pianist, but she faced setbacks getting there. Her parents divorced when she was nine, so she lived with an aunt and cousin in Fredericksburg, VA, where she received schooling and music lessons. She and her mother moved to Washington, DC, where her mother worked as a housekeeper at the Casper Music School so her daughter could finish high school. Carrie accidentally got pure iodine in her left eye, which made her unable to study and keep up at school. But mother and child never gave up their desire for Carrie to have a secondary education. Carrie went to night school at Cardozo High School and completed school in 1936. During a 1998 interview in her Columbia Beach home, Carrie was wearing the class ring that her mother had given her at graduation.

Listening to her interview, one soon grasped that Carrie and the local country people were respectful, helpful, and kind to one another. They were mindful of life's challenges during the Depression and were quick to assist others in times of need. The Golden Rule was evident in actions, and there was a strong consciousness of "the right thing to do" and doing it. Connections to church and Christian believers were a uniting force, and a deep love and appreciation of God was expressed openly.

With high school behind her, Carrie decided to go into the hair dressing business for the Blue Chemical Company, operated by Dr. James E. Blue from British Guiana. Apparently, one of Dr. Blue's sons had a crush on Carrie and must have talked up the opportunities of the company. She became a successful manager for the company, and when Dr. Blue decided to expand the company into Virginia and Maryland, he sent Carrie to sell the products because of her "gift of gab." Every two weeks, Carrie and Rosetta Hyman, the other "Blue" agent and Carrie's friend, "did our canvassing by walking to homes in Galesville and Shady Side and then winding up in Churchton to eat at Blunt's Store." With all of the day's walking and selling, they were in need of a hearty dinner. "At that time colored people didn't have any place where they could eat or recreate themselves except at Blunt's Store."

Blunt's Store had a jukebox, and Carrie liked to "shake a foot"—especially the tango. Her favorite dance partner was Sanky Thompson, who called everybody "Cuz." Besides dancing the tango, Carrie and Rosetta had dreams of attending Howard University for medical careers. Carrie wanted to become a pediatrician. To make money for college, they planned to rent some place where they could cook meals and feed people, perhaps even have overnight guests who would come from Washington for weekends or summer vacation. They had plenty of Washington church friends and acquaintances who would enjoy a country-cooked meal. These folk would also recommend them, because they were already famous for their southern fried chicken, pies, and cakes. Dr. Blue, who happened to be with them on that particular trip, was in favor of their plan and willing to back them. Carrie spoke to Mrs. Blunt, who suggested that a Mr. Crowner, whose wife had died, had a nice big home and only his sickly brother living with him.

Serendipity! Mr. Crowner was sitting over in the corner of the store, so Dr. Blue asked Mrs. Blunt to introduce them. Dr. Blue explained the plan to Mr. Crowner, who agreed he'd rent them the house from the first of May to the first of November, six months, for $300. Fortunately, Carrie had her receipt book in her pocketbook, so Dr. Blue had her write out the receipt to pay Mr. James Edward Crowner on the spot.

It was the most money Uncle Jim had seen in a long time, and it would help him with his debt. His deceased wife had a very kind heart, and if someone asked her to go on a note, she would sign her name and his name. At her death he found out about the notes and had to make good on them. By the time of the meeting with Dr. Blue, he was close to losing his house in spite of having his various water businesses and farm. He told them that the Lord had sent them there just in the nick of time. He invited the ladies to dinner at his house in Shady Side when they returned to sell their products in the area again. An excellent cook himself, he served country food: hams, chicken, guineas, fish, and vegetables. If the young ladies wanted any fancy city food, they were welcome to bring it. Carrie wasn't so sure she wanted to eat a man's cooking, because she felt they didn't wash their hands very well, but "I reached over that thought. He was clean, his house was clean, and Dr. Blue said that we couldn't beat this."

Mr. Crowner was older than Carrie's father, reputable and respected in the community, and it was clear that the working relationship would be respectful and proper. In the meantime, Rosetta and Carrie continued to support the Society of Christian Service by each buying a plate of food for their return trip to Washington at the end of their selling weekend.

Carrie and Rosetta had plans "down on paper" that if guests came, they would go up to the attic to sleep so the guests could use their bedroom. Alas, once "down in Shady Side," Rosetta became ill enough to require emergency surgery, and Carrie was left alone with the cooking for the rest of the summer. Rosetta returned much later in the season.

In the meantime, Carrie coordinated with Mr. Crowner and suggested that she would buy her chickens and seafood from him rather than going to a grocery. In turn, his income would be further enhanced. Mr. Crowner was very grateful for her idea and said, "Miss Bowles, this is your house now, just take over. I see how you act, and you're not someone who is out to get somebody." She agreed that this was not her aim and moved forward with her plans. She learned that people in the area liked desserts such as raisin pie, green tomato preserve pie, and sweet potato pie. "Not to pat myself on the back," Carrie knew her excellent sweet potato pie was no problem, but she didn't know a thing about the other two. Mr. Crowner, an able cook and baker himself, volunteered to bake those.

At that time neither roads nor houses were numbered, so Carrie put up signs and made flyers to let people know the location of her eating establishment, which she named "Terrace Inn." People who came fell in love with all of the foods served at the inn, and she had a "crowded season."

The Terrace Inn is long gone and today two houses forming a right angle now sit on the land owned by Augustine Smith. The newer house was designed and built by Vic Smith for his sister.
Miss Helen Crowner Gorham Collection

Many people also wanted to go swimming at Columbia Beach. During Carrie's first restaurant year, some instructors from the Academy came down with their children for meals. James played his piano and helped the children pick out tunes on it. An untrained musician, he had a gift for playing by ear and could play most requested songs. While he entertained, "I was back there sweating in the kitchen," Carrie laughed delightedly.

Finally, Rosetta, who was like an older sister, returned to the Terrace Inn, and although she wasn't able to work, Carrie was happy they were together again. Again the women talked of their Howard University plans, and Carrie told Rosetta that she had put Rosetta's name on half of what she herself had earned. Carrie believed that because they had planned this together, and because Rosetta certainly couldn't help being sick, it was only the right thing to do. Carrie believed she herself could have been in the same situation.

As it was nearing time for the rental to end, Mr. Crowner said, "Young lady, you are one business person." Carrie gave the credit to her father's family and an uncle who had a store.

James Crowner had a huge square of land that went from Columbia Beach Road to Cedarhurst Road and was bordered by the Dennis and Thompson properties. The original colored schoolhouse sat on the same spot where Miss Carrie was living at the time of her interview. The Board of Education bought the land from Mr. Crowner's father, John Crowner, for $10 for a school. Much later, when someone cleaned out the yard where a locust tree had fallen over, Carrie found a stone under it. Mr. Crowner told Carrie that the stone marked the place where the schoolchildren had to stop if the rag ball was batted into the dirt road. The child waited until "the teacher granted permission to recover the ball" in the dirt road. Before the Columbia Beach School was built, a few colored children were taught in a barn owned by the Lerch family, according to Mr. Crowner.

As the departure time for the women approached, Mr. Crowner announced to Miss Bowles, "I don't think I am going to let you go back."

She said, "Oh? Why?"

"You know I have observed you, and I have had contact with a lot of ladies, but you are the tops. You are the just the type of a person I need."

It stunned Miss Bowles for a moment, "How do you know? We haven't even courted." She believed that people acted differently in a courtship than in a business. "I don't think we have known each other long enough to decide if we are suited for marriage. Let alone, you are older than my father."

"Well, regardless," he said, "I'll be a good husband to you. I'll guarantee ya; I'll be a good husband to you."

Carrie said, matter of factly, "I'll have to write to my parents and ask their opinion." Both parents had met Jim in separate visits. Her father wrote from New York City that he thought Mr. Crowner was too old for her, and he didn't want her to marry an old man. He wanted her to marry somebody her equal. Carrie countered with how nice he was and all of the things she had observed about him. She didn't have to marry Mr. Crowner for a home, her papa reminded her, because he had left her his little Virginia farm and had built her a home on it. She agreed that she enjoyed her home and independence. She called her mother, who was still working in Washington and came down by bus almost every weekend to Wayson's Corner, where Carrie picked her up. Her mother was a very sharp observer, and she said that she would come down again and do some more observing. Meeting at Wayson's again, Carrie told her mother, "He seems to be a nice gentleman. He's old and countrified, it's true, but at the same time he needs somebody." Still, Carrie's mind was set on going to college, and she didn't have any time to waste on a boyfriend.

Mama asked, "What about college?"

Carrie responded, "What about it?"

Mama asked, "What does Rosetta think?"

"Well, Rosetta thinks Old Man has fallen in love with me." Carrie had believed wrongly that he was falling in love with Rosetta! A widowed minister in Washington was interested in Rosetta, who wasn't particularly interested in him.

"Do you love him?" Mama asked.

Carrie replied, "I don't know yet. I love him because he has been very nice, and he filled a gap like a father to me." She had been unable to be around her father much because of her parents' divorce, but she knew her father loved her and would do anything he could for her. Carrie loved to fish, but her father didn't want anything to do with water except for the bathtub. Mr. Crowner regularly took the women out fishing in his boat on the river or into the Bay. Carrie absolutely loved the water, and it was a big draw for Mr. James Crowner.

Listening and thinking, Mama said, "If you think enough of him, and you feel that you could learn to love him, go toward it!"

Miss Bowles went to her pastor, Rev. Middleton, the pastor for both Franklin and St. Matthew's churches, and his wife. Whenever she needed advice, she had made it a habit to talk with them.

Miss Bowles: "Rev. Middleton, Mr. Crowner has asked me to marry him."

Rev. Middleton: "Miss Bowles, what do you think of him?"

Miss Bowles: "I think he's a perfect gentleman, and he turned his house over to me and my girlfriend when we were renting it. He acted like we were the owners, but he was the owner."

Rev. Middleton: "Carrie, that shows you he has confidence in you."

Miss Bowles said, "Yes," to James Edward Crowner. Rev. Middleton married the couple in 1938. Their marriage lasted twelve years, until his death.

During their life together, James ran a fishing business and operated a duck blind. Carrie liked to go out with James and his brother Charles to help with the pound net. Carrie cooked breakfast for the guests before they went out to hunt and had dinner ready for them when they returned. She also fed the men who worked with James: Howard Matthews, his nephew, James Brent, and "Best Friend" who helped James by climbing in and out of the duck blind. People came from Baltimore, New York, North Carolina, Pennsylvania, and New Jersey. The house was filled up all the time, and guests would stay over. While the men slept, Carrie picked the ducks' feathers and had the ducks ready to go home with instructions for cooking. The men didn't want the feathers, so "I made a lot of pillows. A *lot* of pillows.

Carrie Bowles Crowner and James Crowner enjoyed dogs and water adventures.
Helen Crowner Gorham and Doris Crowner Brown Collections

The Crowners adopted a two-and-a-half-year-old boy whose teenage mother didn't want him. Carrie went to Washington to see about getting him, and the mother was happy to give him to someone who wanted a child. When the little boy arrived home, James wrapped him in his arms and said, "Poor little precious thing." The child asked for a hot dog because that was all he knew—to eat a raw hot dog. He never asked for his mother and never showed any signs of wanting to go back, so they legally adopted Tony. Carrie began calling her husband "Daddy" as an example for Tony, and "Daddy" instead of "Mr. Crowner" stuck from that point on.

With Tony's adoption, Carrie asked her cousin to be Tony's godmother, and James chose his cousin Hiram, called Matt, to be his godfather. Privately, and unbeknownst to Carrie, James also asked

Matt to always take care of Tony, Carrie, and her mother in the event something happened to him. Matt agreed to do so.

James told Carrie that she had been a good wife to him and when he was gone he didn't want any more of her life spoiled by an old man. He told her she should find someone "who was more her equal." She told him she wasn't interested in marrying again and wanted to go back to college. James wanted her to follow her dream, but if someone nice offered to take care of her, Tony, and her mother, "I don't want you to pass him up."

James died on December 23, 1950. Carrie didn't know how to tell Matt of James's death. Cousin Matt lived in Boston and was engaged to Eva, who was also from Boston. Unexpectedly, Eva died, and Matt accompanied Eva's family to Virginia for her burial. Before returning to Boston, he stopped to see his Aunt Lorraine at her bakery, and there he learned of James's death. Matt delayed his trip home so he and his aunt could drive to Shady Side and pay respects to Carrie and Tony.

Carrie Bowles Crowner wrote about her loss of her husband Jim. Writing
continues on the back of the card.
Miss Helen Crowner Gorham Collection

Tony and Carrie were away at Johns Hopkins when the two arrived, but they waited for them to return home. When they arrived, Tony was excited to see his Aunt Lorraine's car in the drive and rushed into the house, but it was Matt who first picked him up and kissed him. Carrie followed behind and was surprised to see Matt and asked after Eva. He explained his recent loss. When Matt and his aunt left, he told Carrie he would call her when he got back to Boston and tell her about what Cousin Jim had asked him. Carrie figured that it was about James's old boat or something like that.

When the call did come, Matt told Carrie of James's request that he care for the family. He suggested that neither of them had anyone now, so what did she think? Carrie didn't know where she stood, because all she could think about was the loss of James. It went on like that for several months until she talked to her pastor in Annapolis, where she was the organist. He cautioned her, "You know a lot of these old dudes are looking for nurses. Don't you accept him. There was only one Mr. Crowner and he's gone." When she told her mother, they laughed and laughed about Matt being called an old dude. By then Matt was phoning three times a week to check on them. Carrie told Matt what her pastor had advised, and Matt requested to meet the reverend.

When Matt came down to visit, Carrie took him with her to church, where the two men had an opportunity to talk. Rev. Johnson looked Matt up and down and said, "Young man, you meet my approval." From then on, things were easier for Carrie. Matt's calls continued, and he officially proposed to her over the phone. Carrie turned from the phone to ask her mother, but her mother said Carrie was old enough to decide for herself.

Carrie's mother had worked as a housekeeper in Washington for many years. Her wealthy employer was in the banking business but was moving his family to his estate near Orange, Virginia; he wanted Miss Elizabeth to move with them, but she didn't want to move. While she and her second husband were visiting Carrie, her employers highly recommended Elizabeth to someone else: J. Edgar Hoover. Some of his people from the Justice Department called Mr. Leatherbury's store trying to locate Miss Elizabeth for an interview. Since Carrie's stepfather had always played the numbers, the first thought was that the call was about him! Carrie's mother was hired as J. Edgar Hoover's housekeeper, and she and her husband lived in his home. Thinking he was being watched, her husband refused to stay in the house because of the beeps and peeps and lights going off and on. Miss Elizabeth continued living there until she became ill and was hospitalized. She died from diabetes.

Carrie's positive answer gave Matt and Carrie 44 years of marriage. For a time they lived in Boston. Carrie did get her nursing training, and they lived in Shady Side until they eventually moved to her farm in Virginia. While living there, she worked in a nursing care home in Charlottesville and was then hired to help establish and run a tri-county health center. She stayed in Virginia until her retirement and then returned to Shady Side until her final days. She said that she was always considered a "foreigner" because she was not originally from Shady Side.

Aunt Hattie Nick taught Carrie "how to use my hands that would be helpful to man." Carrie didn't talk about the babies she delivered in Shady Side, but other people talked about her doing so. It is safe to say that Carrie Bowles had a unique, interesting, and extremely productive life. She was remembered as "a smart, educated woman" who was from Virginia.

★   ★   ★

During her Shady Side years, Carrie fostered 37 foster care children, according to one of her foster children, Gerald Thomas. He lived with her from 1949 to 1956 and described "Mama" as a foster mother, historian, and midwife who taught him to respect all people. After serving in the Army, including in Vietnam, he went on to other opportunities and work and now resides in Virginia on his thirteen-acre ranch. His brother, Robert Taylor, moved to Shady Side and now lives next door to the house where Gerald was one of Carrie Bowles Crowner's foster children.

Robert Taylor and all of his nine siblings, including Gerald, were raised in foster homes. Rachel Harried, who lived in Owensville, raised Robert, his own brother, and other foster brothers in a former church that had been converted into a two-story house with an attic. Miss Rachel told the children to NEVER go up in the attic. Robert, about nine, and a foster brother slept on the second floor, and curiosity got the best of them one day when "Grandmother," as they called her, was off to church and they were alone. They removed some boards in the ceiling to hoist themselves up into the attic, where they discovered several dusty wooden coffins. Stunned and afraid, they scrambled and half fell into their room and shakily replaced the board. Having knowledge of the forbidden fruit above their beds, they NEVER told Grandmother the true reason they wanted to move to the floor below them. She kindly complied, not guessing their true fears or motives.

Weeks later their dog, Whitey, was howling and barking incessantly; he finally jumped through a window, breaking the glass in Robert's brother's downstairs bedroom. Looking outside, his brother saw an eerie yellow glow on the yard. He realized that the house was on fire and quickly roused the family. All escaped as the attic fell into the second floor and then down to the first. Everything was lost. Neighbors took them in that night.

James A. Crowner Family

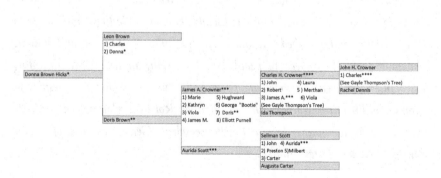

190

When James A. Crowner and his wife, Aurida Scott Crowner, lived on the corner of Shady Side and Cedarhurst Roads, his father, Charles Crowner, and family lived further up the road. In 2011 his daughter Doris Crowner and her husband, Leon Brown, live near James's sisters Helen Crowner Gorham and Daisy Crowner Thompson further up Cedarhurst Road, but the relatives now share many more neighbors in between their homes.

James and Aurida had five young children by 1929: Marie, Viola, Katherine, James Melvin ("Sonny Boy"), and Hughward. George "Bootie," Doris "Nellie," and Elliott "Purnell" came along later. Dr. Hugh Ward delivered Doris in 1933, the seventh child and fourth daughter, surrounded by brothers, three older and one younger. Dr. Dent delivered the four oldest children, Dr. Hugh Ward delivered the next three, and Elliott Purnell was born at Johns Hopkins Hospital in Baltimore. One son was named after the doctor who delivered him.

Doris's father wanted doctors instead of midwives for his wife. Doris Crowner Brown is their only surviving child.

Doris said that Bootie and Sonny Boy got to ride on the horse and wagon and sell produce in the community with their Grandpa Sellman Scott. Strawberries were a popular purchase. Doris spent her earliest years living on the corner of Cedarhurst and Shady Side Roads and remembers her grandmother Gussie living with them after her grandfather Sellman died.

*Aurida Scott Crowner was sister to the three Scott brothers who
drowned in 1929 and the mother of Doris Crowner Brown, born 1933.*
Miss Doris Crowner Brown Collection

Originally, the James and Aurida Scott Crowner family lived in the
corner house when Miss Aurida's three brothers tragically drowned in
the April 1929 daytime storm that rolled through the Bay, turning the
sky black and bringing punishing downdrafts followed by the powerful
winds.

Doris was about twelve and at school when the house was moved
to Crowner property just up Cedarhurst Road, next door to where she
and her husband, Leon Brown, have now lived for 53 years. Her parents'
house was cocooned with additions over the years and was purchased
by new owners.

Leon remembered the day the house was moved: "Cedarhurst Road
was tar on blue chip stone. They jacked up the house and put it on
notched skis so the weight of the house kept it on the wooden skis to get
it over there. The smoke was still coming from the chimney! Three or

four people walked along with the house, set on blocks, that was being pulled by a loader."

For four or five years, Leon delivered ice with Octivius "Shake" Thompson. Getting 25- and 50-pound blocks of ice from Woodfield's in Galesville, the two made deliveries to people's homes twice a week. Ice delivered the previous week usually held until Monday's delivery. They delivered to Ethel Gross, who needed ice for her seafood business icehouse beside her family home.

In 2006 Doris was one of several senior speakers at "Guest Storyteller Day" at Shady Side Elementary School, where she told the children "they were a poor family living in a real small house" in a wooded area where Richie's Grill now stands. Her family property was wooded, with mostly gardens, fruit trees, hog pens, and chicken yards within the perimeter. Doris's family had a radio, and it was the main source of home entertainment, broadcasting music and radio programs. Bingo, dancing, and ball games were community activities.

Her mother, Aurida, often babysat for families, but she always made it clear that Doris would be coming with her. She did not want to leave her at home with the boys. Luther and Amy Leatherbury owned the store on the other corner of Cedarhurst and Shady Side Roads, where they lived above the store. When they were away, they asked Aurida to stay with their daughter, and that is how Doris's long friendship with Carol Ann Leatherbury began. The same age, the little girls played every day outside, in the store, or upstairs. Carol Ann went to Doris's house to get her playmate, and they played dolls, slept together, and slid on the ice in the winter. "The boys were not allowed to play, and we had a good time." On school days, Carol Ann took the bus to her Shady Side School, and Doris walked to her school. During high school, they rode different buses to separate high schools, but the friendship survived, and they still cross paths.

Doris started school when she was five, and like the other Shady Side children, she experienced the cold winter walks to the Shady Side

School for Colored. The big round stove with its coal bucket nearby, stationary desks, the daily school openings of prayers and saluting the flag, and daily exercises and reading, writing, and arithmetic were routines for Doris. She went to Bates for her high school years, and after graduation she went on to college at Bowie State to become a teacher.

Luther Leatherbury had a well dug behind his store and invited his neighbors to use it. Doris's family, Josephine Tongue's family, and the Leatherburys used a pump to get their water. Aurida and Josephine cooked for two families, whose last names began with a B, at Felicity Cove. A third woman worked for the Beebe's in West Shady Side, and the patrons were referred to as "The Three B's."

Doris's older sister, Viola, who was about 10 years ahead of her, went to Bowie Normal (now Bowie State University) for one year, and brother Purnell attended for two years, 1956-1957. Other African American young people who attended college around the same time as Doris were John Fountain, sisters Patricia Nick Gross and Barbara Nick Johnson from Shady Side, and Yvonne Holland Matthews.

Leon Brown, two years older than Doris, grew up in Churchton and went to Churchton School. Like the majority of young men in the area, he quit school to go culling and oystering, but he went out from the Deale county pier rather than Shady Side's county pier. At one point he oystered on Tallies oyster bed between Shady Side and Annapolis, beyond Thomas Lighthouse sailing north. He also went to New Jersey to work on a dredge boat after the local oyster season was over; he worked on the Delaware Bay going up as far as New York and saw Russian ships passing by. In the summers he went clamming and crabbing and worked in Kirchiner's boatyard on Chalkpoint Road across from Galesville.

Doris and Leon met by chance at the old movie theater building on Shady Side Road across from Dent Road. Since he had no car, he borrowed his father's car to take Doris out on dates. Many times on weekends when Doris was home from college, they would go to

Leon's aunt's cook shop. Although Doris had one more year of college, during Christmas break of 1953 they decided to marry at the church parsonage on April 19, 1954, with Rev. Rufus Abernathy, Sr., officiating. They had no transportation and they weren't dressed in wedding attire, but Leon borrowed his dad's car to pick up Doris and they drove to his grandmother's house. From there they walked to the parsonage and wed without wedding rings—but they had $5 and a witness. No pictures were taken; there was no reception and no honeymoon, because they each returned to their separate homes after the wedding. They spent their wedding night apart.

As planned, the next day Leon drove his father's car to collect his bride, and together they drove to Leon's grandparents' house to live with them. That summer Doris worked at a summer camp in Schenectady, New York, to earn money to finish her last year of college, and Leon worked on a dredge boat in New Jersey. Doris went back to college for her final year and graduated in 1955; she taught that fall at Ralph J. Bunche Elementary School on Muddy Creek Road. In the meantime Leon continued working as a waterman, and in the summer he painted.

In the 1960s Doris left Ralph J. Bunche to teach in Shady Side. She taught a combination classroom with the strongest first graders and second graders at Lula G. Scott with Mrs. Alice Battle, principal. When the first grade teacher left, she switched to first grade. Besides having an overhead projector and an opaque projector, she used a controlled reader. This machine was usually used with remedial reading groups of children. Lines of a story appeared on a narrow display, and as the child read, the read words were covered up. The objective was to increase reading speed, so that the child was forced to go on reading at a particular pace. Her students did not receive used books as she had when she attended Lula G.

Mrs. Battle asked her to be a remedial teacher for both Lula G. Scott and Lothian schools, and she agreed to step out of the classroom. Four years later she returned to a regular classroom of first graders at

Lula G. Scott. Ron Holland was one of her first graders, and he enjoys the fact that he is still worshipping with his first grade teacher at St. Matthew's UMC. Doris taught during segregation and integration of the two Shady Side schools and finished her career teaching at the brick school before retiring in 1986.

After their first year of marriage, the couple moved in with Leon's parents for the second year and then into a little house that Leon's aunt had renovated. In 1958, they purchased a small house next to the house where Doris grew up. They have lived there ever since, enlarging and remodeling their home over time. They have been married for 57 years and have two children, Charles and Donna, grandchildren, great-grandchildren, and one great-great-grandchild.

Donna Brown Hicks has a busy daycare center near the Browns, so Doris can still be involved with children whenever she wishes. Three days a week, Doris goes by bus to the Senior Center in Edgewater, and if you call asking for her, Leon reports, "Oh, she's at school." Doris has accrued a tremendous collection of pictures of family, friends, community members, and church members in Shady Side. She was known as the go-to person to learn about St. Matthew's church history. Although she is no longer the church historian, she was invaluable in suggestions and knowledge for this writing.

Doris has belonged to St. Matthew's her entire life, and Leon has belonged to Franklin UMC all of his life and has held leadership positions including trustee. Frequently they drive people to appointments and visit shut-ins. Doris has always loved gardening, and Leon joins her in creating a lovely lawn with beautiful flowers.

A Friend and Neighbor

Josephine Tongue was a friend and neighbor of the James "Nink" Crowner family. Her house sat next to Luther Leatherbury's store on Shady Side Road, but her backyard was diagonal to the Crowner's backyard. A contemporary of Aurida and James Crowner, Josephine's life was one of constant work and taking care of her family, including a grandson. "My mother and I visited at her house, and she made people laugh with her stories," said Doris. "Her children called her 'Ma Phiney,' and I thought that was her name." Years later Doris's daughter played with Josephine's great-granddaughter.

Josephine Brent Tongue's father's farm was about 22 acres on which he both farmed and gardened. Like many of his neighbors, he had chickens, hogs, beans, and tomatoes, and he had a little stand along the road. He slaughtered his hogs like his neighbors, but he had his sausage ground at the store, and he would season it. Instead of precooking his sausages and putting them in jars, he put his in big stone jars that were stored in cases filled with brine. To keep his potatoes, turnips, and cabbages from freezing in the winter, he kept them in a bin covered and surrounded by straw. He went to the mill to grind the wheat and had the corn ground into cornmeal. He hunted rabbits and squirrels but not deer. In the winter he worked as an oysterman for Harry Hallock, Mr. Nieman, and others. "He kept us alive."

Josephine Tongue, called "Miss Sis," reported in her 1984 interview that she shucked oysters for the Heinrichs for four years and got 25 cents for a bucket. She helped Carrie Bowles Crowner with housework and remembered people coming from Washington for duck hunting parties at Jim Crowner's. She was used to working even as a young child, because she picked corn from her father's field. She especially liked to shell vegetables and gather eggs. In fact, the family would pick beans and shell them at night to sell the next day. "Father would carry them to the beaches to sell from his horse and wagon."

Her father owned two horses, but Josephine had to sell them when he passed because she didn't know how to take care of them.

Josephine remembered the feather pillows and feather mattresses: "Mother would cover old quilts and make comforters out of them. You'd just sink down. Mama made biscuits and whatnot on the coal stove, and we'd heat by it." She was very happy when electricity came because she did not have to clean the lampshades or fill 'em up (the kerosene lamps). Josephine peeled peaches and apples and helped her mother can, a skill she continued to use because she loved to have jelly on hand to give to friends.

She and her brothers liked to climb the fence and go over to Mr. Crandall's gooseberry patch and "go pick his berries. He'd get after us, but we'd go back. We loved to pull our shoes off and play in the dirt roads. We'd make fish bones that we put together in the dust." She described the roads as "roads that roll backwards." She said that she used to chase Julius's father's (Joshua Dennis) cows back when they got out.

Her parents taught her to have manners and treat people nice and "if you do that through life you make it." Her father said that if you are nasty to people, these things will come back to you. "Your manners will carry you farther than money, Sister," as he called her. As a child she thought, "I can go a long ways with money," but as an adult she carried her father's words in her heart.

At age 17, Josephine married Roosevelt "Ding" Thompson of Churchton, and they lived with his parents until they moved down on the shore at Broadwater. They had two children, and Hattie Nick was her midwife. "She was a lovely person. If you were sick at night, she stayed with you. She would stay a couple of days longer to help with the children and house. Maybe she was paid ten dollars." When her husband's father took sick, they moved to care for him, but "he passed." Shortly after his death, her own husband passed, and she was left with her "little stair steps" of two sons and a daughter. Later she married Frank Tongue, who worked at the Naval Academy, but he got sick and could no longer work.

In spite of so many struggles Josephine Tongue kept her marvelous sense of humor and went about her life working hard and caring for her family.

CHAPTER 11

BUDDY HOLLAND

Ron Holland Family Tree

		Alexander Holland 1) Blake Alexander***
	Blake Alexander Holland*** 1) Ralph 2) Blake 3) Buddy** 4) Harold 5) Cora 6 and 7) Naomi "Shirley," Joan "Curly"	Cora
Arthelbert "Buddy" Holland** 1) Jeffrey 2) Monya 3) Wanda 4) Ron* 5) Valerie 6 and 7) Carl, Carol 8) Deneen		
	Ruth Adams	
Ron Holland*		
		Joseph Matthews 1) John***
	John W. Matthews*** (Children listed in Jean Yvonne Johnson's family tree)	(Siblings on Yvonne Johnson's Tree)
		Mary Elizabeth Holland
Thelma Matthews		
		William Scott 1) Sarah ***
	Sarah E. Scott***	(Siblings on Olivia Scott Gray Tree)
		Maggie Shaw

B UDDY HOLLAND HAS LIVED in the Shady Side area all of his life except for the years he served in the military. Born July 15, 1933, on his parents' farm on Shady Side Road, he was delivered by midwife Hattie Nick. Named James Arthur at birth, at three weeks his name was changed to Arthelbert after family friends came to visit from New

York. The friends knew of someone named Arthelbert who was rich and successful, and they made a case that having this name would bring the little baby fortune and luck. Thus, Arthelbert is his real name, but friends call him Buddy.

He attended Churchton Elementary School and Bates High School in Annapolis. Besides his service in the military and being an adored father and husband, his life experiences include being a waterman, business owner, welder, mechanic, construction worker, loyal St. Matthew's UMC member, founding member of the Carvers (a men's service group), and cook at the famous Galesville Hot Sox games. Active in the Anne Arundel Watermen's Association, Mr. Holland attended meetings with then—Maryland Governor (1959-1967) J. Millard Tawes at Government House, and he shucked oysters at the National Press Club to bring attention to the group's agenda.

A tall man with kind eyes, he has the deepest love and respect for his wife, children, grandchildren, and family. He is a great storyteller and has a remarkable way of describing how to make or do something, accomplish a task, or imagine an event. Although his health isn't what it once was, he has a spring in his step and an encouraging comment on his lips for every person he passes. A man who has steadily met life's challenges successfully, he responds with gratitude for God's presence and blessings.

The Beginning

Buddy's mother, Ruth Adams, grew up outside Reidsville, North Carolina; she had to leave school after seventh grade because there were no public high schools for blacks. Because Ruth loved school so much, her mother allowed her to repeat the seventh grade. The lack of higher education would have been the same if she had grown up in Shady Side. Even if there had been a school for blacks, there was no transportation to enable students to reach it. Instead, young people began looking for work because higher education was improbable. Ruth moved to Washington, DC, to work for a family. There she met and became friends with Nellie Gibson, who invited her to spend some weekends at her home in Owings. Buddy's father, Blake Holland, was working at Chesapeake Beach, where Ruth and Blake first met.

Ruth Adams and Blake Holland married and reared seven children, four sons and three daughters: Ralph, Blake, Buddy, Harold, Cora, and twins Naomi (Shirley) and Joan (Curly). Their paternal grandparents, Alex and Cora Holland, both grew up and lived in the Churchton–Shady Side area, but the senior Hollands passed before Buddy was born.

In front of their home Ruth Adams Holland is surrounded by her children, from left to right, Ralph, Cora, Blake, Buddy, Harold, and twins Shirley and "Curley." **Ron Holland Collection**

Mr. Buddy's father, Blake, is buried in the Holland cemetery a distance back from Shady Side Road. **Ann Widdifield Collection**

Until they built their own home on Shady Side Road, Ruth and Blake Holland lived with his parents on his father's 20 acres along South Creek. They lived down on the shore near where the Dennis graveyard is today. Buddy Holland's mother often told him a story about his grandmother Holland being on a sailing canoe returning to Shady Side from Annapolis when they got caught in a terrible storm near South River. According to his mother's story, the danger scared his grandmother so much she appeared paralyzed, stopped talking, and was never quite the same after being tossed about in the shrieking storm.

The Blake Holland farmhouse where Buddy was born and raised is still standing. Driving on Route 468 toward Shady Side from the stoplight, the home place is on the right before Dent Road. His dad always had two horses. Two that he remembered were "Coal," who was jet black and the prettiest, and "Cedar." "Dad farmed and worked a lot with small gardening around town. He traveled around Shady Side with his team and plowed up gardens for people or cut their grass. All of his equipment was on the wagon: plows, mowers, harrows, and rakes." In

Buddy's time Julius Dennis and his father were the only two farmers that did such work in the area and would have been in competition. "Everybody else was driving cars and trucks while Daddy and Mr. Dennis were driving horses and a wagon. This was in the sixties! My dad never owned a car."

Buddy's relatives now reside in the two-story white home that sits back from the road. Next to his dad's property, Al Holland, his grandfather's brother, owned 65 acres going up the road almost to Brown's Way.

On the Water

Buddy first went oysterin' with his father on weekends when he was nine years old. At fourteen, he quit Bates High School to be on the water every day with his father and brother Ralph until he went in the military at age twenty. The first time he went out with his father and brother in the wintertime stands out in his mind. "We were out of Deale near where Skipper's Pier is now, and I was standing behind the culling board culling. Dad and my oldest brother was catchin' em. My feet got so cold I thought I would die. At lunchtime my dad went down in the cabin and lit a round oil stove and called, 'Come here, son. Come over to get warm.' Well, I couldn't get over that culling board to get me to him. My legs and everything were frozen. My brother and dad come on each side of me and swung me over to get me into the cabin. I said, 'Dad, my feet is aching. I feel like I'm walking on two cinder blocks.' I only had two pairs of socks and a pair of boots. Dad told me that he would find something that evening to keep my feet warm. I told him, 'Dad, there is nothing that God has made that will keep my feet warm.' An old two-story country store [now gone] sat on the right corner of the last curve on the way to Skipper's Pier. The proprietor was Mr. Johnny Parks, the great-grandfather of the Parks who now run the filling station on Route 258. So we went to that country store on the way home, and my dad said, 'Mr. Parks, do you have a pair of puppies to fit this boy?'

Now, puppies were made out of felt that looked like a giant sock, very thick, that came half way up your knee, and you wore those inside your rubber boots.

"He looked at me and said, 'Blake, that boy is too small. (I probably didn't weigh 130 pounds.) Is he working with you?' Dad said, 'Oh yeah, he's a man.'

"'I don't think I've got nothin' that small,' but he pulled down a ladder, climbed up in the attic, and came down with a pair and said, 'The smallest I've got is eight. These should keep him warm. Put your sock on, but before you put these on, you wrap your feet in newspaper. That will keep you warm and take up the room inside.' Next morning I put those things on with the newspaper, and I could hardly walk because they were so heavy. But that was the end of cold feet! Those things worked like a miracle. It was like somebody had put a stove inside of my boot. The day came when I didn't need the newspapers for size, but I always needed those puppies."

Buddy always oystered with his dad and brother Ralph on the *Augustene.* Later, in 1962, the men bought *Catherine* from Henry Thompson, a boat builder and owner of a marina in Eastport.

Buddy's youngest brother, Harold, the fourth son, and middle brother, Blake, the second son and five years older than Buddy, always worked together on water and land. For them winter was oystering on Blake's *Southern Belle,* and summer was carpentry. Harold was an experienced and accomplished boat builder and lived at the angle of Nick and Scotts Town Roads. There he built his first all-wooden boat, *Miss Amanda,* named after his daughter. (Buddy gave an assist by putting in the motor for his brother.) In 1979, Harold was 80% finished with building a two-thirds fiberglass pleasure craft named *Swahili* when he died suddenly of congestive heart failure at age 43.

The Military

A month before he turned twenty, Buddy Holland was drafted into the military. His older brother, Ralph, served in a segregated Army, but Harry Truman integrated the service in 1950, so Buddy entered an integrated service right at the end of the Korean Conflict. All of his Army instructors were coming back from Korea saying, "I'm trying to save your life. I lost a lot of buddies over there," as they put the new recruits through their basic training at Camp Atterbury near Indianapolis, Indiana. He completed his training at Fort Knox, Kentucky, and was then stationed there in Company C, 701st Military Police Battalion, as a military policeman, an assignment that he loved. A Shady Side friend who was in Company B talked Buddy into reenlisting so they could use the reenlistment money to travel home for a month before being shipped out. When they returned to the post, his pal was sent overseas, but much to his chagrin and dismay, Buddy Holland was transferred to cooking school to replace someone in Company C who was getting out of the service. Against his wishes, "I traded my military policeman's white hat for a cook's white hat." He became very good at both cooking and baking, but left the service as soon as his three years were up. Each company had its own mess hall, and "the cooks fed about 85 to 90 people each meal every day except for some guys who chose sleep over breakfast." Company C was considered the best mess hall on post, so special visitors including congressmen and a three-star general from the Second Army were brought there for meals.

When returning home on leave in 1954, traveling north along Route 256, he was shocked to round the curve and not see his Churchton Elementary School where it had been all his life. Of course, the mystery was soon solved when he learned the school had been moved to Shady Side.

During the cooking phase of his military years, his wife, Thelma, joined him, but they had to live off post and rent a small space from a family in Louisville. Financially it made more sense for Thelma to return to Shady Side, so Buddy returned to the post barracks. He followed her home to Shady Side in November 1956 as soon as he could and returned to oystering with his dad and brother.

On the Water Again

The workboats were kept where Leatherbury's Marina is now and at Woods Wharf, the county dock, right across Parrish Creek from present-day Discovery Village.

The Chesapeake Instrument Company, founded in 1954, occupied the space. The present Discovery Village brick structure was started in the 1960s and by the 1970s was enlarged to contain 90,000 square feet. Starting with about a dozen engineers and scientists, the group grew to about 280 people in the '70s. Their work for the Navy centered on sonar systems: research, development, conceptual design, and manufacture. When the company merged with Gould, Inc., it became Gould, Inc., Chesapeake Instrument Division. In 1978 Gould Incorporated donated the facility to the Johns Hopkins University for the construction of modern laboratories for a marine research center. Formally dedicated in 1981, Bruce Cornwallis, a descendent of Edward Parrish, was the Marine Superintendent at the Shady Side Campus.[1]

Bessie Thompson, who worked for the Chesapeake Instrument Company, remembered seeing what Mr. Holland described: "Those people would watch us go and come. They actually thought we were crazy. They'd see us wearing our rain gear cracking ice to get out and coming back with icicles hanging off our caps. They would be standing on land saying, 'Look at those crazy people!'"

Like a knife through butter, ice cut through unprotected bottoms of the wooden boats. So, watermen would "metal" their boats by putting copper or stainless steel around the bottoms and up the boats' sides. Watermen bought copper flashing, like that put on a roof, at a hardware store and nailed it on the boats. It could weigh as much as 75 pounds. A printer from DC found out the watermen could use the spent metal that had been used for printing newspapers, so he brought rolls from the scrap yard down to Shady Side. Once they were covered, the wooden boats could cut through ice if it were no thicker than two inches. Breaking ice using their boats, boat hooks, and oars in front of the boat, the watermen had to shove the broken ice down and under the stationary ice to the side. They hoped the opened path would remain clear for their return trip home. Thicker ice required stronger efforts. An icebreaker from Annapolis, referred to as the "widener," might be called. The steel boat with twin diesels kept Annapolis open and allowed pilot captains to get out to ships waiting for the pilot to take them to port.

It was not unusual for Shady Side watermen to take their boats up to Annapolis City Dock and leave them there between Thanksgiving and February. During those winter months there might be 50 to 60 boats filling the harbor, so that one could almost walk from Market House to the Harbor Queen on watermen's boats. When the first boats began returning at the end of a day's oystering, they tied up along the wall near Market House. As later boats came in, they rafted up to the first boats. To reach shore it was necessary for many to climb in and out, up and over boats to exit their boat for home. The next morning could be a potential traffic jam if the watermen of the furthest boats out from shore were tardy and blocked those set to go.

From Shady Side four or five guys piled into someone's car and left early in the morning for the trip up to Annapolis. Not everyone owned a car, so riders paid the driver a dollar a day for gas. Parking was free at Susan Campbell Park at that time. If they couldn't find free parking, they parked at a street meter and loaded it up with nickels for a day at five cents a half hour.

Once the icebreaker had done its work, the watermen were free to work on the Bay. In the meantime, during the day the chunks of ice were "slidin' around the shore." Moved around by the changing tide and winds, those hunks of ice started piling up and jacked up on top of each other. Sometimes when the watermen returned, the whole harbor might be closed with ice: "We had a heck of time getting back in to City Dock or Eastport. If you made it to Eastport you'd stay there." McNasbey's Oyster House in Eastport was a selling point, and a lot of men "put their oysters out there" before returning to City Dock. Sometimes watermen sold their oysters at the harbor to captains of "buy boats" like Buddy Shepherd, a white captain who bought there. Ethel and James Gross of Shady Side often sent a truck to buy oysters, and the watermen shoveled their catch into the truck.

One day, Cyrus Gross, K.D. Gross's great-uncle, got caught in a very bad windstorm in the middle of the day. Working with other watermen at White Hall on Hackett's oyster bar between the Bay Bridge and Annapolis, he was headed back to Annapolis in his small wooden boat, which had a one-cylinder motor. A northwester, blowing 40 or 50 miles an hour with stronger gusts of wind, struck his boat, and his motor conked out. Turning his boat with the bow to the wind, he lay down in the middle of the boat, fearing he was going to roll over. The boat was pushed out in the shipping channel, and the waves were so high he was sure he would get swamped. Instead, he was blown all the way across the Bay to Bloody Point on the Eastern Shore. When the wind calmed down, watermen from the western side started looking for him. He was picked up on the eastern side of the Bay and was able to phone home.

Joyce Brown Thompson, interviewed in 2002, remembered her father, Squeeze Brown, telling her about her great-uncles Clark Gross and Cyrus Gross being blown over to the Eastern Shore. "Dad said how he was just really horrified thinking these two brothers were lost out there. But they were found."

Clamming

Blake Holland used to go down to Columbia Beach with a spade and a basket to dig up clams, or "mannose" as they were usually called in the early days. He could go out on the sandy beach and easily fill the basket for family dinner.

Buddy Holland clammed for four or five years during the warmer months, although he didn't have his boat *Catherine* rigged for clamming. Instead, he worked on commission for his brother-in-law, Ellsworth Brown, who ran a clamming business on Parrish Creek. Ellsworth never oystered but worked year round at clamming. He had three boats: one that he worked, a second one that Buddy and his brother worked, and a third one that two other men worked. It took two men to work a clam rig. Ellsworth also bought clams from other clammers and kept them in refrigeration boxes until trucks came to pick them up. Quite often the truck was waiting for the clams to be off-loaded for delivery to clam houses. Clamming was not as big a business as oystering, but Ellsworth Brown had a productive business.

Buddy explained the process: "You have a big motor inside your boat that sucks water up through this giant six-inch pump that blows 60 pounds of pressure into a four-inch head of the clam rig that's down on the bottom. This nipple-shaped manifold blows the clams from the bottom out onto this rotating conveyor belt and brings 'em up. Once they hit the conveyor belt you stand there and pick 'em off as they come by and put 'em in a basket. Everything comes up and that was what we was afraid of. Every time someone jump off the Bay Bridge, we was always afraid, thought about it all the time, that someone might come up. Of course, a body would keep on going off of the conveyor into the water, but you never knew what was going to come up. Whatever that thing passed over it was going to come up."

Bottles and rocks were considered routine stuff to run across on the conveyor. One father and son took advantage of the stones and rocks and carried stone to the shoreline at the point where they lived. At the end of each clamming day, they returned with twenty or so rocks the size they wanted and threw them on the shore from their boat. It didn't take too long to complete the effect they wanted.

One surreal event look place when Buddy and his brother were clamming near buoys on Herring Bay. Buddy was operating the extremely noisy rig. In fact, that was all he could hear as he watched the rig. Suddenly, baskets began flying around the boat and the wind swirled about him. Both men, disoriented by the bizarre disturbance, wondered what was going on. A voice bellowed from above. They looked up, and "there was Howard Shenton of the marine police with his legs hanging out of a helicopter and he's yelling through a bull horn. 'All of you on this side of the line; someone will see you when you get back with your load!'" They were on the wrong side of the invisible clam line. Sure enough, when they got back to Ellsworth Brown's place on Parrish Creek, there was another marine police officer waiting. Unfortunately, the men had broken a clamming law. Because clams don't survive once they have been pulled from the bottom, the clams were already goners. Thus, the fine was that they should take the clams to the dealer, who was alerted to make the purchase check out to the Department of Natural Resources. When they off-loaded the clams, the dealer seemed to relish asking the men, "Now, how should I make out this check?" Buddy's fine was $117 on top of the check for the clams.

Clammers first caught clams that had been ordered by a buyer. Clams not sold for eating because of their size were sold for chumming. As the clams came across the conveyor, the clammer separated them by throwing the larger ones into buckets; these would be ground up and sold later as chum.

Chumming was a way to bait for sport fishing as late as the 1970s. Charter boat captains or buyers at Woods Wharf, Manifolds in Deale, or Rod and Reel at Chesapeake Beach ground the clams in a stainless steel grinder to prepare the chum. Out on the water with sports fishing groups, the captains threw whole buckets full of the ground clams and their oil overboard to attract rockfish and bluefish. Alewives and menhaden were used in the same way. Today, sportsmen use "live lining" as opposed to baiting a hook with night crawlers for bait. Small spot or other small fish are kept alive in a tank on the charter. When the fishing grounds have been reached, a fisherman hooks a grappling hook into the back of the fish and casts off the boat. The swimming spot fish attracts the rockfish.

Dangers in the Family

Blake Holland was working at the Naval Academy the day that Chuck Gross's father drowned. "A lot of people were hurt up there. It was a big job that lasted for years . . . early '60s. They were dredging the Severn River to make the academy field near the water." The area is north of City Dock inside the academy on the far side of Halsey Field House and the Naval Academy Visitor's Center. In the same area, Buddy's oldest brother Ralph's fingers were chopped off while he was working as an oiler on a big crane. That day he was working on gears that swung around, and as he was greasing the cogs, another guy who wasn't paying attention started turning the crane and caught Ralph's glove. "Every finger was cut off just like that," Buddy demonstrated with slices across his hand.

When Buddy was an adult, Blake spent summer nights working on a 100-foot barge owned by the Diamond Company that carried mud and sand to a hole called the "Dumping Grounds." The tugboats and barges were working 24 hours a day. A licensed tugboat captain and his first mate pushed a barge under the Bay Bridge, up the Bay, and to the grounds off the Chester River on the Eastern Shore. Going to the grounds, Blake and another worker rode on the tug, but as they neared the grounds, the two men jumped from the tug onto the barge to be ready to trip the gates at the bottom of the barge. There were three gates in front and three in back. Unloaded, the barge was ten to twelve feet tall, but fully loaded with residue, the barge rode eight to nine feet under the water and appeared almost level with the tug. The jump was doable, but the next part of the job was both tricky and risky. The men walked and worked around the edges of the barge. Arriving at the destination, "Dad used a maul to trip huge gates at the bottom of the barge to release the load of mud." If this maneuver were executed incorrectly, the barge would pop up and flip a person into the dark waters below. Therefore, he opened the middle gates first, then the outer gates in such a way as to keep the barge balanced and stable until all the contents were released. The empty barge sat ten to twelve feet high, and Blake was too high to jump back to the tug for the ride home. There he rode in rough waters until he returned to the naval harbor in Annapolis. The job was not for the faint of heart because of the obvious dangers and the need for balance, agility, courage, and quick thinking and decision making in a short response time.

Over the Water

Buddy Holland worked on the first Bay Bridge, which was named for Governor J. Millard Tawes. "I scratched my initials up under that bridge in many a place, but it's probably painted over by now. Quite a few guys from Shady Side helped build that first bridge. It was built mostly the old fashioned way: poured concrete."

A local guy told Buddy that they were hiring guys for the bridgework, so he went up and was hired on the spot with about eight other men. They went straight to work. "I was scared to death because I'd never been 30' to 40' in the air pouring concrete. We would pour roadbed seven days on the western side of the Bay and then take a ferry to the eastern side to pour concrete for seven days.

"There were some crazy drivers. Trucks like you see on the roads today brought us the concrete. They'd drive up on that bridge with no sides on it, turn around and drop the load. Only bolted bumpers kept the trucks from going over. We'd be above the water 100', 150', and they'd come up, drop their concrete load into motorized Georgia buggies [steel frames that each held a yard of concrete]. We were pouring about 12" of concrete; then 6" of black top on top of that. The second bridge was built using helicopters to bring the concrete."

Under the Water

Buddy worked as a laborer digging out mud for the Baltimore Harbor Tunnel. Three other diggers worked with Buddy, but they were hardly alone. During the day from 35 to 100 other workers might be found welding, using machines, driving vehicles, or directing the construction of the inside of the underwater expanse. While they worked, outside the tunnel new sections of hollow tubes were being added when ready to be received below. These hollow sections, 12 feet between each bulkhead and sealed at both ends, were placed on the bottom of the harbor and inserted in the expanding tunnel. When the next tube was inserted into the tunnel, its end was cut open. During the insertion mud was pushed up between the joining parts, and the oozing mess had to be removed quickly so the welders could seal the two integrated sections. Digging mud three to four feet deep and pitching it into a backhoe bucket was the digger's job. The backhoe driver left for a brief time to off-load and returned for more. When the day's work was completed, Buddy and his crew left the same way they had arrived at their digging area: they walked out. From 80' to 100' below the harbor, they retraced their steps down the middle of the tunnel until they reached the opening back on land. Back home, Buddy was sick every evening.

After three dreary months of breathing in bad air and getting terrible headaches from truck exhausts belching carbon monoxide, Buddy made a decision. One Friday payday he caught his ride home with a guy who dropped him off at Mayo. While waiting to hitchhike the rest of the way home, he decided, "Never, no more. I've got to find something else to do. So, I give the job up." Driving through the tunnel not so long ago, he saw the tiles that vividly reminded him of days during construction.

Near the Water

One June when the clamming season was slow, Buddy checked about work at a little cinderblock garage that sat where the 7/11 in Deale is now. He worked there as a mechanic for two years until business slowed and then switched to the Sinclair station, which is now known as Good Old Days auto repair. For a time he was part owner of the Sinclair station. Ira Nichols, a professional welder who often stopped by the station, taught Buddy welding.

When oystering was out of season, Buddy ran his own welding business during the summer down on Scott Town Road for ten years. The garage is still standing behind the two-story home where his brother Harold Holland's widow lives. His mechanic's shop had a welding machine, and he worked on oyster rigs and motors. "In 1974 this black guy came down looking for Buddy Holland. 'You found him,' I said." The man had heard a lot about Buddy and asked him to work for him at the marina he had bought in Deale. Buddy preferred working for himself, because he had been working for someone else half of his life, so he turned down the offer. Ramon (John) Fountain often hung out with Buddy during the summer when school was out, and he witnessed the man's pleas. One day John recommended, "Buck, you might have a future down there. Why don't you give it a try?" So the next time the man came, Buddy agreed to give it a try, and he never left the job until he retired in 2007. The marina was bought and sold twice, but he stayed on at the marina at Herrington Harbor North for 33 years. In 1974 Buddy completely gave up the water, as many Shady Side men were doing, because oysters were drying up. He sometimes missed the water, but he found his new work very fulfilling, and he liked talking with the many interesting people he met.

Husband and Father

Thelma Matthews, Buddy Holland's wife, was 14 when she met Buddy, who was 17, on a Sunday as she and some of her sisters were walking home after church. He stopped to offer them a ride home on Scotts Town Road.

When Buddy returned from military service, they lived with her family for about a year on Scotts Town Road. They then moved to his parents' house until they bought their home on Cedarhurst Road, where they raised their children, including the twins. Twins seem to run in the Holland family: Buddy had twin sisters, his and Thelma's twins were a son and daughter, and his son Ron and his wife, Mary, had twin sons.

By December 4, 2010, Thelma and Buddy Holland had been married for 57 years. To celebrate their fiftieth wedding anniversary, their children managed to sweep them off their feet, so to speak. The children told the couple to pack suitcases and prepare for a child to pick them up for a family dinner at an Annapolis restaurant, after which they would spend the night at a hotel. To their surprise, a limo arrived to take them and their luggage to the Annapolis Marriott. Staff greeted them and ushered them to their room, and then they were escorted to dinner. Not only did their children greet them, but they also walked into a roomful of cheering, laughing friends and extended family, clapping and smiling while the totally surprised couple looked at each other in astonishment.

Any Sunday that Buddy's children attend St. Matthews, they know that their father will prepare breakfast for them after the service. "I never know if I will have five or fifteen. We have a good time. If they stay on, my wife fixes the supper."

The Galesville Hot Sox

Buddy Holland was a member of a men's service group called the Carvers Club, which was made up of men from Galesville, Annapolis, and Shady Side. They worked to do things for the community. Today, only three former members from Shady Side survive: Cordell Salisbury, Reginald Miller, and Buddy Holland. Their main objective was to bring back and support the Galesville Hot Sox.

Shirley Salisbury surprised Buddy Holland with this picture of the Carvers for his birthday in 2010. The majority of the members were from Galesville, and the rest were from Annapolis, Churchton, Edgewater, and Shady Side. Shady Side's men are Cordell Salisbury (second row far right) and Buddy Holland (second row fourth from right) and Galesville's Raymond "Tuck" Fountain (second row, second from left). **Cordell Salisbury identification of men, Buddy Holland Collection**

In 1915 a loosely organized group of black men in Galesville started playing baseball. When Howard "Leslie" Mackall joined the team in

1924, he began keeping records. A new team formed about two years later with a few of the original players incorporated, but mostly younger men were added. The first organized team appeared in 1926 with Leslie Mackall as shortstop and manager. Most but not all of the Galesville Hot Sox were shuckers and oystermen who worked at Woodfield's Oyster and Fish Company in Galesville. Workers from the Eastern Shore lived in an area called Shantytown. Rules were quite strict for the players: No drinking the day of the game, and a player must practice and attend meetings to play. The players usually donated food to sell at the games, which their wives prepared at home.

In 1928 the games were moved to the Wilson family field, rented for $50 a season until the beginning of World War II, when the rent was raised to $125. A black family whose ancestors had lived in Washington owned the whole property, including the field. Games were played on Saturdays, and admission was 25 cents. On holidays, it cost 35 cents. Hot dogs were a dime. The team got the hot dog buns on credit at Dixons' store on the corner of Route 468 and Galesville Road and paid it off after the game. In 1941 the Hot Sox started playing games on Sunday, but church was first and baseball came later in the day.

Each season the Hot Sox played at least one Negro Professional League team, such as the Baltimore Giants, the Newark Eagles, the Indianapolis Clowns, or the Washington Black Sox. Famous players included Luke Easter, Joe Black, and Willie Wells, who is in the Hall of Fame. In 1929 the Hot Sox were almost undefeated, losing only to the Washington Black Sox. Several area teams took their names from the Negro Professional League, including the Drury Giants, the Edgewater Grays, the Davidsonville Clowns, and the Owens Station Eagles.

The Galesville Hot Sox was one of the best sand lot teams back in the old days. The Brooklyn Dodgers came to scout players and recruited a couple of guys from Galesville. Billie Tiding played on the farm team in the late '50s or early '60s. Attendance averaged 150 to 200 fans on weekends and 500 on holidays, but the record was set with 945 fans.

As the older players died out, the team started going down, and nobody would start it up again or wanted to put out the money to lease the field. The Carvers Club took on the project to revitalize the games. They leased the field and started a brand new team. Buddy Holland welded a flagpole for the field. Doll Baby Dennis's nephew Thomas Dennis, who owned a well drilling company, volunteered to set the 40-foot galvanized pole. Billie Tiding was so proud of what the club was doing that he donated the military flag given to his family to honor his brother, who had been killed in Vietnam. When the flag was first flown during the opening ceremony, many people had tears glistening in their eyes.

Buddy Holland cooked at the games every Sunday afternoon for more than ten years. In his welding shop he had crafted a giant frying pan that held 25 pieces of chicken in quarters. He made a second pan for frying fish. "I'd be there all day, and guys would be helping me to bring wood up for the wood pile to keep the barbecue going." Behind a long trailer that had a refrigerator, they served the clamoring public eager to make food purchases. Several of his children grew up at the games, and his second daughter, Wanda Smith, was an honorary member of the Carvers Club because she sold tickets for the club.

From 1929 to the early 1980s, the Galesville Hot Sox baseball game was the Sunday event for black families, and people flocked to the games. As soon as St. Matthew's church service was over, Buddy Holland's family headed for Galesville. "It was a good part of my life," Buddy said.

"I tell people that this is God's little happy acre here. Most people, when they come here and spend any length of time, they'll always come back. My wife won't live any place but Shady Side."

CHAPTER 12

HOG STORIES

A NY PERSON OVER THE age of 50 who was born in Shady Side probably has a hog story or a memory of seeing butchered hogs hanging on racks in people's yards. Just about every family, black and white, kept hogs. A memory took on a deeper meaning when a child's pet pig was butchered for food.

"We had hogs, ducks, chickens, and goats. Everybody had hogs. That was their meat. Every year they'd come to slaughter, and I used to hate that," said Chuck Gross. "First they used a knife, and then later they'd shoot them," but they still had to be stuck with a knife so the animal would bleed out. "With the knife to the throat, the pigs would be screaming and bleeding as they ran until they fell over."

A female pig, or sow, is extremely protective of her piglets. "They'd eat you up" if anyone interfered with their babies. It was said that if the boar's testicles got really big, it made the meat tough, so males not used for mating were neutered at about five or six months of age. A neutered boar is a barrow.

Only one boar was kept as a stud hog for mating with the sows. A female might have two or three litters of four to seven piglets before she reached the poundage for her demise. Weighing in at 250-300 pounds could be the beginning of the end for a hog that was between two and three years old. Meanwhile, the boar lived a complete, productive life, eating, grunting, wallowing as only a pig can do, and being of service to the sows. But even for him, all good things had to come to an end, because he, too, was meat for the table. The young males were castrated earlier than butchering season when they reached the weight limit. Being spared as a piglet meant he had a few years of bliss, but when his services and term were finished, so was he. Retirement was no celebration for him!

"The worst part was when the stud pig was castrated. Oh my, I never saw anything like that. They would grab the pig and flip him over and cut them off. That pig would walk backwards in pain for ten or fifteen minutes screaming," Chuck explained. "I think the most painful thing for the pig was the salt. They would put the salt on to heal the wound, so it wouldn't get infected." Apparently, a mixture of salt, juniper tar, and turpentine was painted on the hog with a paintbrush. (There is a reason for the expression of rubbing salt in a wound.)

Carla Nick Gross added, "That's how my pet pig died. He started off as a pet, and then he was our meat. I cried."

Carla's oldest sister, Delores Nick Harley, still carries a scar above her eye that she got when she was a young child during hog butchering season. She was outside when one of the hogs got loose from the men, and the barrow came screaming toward her. She started running and fell against the rim of one of the tubs where the hogs were drained, receiving a gash above the eye.

Patty Gross explained in an interview in 2004 that she never got upset at hog killing time in spite of having hogs as pets, "smoothing them down" and feeding and loving them. "I never felt sad because I knew the day was going to happen."

Helen Crowner Gorham well remembered hog killing time. "My brother couldn't stand it when it was time to kill the hogs. He'd leave home." She added, "In fact I had a pet pig when I first got married. We called her Susie. That was terrible when she was slaughtered. We ate her, all righty. We didn't let her live long enough to have babies."

Sisters Helen and Daisy Crowner remembered that their Uncle Jim Crowner "cut 'em up. They'd kill 'em, build a scaffold, and then hang 'em up for a while. They'd make chitlins, sausage, ham, ribs, and pork. Some people made link sausage, but Mama always made patties and canned them. There was a little house where the hams and meat were kept hanging."

One family recommended a way to make link sausages: run sausage through meat grinder; pack ground sausage measuring an inch or more in length into hog's intestine; twist the intestine around and around; continue filling same sized sections and twist until 10 to 12 links are formed. Twist the ends and knot. Take to smoke house and smoke 'em.

In an audiotape interview recorded in1984, Sarah Scott Matthews (1900-1998) told about hogs being slaughtered in the wintertime during her childhood. Her father, William Scott, salted and smoked the meat, and her mother, Maggie Shaw Scott, would make patty sausage and lard. Apparently, Shady Side men had secret recipes for salting down the meat. Sarah's son-in-law, Arthelbert (Buddy) Holland, was interviewed in 2009, and the interviewer may have hoped to hear this family recipe. Sitting on the back deck of his home on a warm, breezy June day, recorder running, she got bad news. "I can't help you with the recipe because I don't know the recipe." Luckily, Mr. Holland had other information.

He told about coming home from school one early winter day in the 1940s when there were three dead hogs hanging upside down on what was called a gallows. "We always killed two or maybe three hogs every year." Imagine two five-and-a-half-foot Y-shaped frames staked in the ground, separated about six feet apart, and three butchered hogs hanging from a pole between the two Ys. From there the story of the winter butchering process unfolded.

The Winter Butchering Process

As Buddy Holland told it: "The men would go in the pen, grab a pig and shoot 'em in the head with a 22-caliber rifle. If they had enough men, they would jump on him, tip him over, and one of the guys, he was always the sticker, he'd stick that long butcher knife in the pig's throat. [Even with the shooting, a pig must still be stuck for the bleeding.] The blood would come whooshing out. That was the quickest way. Sometimes if he got him right, that knife would go right into his heart. Then they'd let him up, and he would wander around until he fell over. They called it 'bleeding out.' In the cold, the blood was steaming. The other hogs would be running around screaming and go over in the corner screaming until the men would go get another one.

"My father, Blake Holland, always had horses because we lived on a small farm. He was a truck farmer. My father hooked a slide on the back of two horses, put the hogs on the slide and then took them over to the scalding barrel. They'd have a scalding pot, or 55-gallon drum, sitting on an angle, so they could slide the hog in and out. The men would have already dug a pit, put wood all around, and started a fire to get the water scalding hot. Next, they took wood ashes from a wood stove that Dad had already saved in a bag, bucket, or pile. They put a ten-quart water bucket full of these ashes right in the water. Called 'shaking it down,' helps, they say, to make the hair come off the hog easier and cleaner. Taking about four or five minutes, three or four men dipped the hog in head first, sliding half of him down the barrel. Then they rotated him around by his back feet, flipped him over to scald the back half to remove that hair, pulled him out and laid him on the platform. Then they'd jump on him with knives to hang him up.

"They did this by cutting behind his hind feet where there's a big leader that's real tough. They'd stretch his legs open to put a prepared stick between them. This stick, about two inches in diameter, had been sharpened on each end and was strong enough to hold the hog's weight.

Then four or five guys would grab and raise him up in the air and put that stick over the bar or pole and attach the other leg. There he'd hang with his nose about six inches from the ground, or just high enough for a small boiler or a number two washtub to stick up under his nose.

"Now, here comes the gruesome part: We'd have a guy that would come to cut him open. Not everyone could do this job, and he was specialized for the job of gutting the hog. He'd cut him up between his legs all the way down to his throat and open him up. Part of his intestines would come out. That is where your chitlins are. They'd stretch him open and clean him out inside. Everything would come down: his kidneys, liver, and heart—all of his innards in this tub. There wouldn't be anything left inside the hog. Then, that tub would go in the house. That's where the women were. They'd clean and separate all the edible stuff.

"An Eastern Shore guy at the marina where I worked in Deale told me that he had learned that we ate every part of the hog but the squeal. We eat the pig's head, feet, almost everything—nothing is left.

"The pigs would hang on the gallows for about three or four hours, but overnight you'd put them in the shed or a barn. You always killed in the winter when it's cold, maybe before Thanksgiving up until Christmas. It had to be cold so the meat would survive. Dad would put the pigs in the meat house on the floor until the meat got cold, not frozen but stiff, and then he could cut him up. I'd sit and watch him, and I still don't know how to do it, but Dad had learned. He'd cut off the shoulders, hams [from the thighs], section them up, he'd cut the middlings, where the bacon comes from [between the shoulders and hams]. He would cut them down and trim the parts." Demonstrating with his hands, Mr. Holland showed how his father would lay out the parts.

"The hog's head was cut off with a knife, and then Dad would use an ax to cut the head right down the middle length-wise. The nose might be cut off with a hatchet. In the head was gristle and gruesome stuff, but he'd clean all that stuff out. You'd salt the head down to get cured.

There's plenty of meat on a hog's head. You'd be surprised! A cook could use the head for cooking and seasoning beans. The hog's tongue is delicious: It's nothing but a big chunk of pure, lean meat. It's some of the best meat in the world. He'd cut his legs off; cut his feet off at the knees. There is quite a bit of meat on pig's feet. There are big hunks of lean [meat], especially at the knee. They have beautiful pig's feet down at Renno's.

"Dad would take the hams and shoulders to smoke in the meat house. Setting on the floor on some bricks, so the bottom wouldn't get too hot, would be a 55-gallon drum cut in half holding usually hickory or cherry wood to make the fire. He'd start his fire and keep putting wood on it until he had a good foundation of fire, and he'd put some water on it or a burlap bag to make it smoke some. Once he got it cooking good, he'd just leave it. Every now and then he'd go in and put some wood on to keep the fire going and putting out heat and smoke. The meat was getting smoked and cooked while hanging on hooks on a beam going across the shed. The beam wasn't too high so you could stand on the floor to get to it. If I'm not mistaken, he smoked it for three days and three nights. That meat would cook hanging up there on those hooks. Dad had the special wood all stacked up, and he'd say, 'Son, make sure you check the wood and the fire every few hours. Don't put too much wood on there now.' That meat was delicious. Mom was telling me that Granddaddy, Dad's father, would pull out a knife and cut a piece off and eat it right there while it was smoking.

"When the meat was finished, Dad would put a gunny sack around it to keep the flies off, tie it up, and hang it back up on the beam. It could hang there for a year. You didn't have to worry about anyone stealing it back then. You didn't even lock your doors.

"Dad made a wooden box about six feet long and three feet tall for the other things like the head, feet, and middlings. He bought table salt in 25-pound bags and lined the bottom of the box with salt about an inch thick. Then he'd put the meat in and lay about half inch salt on it and then layer more meat. The meat would absorb the salt, which is 'salting it down.' It could stay in that box for two years and never go bad.

"My mom cooked the fat that Dad had trimmed off the ribs and the ham—those parts that were too fat to eat. Hog skin is pretty thick, so Mom would take a sharp knife and cut the skin off the meat. She cooked the fat, or rendered the fat to make lard. Then, she would cook the skin and stuff to make soap. I don't remember what else she did besides strain it through cheesecloth and cook it, but she washed clothes with what she made. She cut the lard into blocks a couple of inches long and wide so you could put your hand around it. When I was small, she used a washboard to scrub the clothes. We didn't use that soap on our skin because it was too harsh.

"Back in those days it was amazing how people would preserve things. Mom would make liver pudding. We ground up the sausage, give it to my mom, Ruth Holland, and she partially cook up sausage patties that would fit inside the mouth of a quart masonry jar. So, the patties went in the jar, and after the grease cooled a little bit, Mom poured the grease over the patties to cover them with a lip about an inch deep on top of the sausage. When that grease turned cold, it would turn white. She'd put the lid on top and those lasted for a year or two. She'd put 'em, maybe eight or so jars, on a pantry shelf. On Easter Sunday we knew what we were going to have for breakfast. She'd put the sausages back in a frying pan and cook them some more for us to eat."

An Aside About Hogs and Farmers

"There used to be a hog park where the bank is today," Erwood Avery, then 84 and grandson of Capt. Salem Avery, reported in a 1991 taped interview. "We could get in and out of Shady Side with a horse, but no such thing as getting through with a car on account of the mud and water. You see a few of them little plants come up out of the ground now and that was from the Hog Park."

Erwood, called "Woody," was a lifetime neighbor and friend of Julius Dennis, Miss Doll Baby's uncle. Their farms between Columbia Beach Road and Cedarhurst Road were adjacent to each other, as was true of their grandfathers, Jacob Dennis and Capt. Salem Avery.

An Aside About Sheep

There was a sheep park joining and behind the property where the fire department is now, according to "Woody" Avery in his 1984 interview. It joined part of the old Lerch farm and was in back of Centenary Church at the head of the creek coming off South Creek. Apparently, the sheep park became the source of tick fever. "We lost a number of people with tick fever. They never had anything to help you with it. I think two of the Swinburns died of it, and the sheep was carrying it. The Lerches owned the property, and the University of Maryland and the Maryland Department of Agriculture and all experimented in that quite a bit." This information inspires many unanswered questions, but it is the only uncovered story about a sheep park in Shady Side.

An Aside About Tomatoes

Mr. Wilde said that he made a good living on the farm, adding, "It was 'specially fine for tomatoes." [1]

"The tomatoes that came out of this land weighed about ten more pounds for a half bushel than the higher land tomato weighed. This ground raises a heavier tomato," said Woody Avery during a November 1988 interview. "Uncle Eddie (Avery) sold his (tomatoes) to a colored man by the name of Al Smith."

CHAPTER 13

SHADY SIDE NEIGHBORHOODS

IN THE EARLIEST DAYS, Shady Side was more accessible by water. The dirt roads were terrible, and the oyster roads were uncomfortable to walk on. Two old timers said that you couldn't walk on Shady Side Road because of the oyster shells. According to Erwood "Woody" Avery in a 1988 interview, "The old country road [that] went out here was a path for oxcarts and horses, but they couldn't get out and they couldn't get in." His contemporary and friend, Julius Dennis, at age 97, laughed during a 1992 interview and said, "Oh, ho! Oh my, dust was three or four inches deep. When it rained, oh Lord, . . . mud, mud, mud. We hated to go up that road; it was so muddy." In the late 1920s the first paved roads made traveling to the community much easier for summer people and tourists from Baltimore, Washington, DC, Pennsylvania, and Virginia. Within easy traveling distance was a place where a single person or family could find relaxation, rooms, board, boarding house activities, swimming, fishing, and refreshing breezes away from the cities. Once in the village, visitors discovered a community life that was hospitable, friendly, and kind.

African Americans were able to purchase land that had been worn out by wheat growing. The Prann family owned land near the present-day brick Shady Side School, and the Joseph Matthews family bought property on Parrish Creek. The Scott family purchased land near South Creek off West River Road, and the Nick family originally lived on Hyde family property. John Gross first lived on land owned by Captain Barnard Hallock. Bill Crowner, the father of Saul, Jim, and Charles, purchased land on Cedarhurst Road. [1]

According to Dr. Hugh Irey and Dave Wallace in a 2002 interview, one of the early outsiders, probably the first, was their grandfather, William Wagner, a gunsmith who ran a sport goods store in Washington, DC. He purchased property at the end of **West Shady Side** Road, probably in 1914, according to Ethel Andrews.[2] The men related that in one day's travel, Mr. Wagner took a train from Washington to Annapolis, caught the steamboat *Emma Giles* to Shady Side, where he hopped in a rowboat and was rowed to Cedar Point, owned by Robert Franklin Nowell, Ethel's father. In the meantime, the *Emma Giles* headed toward Galesville for her scheduled two stops before leaving the West River. After seeing the land, Mr. Wagner liked what he saw and quickly agreed to pay $2,000 for the 10 to 12 acres. With the deal sealed, he managed to catch the returning steamboat. Today, Cedar Point is locally called Wagner's Point. In her book, Miss Ethel enjoyed pointing out that her father had originally paid $1,000 for the land, "a fine profit for Papa."

More people came to build summer places of their own along the water. Others bought lots in areas being developed and advertised for summer cabins. For some families Shady Side remained a summertime destination, but for some, like the Wagner family, the children kept the land and became full-time residents.

The young man's name is unknown; however, in May of 1926 he helped dig this trench from Our Place (now Captain Avery Museum) to the new house being built by the Dunn family across the lane. The home's four lights would receive electricity through wires connected to the Club's Remy generator. In 2009 a three-story house replaced this 1926 structure. **The Dunn Collection**

★   ★   ★

Cedarhurst was Shady Side's first subdivision; it was started by the Cedarhurst Realty Company, which was organized in 1924.[3] A 1989 Shady Side Days program reported that William Nowell of Shady Side convinced Washington investors to purchase the farmland for a waterfront subdivision. The transaction was recorded at the Annapolis courthouse in 1921. The original road leading to the property was a cow path, so at some point after 1927 the Cedarhurst Citizens Association, formed in 1926, purchased the "land . . . from Charles Crowner and turned [it] over to the county." Apparently, a leading citizen promised the county commissioner 40 votes if the county would take over the road!

Babe Ruth slipped away to Shady Side to fish and stayed at the Bay Shore Inn (Brick House) in Cedarhurst. Pictured left in 1929 or 1930, Ruth is with Crandall Trott, Frank Owings in the hat and Sam Beard, a friend of the Babe. **Stanley and Glen Trott Collection**

The Cedarhurst name came from the mass of small cedar trees that grew closely together. Erwood "Woody" Avery reported in an undated interview (about 1991, when he was 84) that little "cedar" birds lived among the trees. If the tiny birds were close enough together, "You could clap your hands and with one shot with a shotgun you could get a whole meal off them. That is all gone now." Erwood said that his father, Walter Avery, sold 110 acres of Cedarhurst, including the Brick House, for $950. Cedarhurst was part of the land included in "Rural Felicity," owned by Thomas Norris in 1738.

In 1932, **Avalon Shores** was developed on about 500 acres of Thomas Lerch's (Augustus Lerch's last descendant) farmland, with two original houses on the property. It was desirable land because the river and inlets made for a lot of waterfront opportunities. Edward F. Hines Real Estate Company of Washington, DC, was the purchaser, and it was named the Edward F. Hines Avalon Shores Company. Eventually, William H. Thomas of the Thomas Lumber Company held control of the company with Mr. Hines and Edward Moul of Washington. In 1936 Avalon Manor and "Westelee," a meadow Mr. Lerch had used as a quail preserve, were developed by Avalon Shore, Inc., to the west of Avalon Shores.[4]

The Avalon Shores Volunteer Fire Department started in 1944 with one truck. They saw their first action when responding to a fire at a Franklin Manor house that had been struck by lightning.

Traveling along Snug Harbor Road and turning north onto Idlewilde Road, one reaches the subdivisions of **Idlewilde** and **Felicity Cove**. Travelers reach the Felicity Cove area by turning east on Bay Road, or they might continue on Idlewilde Road where it dead-ends at Idlewilde. Robert Carswell of Baltimore originally purchased the Idlewilde land for $20 an acre at the turn of the century, but by 1976 it was selling for $1,200 an acre for building lots. William Coleman of Washington and William G. Nowell of Shady Side developed Idlewilde, and Nowell named the area.[5]

For a time Mr. and Mrs. Nowell owned and ran a hotel on the shore, but they sold it, and the business went through a string of owners. Supposedly, one owner, Mr. Gaither, cut down all of the oak trees to make a sand field. One hotel was called Danes on the Bay, so named by someone who raised Great Danes.[6] The hotel and name remained though the owners changed, and people living today enjoyed going there for dinner, music, and the view. The musical group LeRoy Battle and the Altones played at Danes. A big wooden sign bracketed with two large Great Dane heads rested on the roof and was lit up with lights announcing Danes on the Bay. "For years the sign was just laying on the ground. I don't know what happened to it," said a long-time resident. Today, owners of a newly built private home reside where Danes' customers once dined, and they enjoy the ageless view.

A.W.Andrews, who had bought the property from Robert F. Nowell, developed Felicity Cove. Ross Fryer bought property in 1929, and later his widow sold lots to Mr. and Mrs. Frank Wilde of Shady Side.[7] In 1953 there were 17 homes, and by 1989 there were 27 homes.

Snug Harbor, another waterfront development, is at the end of Snug Harbor Road. Percival Whipple of the Kentview Land Company bought the property from the Lerch estate. By the summer of 1953, the land company deeded the remaining public lands to five trustees, all property owners. In 1976 there were 70 property owners and 47 dwellings. [8]

★   ★   ★

Only white people bought into and lived in these developing subdivisions. Blacks from the community frequently found jobs doing housework, cooking, babysitting, ironing, collecting trash and garbage, doing yard work, plowing gardens, and taking care of odd jobs in the new developments

"Miss Sis," Josephine Tongue (left) and Aurida Crowner pose outside a Felicity Cove home where they worked for white families in the new developments. Aurida's children called Josephine "Ma Phiney."
Doris Crowner Brown Collection

Two groups were not welcome on "white" beaches: Jews and blacks. But these groups found another way to enjoy the Chesapeake Bay, the Maryland countryside, and Shady Side. In the early 1920s, a group of Jewish Masons purchased a home on the West River on East West Shady Side Road for a clubhouse for their families. They soon enlarged the house and named it "Our Place," and it became a summer retreat for swimming, boating, and socializing with friends. In 1989 the Shady Side Rural Heritage Society, Inc., purchased the property with the goal of preserving the local history and artifacts of the area. Now it houses a waterman's museum and extensive library and is a gathering place for community activities. According to a local person, there was also a second, unrelated Jewish family group, off West Shady Side Road.

★   ★   ★

In a 1984 interview, Charles J. Coates, Sr., born in 1916 "back in the field," described the housing developments as the major change he had witnessed when he retired in Shady Side in 1972 after his years of being away.

But where was **"Back in the Field"**? Every black person growing up in Shady Side would recognize the area as the one behind the Lula G. Scott School, but white families also live on the road. For a long time, the dirt road leading to various homes didn't have a name; eventually it became known as Shady Rest Road. Families of Charles and George Thompson owned properties and have continued living on Shady Rest Road, as did Eddie Nick and the Salisbury families. Cordell Salisbury and Jant Thompson, who grew up together as classmates and friends, called their area the "Hood," short for neighborhood. "That was long before Hollywood came up with the term," said Cordell Salisbury. John Fountain grew up in the field, as did Charles Coates, Sr., who married Kathleen ("Kay") in 1941 in the family house that burned down. Kay said that she fell in love with Shady Side when she first came down to meet Charles's parents, and she and Charles "always planned to return here," and they did.

Charles was the last child born to his parents, Chesterfield and Rachel Etta Coates, who already had Everett, Kathleen, and Alverta. Chesterfield named his boat *Alveretaleen* after his wife and daughters. He was in the Navy for 20 years and then was an oysterman. When his wife, Etta, was away helping new mothers or sick people, he was able to take care of the family because he was a cook while at the Naval Yard. "But he couldn't bake bread," recalled his son, because he had not been taught that skill.

234

"Any illness came and Momma would stay for days in the home to give assistance." Having no transportation, she walked. When Charles, who was the post commander's chauffeur, happened to be driving down from Ft. Meade with the commander, they saw his mother walking down the road to help a lady in Churchton. Charles said that his mother was on her way to a lady in labor, so the commander had Charles drive her to the lady's home.

Chesterfield Coates, his father, was described thus: "When we think of community leaders, our minds immediately go to Mr. Chesterfield Coates, who is actively in anything worthwhile. He is president of the Shady Side-Churchton P.T.A., past president of the county P.T.A., active in his lodge of the Masons, active in St. Matthews Church and a civic minded individual in general."[10] *Discovering Our School Community*, written in the 1952-1953 school year, noted that "the school serving the colored has four rooms . . . . This year the consolidation of Churchton and Shady Side got underway."

Charles Coates was the first Negro to go to college from Shady Side; he majored in mathematics and science and graduated with honors from Morgan College in 1938. He taught for two years at Salisbury High School until he was drafted into the Army for six years. He went from private first class to major during World War II, serving in a segregated unit as an engineer building bridges. He served in the European theater for about four years and elected to stay in to serve on troop ships that carried servicemen to the South Pacific. After the war he got his master's degree in vocational guidance and became a guidance counselor. First a high school principal for 600 Negro children, he later became a principal in an integrated high school with 400 white children and 200 blacks.

As he was growing up, his mother always told him that when he finished elementary school, no matter how far away high school was, she would see that he could go if he wanted to. His thought was to finish elementary school and go out on the water with his father. His father got top pay of 25 cents for a bushel of oysters, and he caught anywhere from

20 to 25 bushels a day. His dad kept his boat at Walter Matthews's house on Parrish Creek. Charles went on the boat with his dad on Christmas Eve and got so sick that it was his last time. When he got home, he told his mother he was ready to go to high school. High school was then at Stanton High School on Washington Street in Annapolis. He moved to Eastport to live with his cousin, and the last year he stayed "at Mrs. Jackson's on Carroll Street. The dirt roads from Shady Side to Annapolis were so bad and the water so high that Poppa got stuck in Annapolis for two days with the horse and buggy."

★   ★   ★

Continuing to describe the Shady Side changes, Charles Coates, Sr., mentioned the white neighborhoods of Felicity Cove and Avalon Shores and the "settlement of Negroes from Washington who bought up Bay Shore, which was right on the Chesapeake Bay. They built a number of homes on Bay Shore and named it **Columbia Beach**." Its name comes from the District of Columbia. The Dennis and Crowner families originally owned the majority of the land.

In 1940 Columbia Beach was formed on about 88 acres as a black vacation community, like Highland Beach near Annapolis. Affluent people from Washington and Baltimore bought 20-by-100-foot lots for as little as $60 and built vacation cottages along Bay Shore between the Chesapeake Bay and the marshy flats of Flag Pond. Property costs soon skyrocketed.

The first cottages were small and lacked insulation or heat, as did the ones first built in the Cedarhurst and Avalon Shores communities. The summer cottages were not meant for winter living, but over time all the developments experienced the conversion of summer cottages to homes for year-round habitation.

Because Columbia Beach was a private beach in its earliest years, the local families stayed over on the public Bay Shore side near the ninety-degree turn into the Columbia Beach property. Ethel Gross had her cookout shack on the Bay Shore side, where ice cream and hot dogs could be bought in addition to crabs. "Rich black people were at Columbia Beach, and we were not to go there," said one of the younger local women. "But the kids went up to Renno's, and we got to meet, talk, and know each other and un-privatized the place! We were invited to the Regatta. Reggie and Ronald had the fastest boat there. We were there for the queen's coronation." Columbia Beach probably peaked between 1958 to the early '60s

A baptismal service took place at Bay Shore in August of 1955.
Doris Crowner Brown Collection

Shady Side's colored families had been enjoying this area before 1940. Josephine Tongue, born in 1907, recalled going to Bay Shore to go swimming. The wide sandy beach was perfect for wading and swimming, and older generations remember going down for swimming, picnics, and gatherings with friends and relatives. Doris Crowner Brown's mother, Aurida Scott Crowner, often took her four youngest children, Hughward, George, Doris, and Purnell, to swim at Bay Shore before it was renamed Columbia Beach. They could wade "way out" on the sand and "loved it" because they didn't have any water near their home. "The water was crystal clear," remembered Doris. "I was considered a child up to age thirteen or fourteen, and I could not go anyplace by myself."

Florine Thompson said that in the late 1940s and 1950s there was plenty of space for parking cars near the beach. People waded in water up to their knees on a sandy bottom a good distance away from the land.

Many parents took their children to Bay Shore, especially on a Sunday evening, and the families swam, ate, and had a delightful time. Crab, seafood, and other delicious food could be purchased from Ethel Gross's seafood hut. Teenagers especially looked forward to the return of the summer people because of established friendships and the opportunity to meet someone new.

The newcomers loved the area for their families because it was relaxing, peaceful, and quiet. The water offered recreational opportunities and the catch of the day for dinner. On clear days you could see six miles across the Chesapeake Bay to the Eastern Shore. The summer season usually ran from Memorial Day weekend to Labor Day weekend. Families and couples arrived on Friday nights and returned home on Sunday evenings. Sarah G. Jones, a retired elementary supervisor for Anne Arundel County's black schools, lived in Baltimore and had a summer home on Columbia Beach.

The highlight of the season was the annual boating regatta, which was held once each summer. Hundreds came for the boating regatta, to watch the boating competition, and to see who would be crowned Columbia Beach Queen. Men in the boating club wore white slacks, shirts, and caps.

Originally advertised as "The Gem of the Bay," the gated community can still be found by taking a right off Shady Side Road onto Columbia Beach Road, traveling to the road's end, and looking on the east side of the road. Turning left, there is one way in and several ways out. Any traveler may enter, passing other homes to reach the gated area. As late as 1979, Columbia Beach, which was 98 percent black, was thought of as a community within the community of Shady Side. Today a visitor finds both whites and blacks living comfortably as neighbors and enjoying the Bay.

Without bulkheads the sandy beach was quickly eroding away in the late 1970s. Each big storm ravaged the wonderful sandy bottom and beach. Leon Brown remembered the beach going out about a mile when he was young, but it has continued to erode away during his lifetime. Erosion is a continuing problem for the community as it is for anyone living on the water. Bulkheads and riprap are now in place to defend the vulnerable shore.

Three Friends Who Played "Back in the Field"

Owen "Smack" Scott, whose father drowned in 1929, arrived "Back in the Field" when his mother married George Thompson. Owen preferred to live at his Uncle Charlie Thompson's home, in part because his cousin Rupert "Josh" Thompson was there. Hughward Crowner rounded out the threesome of lifelong friends who were always together.

Josh came home from World War II and reenlisted during the Korean conflict; he received a Bronze Medal and a Purple Heart. "He was 5'3" and played a great big tuba," reported his baby sister, Darlene Washington, "and he marched and played in the 1st Army Band."

Smack was drafted into the Army and was stationed at Fort Meade, but he came down home every weekend, and the MPs had to come down to get him and take him back to the post. The story goes that he pretended he was crazy to get out of the service. To test him, a psychiatrist asked him what color was George Washington's white horse?

Smack's answer: "Blue." The doctor said that he was crazy, and he was able to get out of the Army.

Hughward Crowner had been honorably discharged from the Army in April of 1956, so he and cousin Smack went out driving together. Heading from Churchton home to Shady Side, they didn't take Dead Man's Curve safely. Their black and white car turned over in the ditch, and both men were killed. The friends' funeral was conducted in one service at St. Matthew's Church. Darlene Thompson Washington, about 13 at the time, remembered her brother Josh standing between the two coffins at the front of the sanctuary and telling their stories. The memory is vivid still.

A Destination Up the Road from Shady Side

Not in Shady Side but within a reasonable reach were two extremely popular beach sites, making them a destination for African Americans during segregation: Carr's and Sparrow's Beaches. North of Shady Side, across Back Creek south of Eastport, the beaches are located today by taking Aris T. Allen Boulevard, to Forrest Drive, to Bay Ridge Road, a left turn on Edgewood Street to the end to Bembe Road to the former locations.

Two African American sisters, Elizabeth Carr Smith and Florence Carr Sparrow, inherited the land and opened the two beaches in 1927. Carr's Beach had more entertainment, like Atlantic City, and Sparrows Beach was more family-oriented, like Ocean City.

Mrs. Olivia Mae Dennis Scott sits between her daughters
Olivia Lorraine Scott (left) and Shirley Mae Scott at Sparrow's Beach.
Olivia Scott Gray Collection

Bates students and their parents have fond memories of days spent on their shores. In fact, smiles cannot be kept out of their voices as former attendees recall those fun-filled days. There were amusement parks, swimming, fishing spots, arcades, slots, dancing, food concessions, places to picnic, bandstands, and a nightclub. Performers included Lionel Hampton, Ray Charles, Chuck Berry, Ruth Brown, James Brown, Pattie La Belle and the Bluebells, Otis Redding, Little Richard, The Temptations, and The Supremes. Carr's Beach had a larger pavilion and could draw the more popular performers. Sparrow's Beach tended to be more church—and family-oriented. At the Banneker-Douglass Museum off

Church Circle in Annapolis, there is a floor-to-ceiling photograph on a wall in an exhibit room that gives a view of how it was. The beaches' popularity waned in the late 1960s, with integration opening up other places to go, and the beaches closed in the early 1970s. The beaches are gone now, and the land is populated with homes and businesses.

A floor to ceiling photo of Sparrow's Beach at the Banneker-Douglass Museum gives one the feeling of what it might have been like "back in the day."
Collection of the Maryland State Archives

In 2011, Olivia Lorraine Scott Gray stands where Sparrow's Beach used to be.
Ann Widdifield Collection

CHAPTER 14

ATHLETICS AND RECREATION
IN SHADY SIDE

A NNE ARUNDEL COUNTY LITTLE Leagues were not integrated in the
early 1960s. The county had one department of recreation, but it
had two leagues: one for whites and one for blacks. Shady Side had one
of four black teams in the southern part of the county. The other teams
were from Galesville, Edgewater, and Lothian. LeRoy Battle organized
the Lothian Clippers to even out the original three competing teams.
Maurice "Bernard" Powell, cousin of Charles Coates, Jr., coached the
Shady Side team, which wore red and white uniforms. Each team's
colors were white and another color. This was as close to whites as
the teams could be at the time, because Little League schedules did not
include black teams, and many local white fields prohibited black and
white teams from playing together on them. The black teams formed
the Southern Anne Arundel County Athletic Association (SAACAA). [1]

Each spring the SAACAA held a parade in Galesville to kick off the
baseball season. Three key people worked at the parade: Harriet Hull,
Theresa Fountain from Shady Side, and Melvin Booze. Accompanied
by a drum and bugle corps and decked out in their uniforms, all
four baseball teams marched in the parade, which included others on

decorated bicycles, pushing baby carriages, or driving convertibles. Besides children's games after the parade, refreshments of hot dogs, ice cream, and sodas were available at the community center. In the evening adults returned for a dance with a live band. All of the money taken in was divided evenly among the four teams. [2]

Lot baseball and pick-up games with kids getting together after school and during the summer had been happening around Shady Side over the years. In June 1964 the Boys Club was founded to provide supervised recreational opportunities for boys ages 8 to 14, open to all members and friends. Girls were added soon after. This was before integration in the schools, but no child was ostracized. Membership was open to any interested adult, civic group, or business that wanted to support the program. In 1966, 59 individuals were regular members at $5 each, 25 were contributing members at $5.01 and up, and 9 were sustaining members at $25. Open meetings were held twice a year.

Audrey Matthews was instrumental in the integration and involvement of women and girls in sports in Shady Side. Her daughters, Deborah and Darlene, played for the Girls Club, and later her son, Herbert, played for the Boys Club, as other black families' children joined the clubs. Audrey Matthews worked closely with Beebe Castro, the first female supervisor (1969) with the Anne Arundel Recreation and Parks Department, and the two women were friends. Audrey was also a faithful, active committeewoman for the Old Fashioned Community Day celebration that occurred during summers for ten years or so in Shady Side. Now the Fourth of July parade is held regularly.

The Kiwanis Club, with the help of the Boys' Club, developed an athletic field behind the community center on Snug Harbor Road. The present Shady Side ballparks had not yet been developed, although a makeshift baseball backstop had been in the same location as today's backstop for as long as anyone could remember. A plea was made for more members, coaches, drivers with automobiles, spectators, and money. "There does not seem to be a shortage of children," stated a newsletter.

Funds for baseball, basketball, and football came to a total of $860.40 for the franchise, equipment, and uniforms during the 1964-1966 seasons.

Supportive football coaches such as Dale Crowner, Sr., and Elbert "Erby" Thompson backed up athletic directors Jack and Beebe Castro and Frank Goldbach. Originally Dale and Erby played on the team but returned as coaches when they graduated from high school. Jack Castro, who had once been a professional ballplayer in the Cleveland farm system, was naturally talented and staunchly committed; he coached all three Shady Side sports. He and his wife, Beebe, left no stone unturned to get uniforms for the kids. Their names were synonymous with community action for Shady Side's young people, and later Beebe Castro led monthly senior citizens' bus trips.

Several adults recalled attending the Annual Awards Night at the Kiwanis Club/Community Center as children, when winning teams received trophies, special awards were given to outstanding players, and certificates of participation were presented to all children who had participated in a sport. Guest speakers from the Baltimore Colts, the Washington Redskins, and the Washington Senators and Anne Arundel officials were also highlights of the evening. The Farm League was for 8 to 10 year olds, Little League was 10 to 12 year olds, and the Pony League was 12 to 14 year olds, recalled a former player.

Jack Castro is photographed with the Shady Side youth who participated in local sports and attended the Annual Awards Night at the Kiwanis Club on Snug Harbor Road. Front row (left to right) Paul Walter, Scott Miller, Calvin "Lil Fella" Thompson, Jeff Unknown, and Glenn Thompson. Second row left Joe Harrison, John Thompson, Unknown, Joel Sasano, Unknown, Bob Holman, Unknown, Jeffrey Holland, John Lowe and Howard Schaffner.
Jack and Beebe Castro Collection

Darlene Washington remembered seeing Jack Castro driving his huge Ford station wagon "that went on forever" filled with kids hanging out the windows on their way to a game: "There was this white guy with a bunch of black kids." Ron Holland was one of the kids who played on the Shady Side team and rode in the car. Spacing his hands about eight inches apart he chuckled, "That car's bumper was about this far off the ground." Vic Smith, telling his station wagon story, laughed at the memory, too. "I'll never forget. Mrs. Castro was having a problem with the transmission when she started to drive. It would drive slow and then bump, it would catch. She told us, 'Now you guys have to lean forward and sing loud to make this car go.'" So a station wagon filled with twelve or so black kids leaned forward and lustily sang, "Cherokee

People, Cherokee Tribe, So proud to live, so proud to die" (made popular by Cher) while a white lady driver lurched and laughed down the road. He added, "The Castros were good people."

Once, when Beebe Castro took a group of kids into McDonald's because of a delay in game time, one of the kids came up and loudly reported, "Mom, So and So ordered more French fries than he was supposed to!" The whole line of kids and Beebe laughed as some strange looks came from other patrons.

Coaches Jack Castro (left) and Glenn Cleek (right) stand with the Shady Side football team in the 1960s. **Jack and Beebe Castro Collection**

Originally, the various baseball and football teams played behind the community center before the county built the Shady Side Park fields in 1972. The county bought the lopsided land of scrub trees, cattails, and grasses, filled and leveled it, and created three ball fields, two tennis courts, and two basketball courts. There was talk of a boat ramp and picnic area, but they did not materialize. Improvements and changes, such as a playground and the demise of the tennis courts, have evolved since then, and the fields are used regularly for baseball, football, and soccer and the courts for pick-up basketball. Before the county bought the property, the land was going to be a housing development called Oyster Harbor. A road ran through the middle of the land to reach the plats, but three lots running along the edge with a right of way to Parrish Creek were the only lots purchased. Today, one house with a white picket fence and garage are evidence of that stage.

Summer School Playground

Thelma Holland followed Rev. Melvin Booze, who then headed the playground program in Galesville, as the coordinator of Shady Side's summer playground program at Lula G. Scott through the county parks and recreation department. When the new brick school was built, the program continued there. It cost $1 to register for the recreation and parks program, and the county supplied everything. Children had daily activities planned for them from 9:00 a.m. to 2:30 p.m., including sports, volleyball, and preparation for a future track meet, checkers, games, pottery, and arts and crafts. Kids brought their own lunches or bought something at Shady Side Market. There was one field trip each year where the children might go roller-skating, go to Lake Shore amusement park, or attend a Baltimore Orioles baseball game. Miss Thelma, a licensed school bus driver, drove the school bus, and one parent chaperoned every five or six children. There was always a good turnout at Southern High School for the track meet of all of the summer playground communities in South County. Ribbons and trophies were presented to the winning competitors and teams. North and South County winners competed at Anne Arundel Community College.

The Shady Side Drum and Bugle Corps

Shady Side children could participate in the Drum and Bugle Corps under the guidance of Charlotte Alderson in the 1960s. The organization owned the instruments, and the integrated group practiced at the Rescue Squad building. Ron Holland and Junior Fountain played the Tim Toms, and Darlene and Debbie Matthews were majorettes. The name was changed to Shady Side Model T's for a period of time. Other communities, such as Annapolis, Eastport, Chesapeake Beach, and North Beach, also had drum corps. The various groups competed at carnivals and parades and before a judges' stand to earn trophies.

Lustine Holland led another marching group called a Swat Team that included boys and girls from Churchton and Shady Side.

CHAPTER 15

MATTHEWS FAMILIES

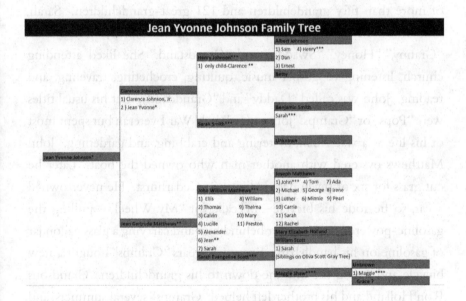

Jean Yvonne Johnson Family Tree

ORN MARCH **28, 1926,** Lucille Matthews Nick Brown was between Miss Doll Baby and the Crowner sisters, Miss Helen and Miss Daisy. Lucille was three years old when the three Scott brothers drowned and too young to understand the tragedy. She was the first daughter to join three brothers in the family of Sarah Scott Matthews (September 9, 1900-1998) and John William Matthews (August 26,

1896-1976). Hattie Nick was the midwife who delivered Lucille. In the following years more siblings arrived, giving the family a total of six sons and five daughters. The brothers were: Ellis, Thomas, Calvin, Alexander, William, and Preston; the sisters were: Lucille, Jean, Sarah, Thelma, and Mary.

Both of Lucille's parents were born in Shady Side. William and Maggie Scott were her mother's parents, and Mary Elizabeth Holland and Joseph Matthews were her father's parents. The Matthews grandparents lived on Parrish Creek on the property that is next to present-day Discovery Village. The Scott grandparents lived at the end of Scott Town Road next to the cemetery.

Sarah and John Matthews married in 1919 and were progenitors of more than fifty grandchildren and 121 great-grandchildren. Sarah, known as "Miss Sweetie," also answered to "Momma," "Grandma," "Granny," "Honey," "Swaddy," and "Grandstand." She liked attending church, listening to gospel music, quilting, crocheting, traveling, and reading. John was called "Daddy" and "Granddaddy," but his usual titles were "Pops" or "Gramps." John was a World War I veteran but spent most of his life as a waterman, oystering and crabbing, and gardening. John Matthews oystered with another man who owned the boat. Later he cut grass for six or seven people living in Cedarhurst. He never owned a car, so he rode his bicycle—he called it "My Wheel"—pulling the gasoline-powered push mower behind him and carrying a glass gallon jar of gasoline on his handlebars. Every few years "Gramps" bought a new bicycle and passed the old one down to his grandchildren. Grandsons Ron Holland and his brother Jeff helped "Gramps" several summers, and they were supposed to jump on their bikes to follow him as he honked his horn and flew by. "He never stopped," said Ron.

In the beginning of their marriage, Sarah and John Matthews lived at her mother's house, and they later moved to their own home on the south side of Scott Town Road—a one-story, four-room house for the family of eleven children. The children went to bed before their parents and had no trouble going to sleep because of all the school lessons and chores they had accomplished earlier. "When we were kids, three or four of us slept in one bed," chuckled Lucille. "We prayed every night before bed down on our knees." They had a wood stove, outside privileges, and a water pump outside to get drinking water, to bathe, and to wash laundry. They had no pump, no electricity, and no radio. They had kerosene lamps, and the boys carried a two-gallon oilcan over a path through the woods to buy kerosene at Mr. Crandall's store on the right corner of Dent Road where it meets Shady Side Road. (Crandall's was a two-story building where the Crandall family lived above the store.)

Walking past their Scott grandparents' home and down a gravel lane past two more houses, the Matthews children could reach the water. They might play or swim in the water—except they weren't supposed to "steal away" down there. Sometimes they would take a seine, or vertical fishing net, with one sibling on each side holding a pole and dragging the net through the water to catch soft shell crabs. "The water was clear and nice, and you could see all the way to the bottom."

Lucille's father and brothers raised chickens and kept hogs, and the family had a garden so they didn't need to buy many things at a store.

Growing up during the Depression, Lucille remembered standing in line for food brought by the county or state that would be distributed at churches or schools. She remembered the food coupons and little red coins that were used during rationing. On her living room wall hangs a large portrait of her father in his World War I uniform.

Younger sister Jean Matthews Johnson said that her father was a great ice skater. "He'd put money on the back of his coat and tell us we could have it if we could catch him. He was so fast we couldn't catch him. Mother could skate, and they wore skates that you'd screw on." The children had shoe ice skates. Some people used to tie corncobs on their shoes to ice skate. Jean remembered her father leaving in the morning to go oystering on the water and coming home in the freezing cold.

In the summertime, "We played in the water all the time, but we couldn't swim. We'd steal down to the shore where the oystermen tied up and go out in the river in anybody's boat. We were lucky we weren't drowned. We had no business down there."

Jean remembered that as little children she and her siblings would help elderly folks such as Cousin Big Grace or their grandmother by cleaning their homes. Laughing, she said, "We were rascals. Our grandmother would tell us to watch her house while she was gone to Annapolis or somewhere, so we'd clean the house. Then we'd get ourselves a crab net to catch a chicken. We'd kill it, pick 'em, and have Lucille fry it up for us." The fried chicken was not for their grandmother's return. "Yeah, we were getting it ready for ourselves to sit down and eat! She would be off shoppin' and we'd be home eatin'. She never missed a chicken. They had chickens, ducks, turkeys, and guinea keets. They didn't sell eggs; they gave them away."

Jean Matthews Johnson sits at home and holds Miss Ethel Remembers as she tells of her own growing up years in Shady Side. Miss Ethel mentions Miss Jean and Jean's sister Thelma in her book. **Ann Widdifield Collection**

For playtime the children made their own dodge ball with rags and stockings and played with anything they could get their hands on. Outside they ran up and down the road keeping a wheel balanced and going with a stick or played caddy, and inside they played jacks, dominoes, and marbles. Trading marbles was an important transaction.

Adults played tricks on the children and "scared us to death. When you went out to get a drink, they'd put a sheet over their heads. One night we were walking down the road and saw a man on a horse with no head. It scared us. They would laugh at you." A friend said that she was told she should get home because the "Boogie man will getcha." There was some retribution. Some men wearing big high-laced boots were sitting with their legs crossed underneath the Matthews' family table. One of the kids crawled under the table without being seen and removed all of the strings from the boots. Discovering the lack of laces, someone exclaimed, "I'm going to kill those children!" The delighted children had no worries and survived with much laughter.

Jean remembered that the siblings never bothered anybody and played among themselves because there seemed to be enough for play with eleven. The family had an old Model-T Ford, and one sibling got in to drive the car up the road while the rest pushed the car from behind. Reaching the intersection to Shady Side Road, they turned the driver around and pushed him back.

As the older children married, they brought their spouses home to live with the family at first. Some more rooms were added on to accommodate the growing family. Once on their feet and able to get their own place, the wedded couples moved from the family home.

Sarah "Miss Sweetie" Matthews is surrounded by her children at a 1991 family reunion at the Holiday Inn. Clockwise from the back (left) are Sarah Thompson, Jean Johnson, Preston Matthews, Mary Tyler, Thelma Holland, Lucille Brown, Alexander Matthews, Miss Sarah and Calvin Matthews. **Jean Matthews Johnson Collection**

In Lucille's day everyone knew everyone else in Shady Side. When she walked to the post office to get the mail, she didn't have to say her name because she was known. The mail was taken from little boxes behind the counter and handed over. She remembered mailboxes for the Hallocks, Leatherburys, Proctors, and Parkers and knew of the Parrot family on Columbia Beach. She remembered the rooms above the post office that were rented out to overflow guests from the Andrews Hotel.

Like Florine Thompson, Lucille went to Gustav Heinrich's store on the West River, but in her case it meant cutting through the woods between her house and the store. In the wintertime she watched people drive an old Model-T Ford across the frozen river to Galesville and back after taking a spin in the village. Roads were mud when she was a child growing up, and snow was so deep that she couldn't see out of the house windows. A crowd of men would get together to dig the way out to the road. "People would help each other." Her family didn't have a car until they were able to buy an old used one.

For Christmas they cut a cedar tree from the woods and decorated it. There were no gifts on Christmas Day because there were so many children that gifts were not affordable. The children would go to their grandparents' houses, and there would be cakes, candy, jenny snaps, apples, and oranges ready. "We'd go from house to house, and the grandparents had filled little brown paper bags with all of the treats lined up on the table for the kids. We were just as happy as if we had a hundred dollars," Lucille reminisced.

For Easter they dyed eggs from their own chickens and had an Easter egg hunt. Other holidays were given little attention. For New Year's Eve the family walked to church for Watch Meeting Service to watch the old year out and the new year in. "We'd be on our knees at one minute to twelve praying that we would see another year." For birthdays, "We'd say 'Happy Birthday' and that was it. You couldn't waste no sugar to make a cake. You had to use sugar to eat," Lucille explained.

Sundays were the most important day for the family. They had breakfast together and walked to and from St. Matthew's Church for Sunday school and the morning service. Sunday school classes were held in the sanctuary before the worship service. Lucille remembered having a catechism book about the size of a deck of cards, and from it they would memorize Bible verses, recite poems, and learn hymns. Because Franklin Chapel and St. Matthew's shared the same pastor, St. Matthew's had the earlier service so the pastor could leave for a later service at Franklin in Churchton.

Home for Sunday dinner, the family spent a quiet afternoon until it was time to walk to Franklin if there was an evening service. They used a path cutting through the woods to reach Shady Side Road and from there walked along the side of the dirt road and avoided the very deep ditches. Some cars might come along, but those who had them were considered rich. If someone was seen on the road, each knew who the other was, black or white.

On Mondays, laundry day, Lucille and her sisters had to get up earlier, about 6:00 a.m., to wash the clothes and hang them on the line before they walked to school in rain, flooding, snow, ice, hot sun, or beautiful weather. The girls carried the water from the outside pump to the inside wood stove for heating. Once it was hot, the water was poured into two large tubs, the temperatures were balanced with cold water, and one sister began scrubbing clothes on a washboard with homemade lye soap. To whiten clothes a small block of bluing was placed in some cloth, tied with string, and dunked for a second in the rinse water, turning it blue. The second sister rinsed and wrung out the clothes. When the third sister hung the clothes on the line, the pieces were as white as snow. In the winter months, "the clothes would get stiff and freeze before you pinned them on the line." The sisters rotated the positions if someone got tired of a particular job. When they returned from school, the sisters brought in the clothes. There were never any arguments over the trading of jobs. In fact, discipline and routines were so organized that her parents only had to look at the children and the children knew what to do. That included going to bed without being told. "We would look at the clock and know it was time."

If the children were working, they did not wear their school clothes, because only certain clothes were to be worn for school. The girls sewed children's clothes and everybody, including the boys, had to sew patches. The girls did the ironing. Five or six irons were heated on the stove, and the irons would be rotated as the one being used cooled down. The ironing board was a piece of wood covered with cloth and shaped like ironing boards of today. The difference was that the piece of wood was placed between two chairs to support the board. Collars had to be starched, so someone made the starch by cooking a block of starch on the stove. "I enjoyed what I was doing because I had no other choice. In order to make it in life you had to do that," said Lucille.

"The bigger children took care of the younger ones. We all had to work." Bread was made at home. If extra bread was needed, someone could go to Swinburn's, where a half a loaf could be purchased. The children, boys and girls, brought in wood from the pile in the morning and stacked it for their mother for the day so she wouldn't have to go out for it, and they repeated the job again in the evening for the night wood. Two or three times a week limbs and such were gathered from the woods and sawed into pieces for the woodpile. To saw the pieces, one child would sit on a large piece and two others would run the cross saw back and forth to cut it to size.

Jean Matthews Johnson described her brother Calvin's garden. "He had the beautifulest garden you ever seen in the summertime with every vegetable you can name: huge cabbages, corn, tomatoes—he gave most of it away. He had chickens, ducks, geese—those geese would run you. Man, I was so scared of those geese I didn't know what to do. They'd be eatin' nice not payin' you no attention and as soon as you walk toward the house, they'd come right at 'cha. They had their wings open and hissing and scare you to death. Calvin even had a goat and even a miniature pony. When they'd have a picnic, then kids could ride the pony."

Up at 7:00 a.m. and due at school at nine, Lucille went to Shady Side Elementary School from the first to the seventh grade when it was a two-room school with the potbelly stoves and "outside privileges." Mary B. Wiseman was the principal and teacher for fourth, fifth, and sixth grades in one room, and Lilyan Burrell taught first through third in the other room. Each teacher had twenty to twenty-five students. "Kids might throw spitballs or pull a chair out from under you," but those were the most serious offenses. Doctors came in to give shots, and dentists came to check their teeth. "Sometimes they'd pull 'em and give you a fit," Lucille laughingly explained.

Jean's school experience was like Lucille's, but she added that Miss Wiseman "was very strict, and you'd better listen, or she'd crack your knuckles with a ruler. You know how they whack your fingers." Jean remembered that the teachers got the students to bring in a pack of this or a can of that. The soup was started in the morning and ready by lunchtime. "Each person had a cup with our names on it and a cup holder. The soup was delicious. It was good, I can tell you that." Other days everyone brought their own lunches, and the teachers, both from Annapolis, liked to trade with the children. A child's parents may have butchered a hog and fried up ham for a sandwich.

For seventh through twelfth grades, the Matthews children caught the Bates bus south of Scott Town Lane when the bus was on its way out of Shady Side. Jean said, "I had a friend that we picked up in Mayo who always wore a flower in her hair. I'd call her 'Lena Horne' and she'd get on the bus and ask, 'Can I set with 'cha?' I'd say, 'Come on, set down,' and then I'd slide all the way over to the edge 'til she'd fall on the floor. She'd say, 'Girl, I'm telling you; you're somethin'. I'll remember you if I live to be a hundred years old!' She always wanted to sit with me. Some of the kids from Annapolis were nasty because you were from the country, and they'd call us 'country mouse.'"

If a child got sick, the parents fixed up something they thought would help them feel better. Dr. Dent was the only doctor available, and there wasn't money for a doctor. A mixture of whiskey, sugar, and honey might be given for a cold. If a temperature was the problem, onions were cut up and placed in a piece of cloth, and tied around the ailing person's waist: "The onions would dry up just like they were fried and you would feel better." They might be given a medicine such as Scott's Emulsion, castor oil, or Three Sixes (666), which tasted bitter.

Eventually, a gas stove replaced the wood stove, and a refrigerator replaced the icebox, where the water had overrun the drip pan "many a day." Jim Gross and Shake Thompson were icemen who drove ice trucks and sold ice at local homes for 50 cents or a dollar for a large piece of ice. The consumer told the driver how much ice she wanted, and the iceman cut off the size and used ice tongs to carry the ice block into the house's icebox. The ice had been made from well water that had been frozen in tin cases, or frames, at Woodfield's in Galesville.

After Lucille graduated from Shady Side, a childless couple with a summer home in Cedarhurst asked if Lucille, then thirteen years old, could work for and live with them in Washington. The response was yes, so Mrs. Quiggly enrolled Lucille in Garnet Patterson School in Washington, DC. As soon as she finished her homework, Lucille might do a job for Mrs. Quiggly. Lucille graduated from Garnet Patterson School and completed one year at Cardoza High School. Lucille saw her own family when she and the Quigglys returned to Cedarhurst during the summers. Her sister Jean remembered Lucille coming home on weekends and the summers with the Quigglys. But Lucille's mother decided that Lucille should stay in Shady Side, and although Lucille saw the Quigglys in later summers, they lost contact over time.

Jean left high school to help her mother. She knew the Cline family from Shady Side, so when she turned seventeen she left to live with and work for the Cline family in Washington, DC, where she took care of Ruth Cline's two boys for about two years.

At nineteen she married Clarence Johnson, then twenty-four, who had a son, Clarence Elsworth Johnson, Jr. Five years later, in 1953, their daughter, Jean Yvonne, was born. Yvonne had a fiftieth wedding anniversary party for her parents at Davidsonville in January 1998. Clarence and Jean had fifty-six years of happiness until his death. Yvonne has an oil portrait of her father in her living room.

Clarence graduated from Bates High School in 1941 and attended Hampton Institute, where he majored in sheet metaling and ran track. He became a junior clerk in the General Accounting Office (GAO), but he left to serve in the Army from 1943 to 1946. Earning several medals and ribbons, he was honorably discharged and returned to the GAO, retiring as a GS–11 after completing over thirty-five years of government service. His nickname was Doctor Snake because he arrived faithfully with his medicine bag to visit the sick and shut-ins.

Eventually, Lucille left Shady Side again to work for a Washington lady. From that job she became the housekeeper for Nancy Dickerson, an NBC reporter, for several years. Sometimes she traveled with Ms. Dickerson; however, a more permanent change was to take place.

Ellsworth Brown, born in 1922 and a graduate of Churchton Elementary and Bates High School in 1939, was in the Merchant Marines for nine years. He and Lucille met after he returned to the area. They dated for about five years before they married in 1964. They moved into the house where she has lived for over forty years on Parrish Creek. Originally owned by Missouri and James Matthews, the house was bought by Alexander and Helen Dennis, who left it to her daughter, Matiel Dennis Carter, who ran a boarding house there. When Matiel went blind, she couldn't keep the house up any longer, but she wanted to keep it in the family. Ellsworth's mother and Matiel were related, so he was allowed to buy the property. When Ellsworth and Lucille moved in, Neal Groom, who turned 100 in 2010, and K. D. Gross were their immediate neighbors on Atwell Road. Lucille's clearest memory of working at the Chesapeake Instrument Company was the traffic. It might take her five or ten minutes to get out of the driveway!

Lucille and Ellsworth Brown bought Matiel Dennis Carter's boarding house on Parish Creek. Mr. Brown, often called "Mr. Clam," ran his very successful clamming business from there.
Lucille Matthews Brown Collection

On July 14, 1977, the *Arundel Times* carried a story titled "Fishable by 1983?" with a picture of Ellsworth Brown standing on a pier on Parrish Creek with several boats in the background. His clamming story was reported and the decline of clams and water quality discussed. He said that Hurricane Agnes had ravaged the Bay in 1972, and clams had made an admirable comeback by themselves, but "Nature can't put it back as fast as man takes it away." He was a member of the county's Coastal Zone Management Commission, an eleven-member panel concerned with Anne Arundel's waterways and shoreline.

As a waterman, Ellsworth Brown planted seed oysters, but his main living was made from his softshell clam business, which turned into a large operation. He woke up around 4:00 or 4:30 and fixed his own breakfast and lunch. In the early days, there was no limit on the amount of clams that could be caught, but laws were passed to limit the number of bushels caught per day, a time was set when boats had to be in, and another law required refrigerated boxes to be on the boat. When Hurricane Agnes came through and brought a red tide, clams were gone for a while, as was other seafood. But Lucille remembered 1978 or 1979 as good clamming years.

Ellsworth, known to many as "Mr. Clam," started out selling clams in the neighborhoods and to local restaurants such as Pirate's Cove. The business grew and he sold in Annapolis, Mayo, the Eastern Shore, Washington, DC, and the New England states. Every Saturday there was a refrigerator truck that was dedicated to delivering clams from Shady Side to New Hampshire. Ellsworth had his own three boats for clamming, and about ten other watermen sold their clams to his operation on Parrish Creek. Some of these watermen were from the Fountain, Gross, Groom, Cheetam, and Wilde families. Each waterman had a license number, and his boat had a number. Every basket had to have a cardboard tag stapled to it stating the waterman's name, license number, boat number, and date. There were refrigerator boxes at their place. If there were any spoilage or health problem, the source could be tracked by the tags. Only one basket was used from the filling of the basket at the water to the delivery of the clams to the customer. Baskets could not be reused. Baskets were ordered by phone from a Virginia basket company, and a trailer would deliver between 4,000 and 5,000 baskets at a time. The tags were ordered from another company.

Businesses called in to order clams from Lucille, who took care of the telephone business. She would tally the number of orders for the day and relay the message—"500 bushels"—on the radio that worked between the house and watermen's boats. Then she would make up the tags while the watermen were out and attach the tags to all the baskets when the watermen returned. On occasion she would even deliver clams for Ellsworth.

He was the only clam dealer in the area, and he worked the business for about thirty years, six days a week. Sundays were for rest and church. Occasionally, the Browns would take a trip to Atlantic City, where he would play cards and she would shop on the boardwalk.

Lucille prepared fried clams, clam chowder, and steamed clams for her family. Crab cakes were a favorite dish; they put pots out from their pier to catch crabs for their own needs, not as a business. As for recipes, she cooked like her parents did with a little of this and a pinch of that—whatever was on hand.

People have rented slips in front of her property for years, and watermen continue to keep boats there. Lucille has plenty of company besides the watermen and her daughter and family. Her two Shady Side sisters join her every day to watch their favorite soaps. Family comes regularly for Sunday brunch after church.

Friends and relatives from out of town stop by, but someone new surprised her several years ago. Mrs. Quiggly's son Jimmy had been searching for her because his mother talked so much about Lucille from the time Jimmy was a little boy. He was looking for a Lucille Matthews. Lucille Matthews Brown didn't know that he was searching for her. The connection was finally made, and the right question asked during Jimmy's visit with Benjamin Dennis, son of Julius Dennis. Now Jimmy, too, is a regular visitor to Lucille's home on Parrish Creek.

Obituary

I will never leave thee, nor forsake thee. Hebrews 13:5

Sarah Evangeline Matthews, or "Sweetie" as she was known to many, was the daughter of the late William and Maggie Scott. She departed this life on Saturday, September 12, 1998, at Anne Arundel Medical Center in Annapolis, Maryland.

She was born on September 9, 1900, celebrating her 98th Birthday on Wednesday. "Sweetie" came from a family of four children, three girls and one boy, of which she was the last to depart this life.

"Sweetie" attended school in Shady Side where she received her formal education. She lived her entire life in the community of Shady Side. Sweetie joined St. Matthews United Methodist Church at an early age and remained an active member throughout her life. In her earlier years she served on the Usher Board, was a church steward and an active participant of the Church Prayer Group. She remained an honorary member of the United Methodist Women until her death.

She married the late John W. Matthews on March 3, 1920. From this union were born 11 children: Ellis (deceased), Calvin, Alexander, Thomas (deceased), William (deceased), Preston, Lucille, Jean, Sarah, Thelma and Mary.

Sweetie enjoyed quilting, crocheting, listening to gospel singing, reading, and traveling with her children. She was dearly loved by her family and was a mother to everyone she met.

She leaves to cherish her memory eight children, three boys, Calvin and Alexander of Shady Side, MD, and Preston of Churchton; five girls, Lucille Brown of Shady Side, MD, Jean Johnson of Shady Side, MD, Sarah Thompson of Churchton, MD, Thelma Holland of Shady Side, MD and Mary Tyler of Annapolis, MD; Over 50 grandchildren, 121 great grandchildren, 64 great great grandchildren, 11 great great great grandchildren; three sons-in-law, Clarence Johnson, Lionel Thompson and Arthelbert Holland; three daughters-in-law, Credella Matthews, Geraldine Matthews and Yvonne H. Matthews; nieces, nephews, cousins and a host of relatives and devoted friends.

Jean Matthews Johnson Collection

Matthews-Scott Family Reunion 2000

Pops	Granny
1896-1976	1900-1998

In loving memory of Sarah and John Matthews.
From the Matthews-Scott Family.
May God keep you in perfect peace.
We Love You.

115486

Jean Matthews Johnson Collection

Chapter 16

Thompson Families

Florine Booze Thompson, born to Walter and Elsie Harris Booze, was raised in Galesville and moved to Shady Side when she married Gerald Thompson. They always looked forward to a good evening at the Sunday Hot Sox games. "The gates opened up, and everyone paid to come in. The games brought black and white people from all over. Shady Side patronized the games in full. They all loved to go to Galesville and watch the team play." Buddy Holland's chicken and fish were "something you would just never forget." A lady had a concession where she fried up crab cakes. None of the volunteers received any money, and everything, including admission, went to keeping the club functioning. The club also sponsored cabarets with live bands, tap dancing, and dancing for attendees at Early Heights Fire Hall in Severna Park.

"The games drew people from everywhere—Annapolis, Brownswood, everywhere—so you met a lot of people from other communities. Everybody knew everybody and everyone rooted for Galesville," said Florine. "My brother, Joseph Booze, played right field. He didn't miss any balls, and when he was up to bat we looked for a home run. It was just wonderful! The baseball field was all fenced in, and the ball would go over the fence out into the road.

"In Galesville when I was growing up there wasn't a whole lot of prejudice because the whites depended on the blacks to make money for them. And that's what they did: They made money for them. Everybody worked for them. It was one big family community. Everybody knew everybody else, but now it's a new Galesville because all of those people have gone on."

Florine felt that Galesville had more social opportunities for blacks because of the Hot Sox and a lunchroom called Mag's Cook Shop, the only local restaurant owned by a black person. Patrons could get food and play music on a jukebox for a nickel a song. With a smile in her voice, Florine said, "It was a small, tiny little house, but there was all kinds of music." Mag Crowner, her mother's good friend, sold a variety of meals: chicken, pig's feet, hog chitterlings, bean soup, prune pies, and white potato pies. "She packed lunch for my brother and me when we went to high school because we were so poor." Florine's father died when she was two, leaving a family of seven children, five girls and two boys.

Mag Crowner cooked, and her daughter packed a basket with food and sold lunches at Woodfield's Oyster House. Men who came from the Eastern Shore to shuck oysters during the oyster season lived in rows of shanties built by Woodfield's located in the black section of town. A few Shady Side women shucked oysters at Woodfield's, which was a much bigger operation than Leatherbury's Oyster House. (In the spring Mag's daughter sold lunches to tobacco packers in Upper Marlboro.)

There were no black-owned stores in Shady Side except Ethel Gross's Seafood, which also sold penny candies. Florine Thompson's childhood connection to Shady Side stores occurred on Sundays. If Florine was good during Sunday school and church, she was allowed to go by boat across the West River with Benjamin Crowner, Sr., Mag's husband. (Mr. Crowner was Florine's oldest sister's father-in-law.) He packed in as many children as the boat could carry, so the children could have an adventure and see friends while he visited his wife's brother,

Eddie Hicks, who lived on the Shady Side shore. Once the boat was securely tied, Florine and her friends hurried into Gustav Heinrich's store at the end of West River Road. She bought Squirrel Nuts and Mary Jane candies, five for a penny. She and her friends enjoyed the precious bags of candy while walking up and down West River Road, sometimes turning to walk on Shady Side Road. Ruth Crowner, her first cousin, Billy Tidings, Kathryn Diggs, Florine, and her brother Melvin enjoyed seeing their friends for a few precious hours, but they were always back in time to board the boat for Galesville.

In Churchton blacks could go to Blunt's Beer Joint, which was located where the laundromat and Chinese restaurant are now. It occupied the whole building and sold food and beer. Later, a lady had a grocery store where the Chinese restaurant is, and she sold all kinds of pork, including pig's feet, pig's tails, and hog chitterlings. "If my husband and I was going out on a Friday, my mother would ask me to pick her up some hog maws—that's the stomach of a pig. I'll never forget; it was January 21, 1956. I was in Galesville, and it was so cold and icy, and my mother asked me to pick her up some hog maws if we went shopping. That Friday night we went to the store, but they were out of them, so I bought her some pig's feet.

"My brother Melvin had come home from Bowie College like he usually did on Friday, but I wondered what he was doing coming over so early on a Saturday to my house. I saw him coming around the corner of my house, and he was crying to break his heart. I said, 'Oh, Melvin, why are you cryin' for?' He said, 'I think Mommy's dead.' And she was," remembered Florine. Their mother had awakened early that morning, put her teakettle of water on to make coffee like she always did, but then said that she was going to lie back down. Soon she was snoring so loudly that Melvin went in to tell her to change her position, but she didn't respond. He phoned for help, but she had already died from a massive heart attack. "She was buried on my husband's birthday, January 24th," remembered Florine. "After she died Melvin came to my house and brought his college friends with him. We were poor as church mice, but we always had plenty to eat. I'd fix fried potatoes, pork chops, stewed tomatoes, biscuits—oh, Lord, those chil'in thought they was eatin' high on the hog. I always tried to have something good for 'em. He'd bring all kinds of young men here. Nice as they could be. His friends called me 'Betty Crocker,' because every time they came I always had something good to eat: home baked pies, bread pudding, all kinds of stuff." Some of his college friends still keep in touch with her; she is home alone since her husband, Gerald, died. One of Melvin's classmates and his wife came from Aberdeen to visit Florine and pay their respects.

Although Florine was named after her mother, she didn't like her first name, Elsie, so she renamed herself and took her middle name when she started high school. Florine made new friends while riding the bus to and from Bates High School. She walked from Galesville to the corner of the Old Quaker Burying Grounds on Route 468 to catch the bus coming from Shady Side. Sisters Jean and Sarah Matthews, Doris Crowner, Virginia Nick, and sisters Puddin' and Doll Baby Dennis were probably on the same bus.

One friend was Geraldine Thompson of Shady Side, and Florine sometimes visited Geraldine's home on weekends. Geraldine's oldest brother, Gerald, had been in a bad accident and was in a cast from his waist to his neck. Recently home from Johns Hopkins, he was laid up recovering with three broken bones in his neck. Florine has always liked to help people, so she naturally did so while visiting the Thompsons. If Gerald's mother had made some Jell-O or something soft to eat, Florine delivered it out on the porch or wherever he was and helped him. During this time the two young people got to know each other.

Once he was well, the two started seeing each other and going to movies and ballgames. They went to Hampton Institute for Geraldine's homecoming and graduation from college. One hot Sunday on Columbia Beach, Gerald asked Florine to marry him, and, happily, they became engaged. "He gave me a tiny little engagement ring about a month later."

The newly engaged couple stood up as witnesses for Florine's best friend, Christolyne Scott, and her husband, Arnett Scott. After a parsonage wedding in Churchton, the two couples went out riding in Gerald's brand new 1948 baby blue Desoto for an evening of fun. "We stopped at a restaurant."

About a month later, Florine and Gerald had a quiet afternoon wedding at the parsonage near Franklin UMC with Rev. Middleton officiating and Gerald's mother, Mrs. Myrtle Thompson, and their brothers, Rupert Thompson and Melvin Booze, attending. The reception was held at Mag's Cook Shop, where family members celebrated with the newlyweds and wedding party.

Gerald's parents, Charles McKinley and Myrtle Marie Matthews Thompson, had only one young daughter, Darlene, living at home, so they had fixed their upstairs as living quarters for the couple until they built their own home on Shady Rest Road. At the end of the reception, Gerald and Florine returned to their upstairs rooms for the wedding night. "We didn't have no other place to go! We didn't go to the motel," Florine chuckled at the memory.

Charlie and Myrtle Thompson

Florine and Gerald Thompson were not the only people who found refuge in the senior Thompsons' home. Additional family members and friends were welcomed into their home over the years. Their son Calvin, newly married to Ruth Crowner, Florine's first cousin, lived with them until they were on their feet and able to build their own home. Nephew Owen "Smack" Scott stayed; Charlie's maiden sister, Deadia, stayed until she died; an ill friend's child, "Bootie," stayed; and Myrtle's brother, Walter, who had lost his wife, stayed until he died.

When Gerald and Florine moved up the road into their new home three houses away, their son, Charles, wanted to stay with his grandparents. Although his own parents took care of his needs and Charles came over to see them every day, he slept at his grandparents' house. Two other couples, each couple with a child, lived with them at different times, and a granddaughter and her child stayed for a while with them. Cousins and friends came from Baltimore for summer vacation. Charles Thompson took seriously the Bible lesson that he was his brother's keeper.

Charles (Charlie) McKinley Thompson (1901–1980) was the eldest son born to Charles Lee (February 1878–January 1958) and Mary Virginia Jenkins Thompson (February 1882–March 1954). Charles married Myrtle Marie Matthews (1904–1984), daughter of Harry and Alda Brown Matthews, on January 21, 1924, and they started married life in Churchton. In 1924 Charles's parents moved to Eastport, where they had a family boatyard.

Charlie and Myrtle Matthews Thompson's children began arriving with Gerald first in January 1926, followed by Rupert (Josh) in May 1927, Calvin in September 1928, and Geraldine in December 1929. The Thompsons regularly attended Franklin Memorial Methodist Episcopal Church, where Charlie's grandfather, Rev. James H. Jenkins, was pastor, as well as at St. Matthew's M.E. Church, from 1901 to 1906.

Charles started oystering in his father's boat at age thirteen and kept saving until he had enough money for his own boat. He and his dad built *Myrtle* at the Eastport yard in the late 1930s. Unfortunately, they had to rebuild *Myrtle* because a careless smoker "slept one off" on the boat, and it burned to the waterline. Charlie knew who it was, but he never accused him. He just started rebuilding.

Aunt - Catherine Turner Thompson   Grand Father - Charles Lee Thompson
        Mr. Dan Johnson   Mr. Oregon Dennis
                                Mr. Ben Smothers

GRANDADDY CHARLES LEE THOMPSON'S EASTPORT BOATYARD
WITH BOAT BUILDERS:Dan Johnson, Ben Smothers, and Oregon Dennis
HIS DAUGHTER-IN-LAW CATHERINE PRESENTING A CERTIFICATE

Charles Lee Thompson, far right, checks out his boatyard. Many of the
Thompson family spent summer months working in the Thompson Marina in
Eastport. **Darlene Washington Collection**

When their Churchton house burned in the early 1930s, the family moved to a rental in Shady Side. They then joined St. Matthew's M.E. Church and never missed. Charlie was the church's sexton, or trustee, from 1957 to 1973. He did not allow his children to play cards, dance, or have parties on Sundays. The ironing board should not be up for last minute pressing on a Sunday morning either. "No foolishness," laughed Florine, "but when they were grown, they got higher than a Georgia pine tree with some beer." Gerald's mother, Myrtle, always cooked Sunday dinner on Saturday night so that Sundays weren't spent working in the kitchen. Sunday was a day of church and rest. Saturday evening preparation of Sunday food was typical of many families of that generation, and some later generations have tried to keep the tradition.

By 1941 Charlie and Myrtle had purchased the rented house and some land that had been owned by Captain Salem Avery until 1876. They built a new house on Shady Rest Road, and there they stayed.

Charlie was a boat builder and waterman. Going out of Parrish Creek, he docked at Captain Howard Shenton's pier from 1939 to 1979 free of charge. In return Charlie took care of the grounds around the shore and kept the boats pumped out. In May and June he got a crew together to work on oyster boats, dredging for oysters out of Port Norris, New Jersey. He was the chef on the boat. In 1979 he sold *Myrtle* to a man on Kent Island for $800. In Charlie's final days, his friend Captain Howard and other long-time watermen friends and family came faithfully to visit him until the end.

Charlie Thompson and Josh Thompson bring their boats into Parrish Creek in Shady Side. **Darlene Washington Collection**

Like so many men in the area, Charlie had other endeavors when oyster season was over. In the 1930s he ran fishing parties for Norman Hazzard and fished with pound nets for brothers Captains Bernard and Edwin Hallock for a few summers. He spent July and August working at his father's Eastport boatyard. With his sons, Gerald, Josh, and Calvin, and other family members, he built boats and hauled, scrubbed, painted, and repaired both workboats and pleasure boats. He taught his sons the trade at an early age.

When Charles Lee Thompson died, he left his boatyard business to his sons, Charles McKinley and Henry; however, Charlie gave up his rights, so his brother, Henry Thompson, retained the boatyard.

Charlie often helped his son, Gerald, and Florine build their house after his own work and on Saturdays to help them save money. Leonard Nick was hired to build the house, but an extra pair of hands helped to cut expenses. Charlie and Leonard also built son Calvin's house, and he gave land to his daughter, Darlene, to build her house on. When her builder skipped out, Charlie finished the hardwood flooring, trim, and steps. Gerald and Calvin helped with the staining and varnishing.

For about five years in the summer, Charlie worked for Mr. McKinley for $9.00 a week. Finally, he told Mr. McKinley that he couldn't support his family for that amount of money, so he was going to go crabbing. The sarcastic response was that he hoped Charlie would get rich. Going crabbing on his Uncle Ollie Thompson's boat didn't make him rich, but Charlie certainly did a lot better. He earned $35 his first week crabbing. Ollie's boat was a canoe with a motor on it. The men worked on the West River and ran a trotline using eel for bait. Perhaps there is some irony in the story, because Charlie made more money working *on* the West River than working beside the river. Mr. McKinley's property was on the shore of the West River, and if he looked out his window, he might have recognized Charlie getting richer and providing for his family.

If Charlie told his family that he was going to rest, he probably was off to hoe the family garden. Although sugar, flour, salt, pepper, tea, and his favorite, A&P 8 O'Clock coffee, came from the store, Charlie raised just about everything else: corn, white potatoes, sweet potatoes, lima beans, string beans, peas, cabbage, kale, and tomatoes. He raised white turkeys, chickens, and hogs for his family and the Eastport relatives. His children were taught to hoe and help with all of the jobs. Myrtle canned and worked as a helpmate every step of the way. Hog meats were cured and hung, and sausage meat was taken to Swinburn's to be ground, but Charlie seasoned it himself. Apples, pears, plums, grapes, and blackberries were available in the neighborhood.

In a 1984 interview, Charles Coates, Sr., told an amusing story about the Thompsons. Arriving home on leave from the Navy in 1944, Charles expected to see both of his parents, Chesterfield and Rachel "Etta" Coates, but only his dad was there to greet him. Etta, a midwife in the community, was out assisting at a delivery. "No, she's not home. Myrtle Thompson's tumor has come to life," his dad reported. The word going around the neighborhood was that Myrtle was getting bigger because of a tumor. Adults didn't want the older children to know about the pregnancy. A second sister joined the family when Geraldine was fifteen. Of course, the tumor story was still fun to repeat years later.

Myrtle and Charlie Thompson welcomed everyone into their home, often on a full time basis. Everyone in Shady Side and Churchton knows their youngest daughter, Darlene Washington, who usually has an idea or the answer to a question. **Darlene Washington Collection**

Florine added some details to the story. "Dr. Richardson from Annapolis delivered my mother-in-law's baby, but he had to leave soon after because another mother was ready to deliver. He had been going back and forth between the two mothers' homes. Miss Etta would usually assist in deliveries. Carrie Bowles [Crowner Matthews] was the main midwife. When I had my baby, Miss Etta brought me a basket with jellies, sheets, peanut butter, and useful things like that."

Even older children sometimes didn't realize their mother was expecting a baby, because women wore smocks so loose that it wasn't noticeable. Many children were not told the facts of life, and when a mother "got sick," a midwife such as Hattie Nick or Carrie Bowles arrived. Dr. Wilson, a white female doctor "who drove an old beat-up car," also delivered babies. One woman "felt kind of sorry for her because she might not get paid, but she never let anyone down and came to help." Dr. George Dent and Dr. Hugh Ward, white doctors, also delivered local women's babies.

In the late 1920s and 1930s, it seemed to go as follows: A midwife or doctor disappeared into the mother's bedroom, and eventually the family would hear a baby crying. The mother stayed in her bedroom for a few days to a week with the curtains down. A mixture of chewed up crackers, tea, and a little sugar were tied in a little cloth teat for the baby to suck on until the mother's milk came in to breastfeed her baby. Neighbor ladies came in to help the new mother and her family in the early weeks following a birth. "There was a lot of love and people helped each other. It's not like what you see today," said a senior lady from the community.

As for Myrtle's 1940s baby, Darlene Myrtle Virginia Thompson Washington now lives in West River. Called Darlene by friends and family, or Aunt Tutney by many relatives, she is the widow of the beloved Rev. Johnnie Washington. Darlene is a certified lay speaker, a former recreation supervisor, and currently the Franklin UMC administrative assistant and a respected leader in the community. She is the administrator of a yearly $15,000 grant from the Har-Pearl Spurill Foundation for children's language arts and math Summer+ Enrichment camp that is held at Franklin United Methodist Church each summer. During the camp, the children go on weekly field trips and have outside speakers that she schedules. In addition to this camp, she works as the administrative assistant for four other summer enrichment camps funded by the Har-Pearl Spurill Foundation. (The Spurills were both teachers at Bates High School and used their money and land investments to fund their philanthropy. They also gave land for Sojourner Truth College.)

Darlene (third row far right) in braids stands next to Miss Battle. Among other children pictured here are (back row second from left) Quinton Dennis, Edward Foote, Anthony Matthews, Vernon Turner, Cordell Salisbury and Jant Thompson. Third row (left) Frieda Matthews, Delores Nick Harley, Velma Nick, June Nick Smith, Evelyn Medley, Unknown, Dorothy Dennis and Darlene Thompson Washington. Second (on left) Kaddie Dennis, Gloria Matthews, Sylvia Brown, Diane Nick, Unknown, Martha Dennis, and Constance Offer. First row (left) Roger Brown, Unknown, Leon Nick, James Nick, Gilbert Turner, and Jimmy Nick. **Darlene Washington Collection**

When Darlene was a little girl, her mother, Myrtle, worked as a maid for the Goodmans, who kept a weekend home in West Shady Side. She was also a link to Gerald's becoming the Goodmans' chauffeur. The Goodman family went to Florida after Thanksgiving and returned before Easter. To earn extra money to pay for Geraldine's college, Myrtle went with them to keep house. Her husband, Charlie, didn't mind because he was a cook anyway, and he could keep house and iron. Darlene's cousin Kathleen "Pickle" Thompson stayed overnight so Darlene had a friend. Darlene's Aunt Margie, Pickle's mother, fixed Darlene's hair and got her ready for school each day from 1950 to 1953. This story is only one reminder that no children were ever left alone while parents were working or away. Families and friends traditionally helped one another in every way. Arrangements were always made and continue to be made to ensure that children have necessary care and companionship.

Holding hands, cousins and best friends, "Pickle" (left) and "Tutney" stand next to Charles Thompson "Back in the Field."
Darlene Washington Collection

In the same spirit of helping Geraldine go to college, her brother Rupert ("Josh") faithfully sent his military pay home each month to help pay for her schooling.

As a young man, Charlie Thompson was one of the ice skaters traveling on the West River from Shady Side to Galesville. He reported that his sister-in-law, Cordellia Matthews, was a great skater.

Blake Holland, Buddy Holland's father, and Charlie liked to play the nickel slots at Swinburn's in Shady Side and Captain Kidd's in Deale. Charlie's first television set was a Philco that his father gave him in the 1950s. He watched the Gillette Friday Night Fights, Amos 'n' Andy, and Ed Sullivan, and he loved watching wrestling matches with his brother-in-law, George Thompson. He was a member of Joppa Lodge #94, P.H.A. (Blue Lodge), and the Anne Arundel County Waterman's Association.

★　★　★

Gerald was always a boatman except for the years he chauffeured for Mr. Goodman, who was president of the Government Employees Insurance Company (GEICO) in Washington, DC. He drove for Mr. Goodman in Washington, and he drove the family to Florida. When he took the job, Gerald and Florine were living in their new home and had started a family. "We were so poor. We didn't have that money for him to commute home every day, so he lived in Washington with a black family we knew that had a summer home in Columbia Beach. They let him stay with them free of charge. I picked Gerald up on Fridays so he could come home for the weekends. He grew tired of being gone from the family, so he went back into the boat business as a boat finisher in Deale until he retired. He was still working on boats, always had more than he could do, until he died in 2000." He is buried at St. Matthew's UMC cemetery.

In January 1960 Florine began working at the Crownsville Hospital Center (1911-2004), formerly the Hospital for the Negro Insane. She recalls that she was hired over a white woman. Florine's drive required her to leave home at 6:00 a.m. to reach her job in Crownsville. She often picked up other riders, such as the father of a family living in the Shady Rest Boarding House, because they had no transportation to reach work.

For the first eight years she worked in patient placement. In 1960 the hospital census was 3,200 patients and 688 employees in all departments and shifts. Florine was selected to train in a one-year health assistant program under the Department of Mental Hygiene, and then she moved into psychology nursing. She prepared the room for people receiving shock treatments, and she noted with amazement how much the treatments helped one woman in particular. Shock treatments were discontinued and out of favor for a period of years but returned as a proven method to improve mental health issues. Of her more than thirty-four years at Crownsville, she spent her last ten years there in the geriatrics unit, which prepared her to care for the elderly when she retired. She and others cared for thirty-two male and female patients. If a patient were sent to another hospital, she would be driven from Crownsville to the hospital to be with that patient until her shift replacement came. Each patient had to be covered by Crownsville staff. Crownsville was closed down five years after she retired.

Crownsville Hospital Center was a mental institution for black patients, yet until 1955 only white people were hired as staff, service, and hospital workers. Here as elsewhere, blacks were kept out of the job market, although they had the education and skills to work. That they could not work with their own people, so to speak, adds to the irony. Students of civil rights know that blacks were repeatedly locked out of jobs in the both the North and South through dozens of laws and methods that maintained the status quo.

A recent bestseller, *The Immortal Life of Henrietta Lacks* by Rebecca Skloot, is a biography of the woman whose remarkable "He La" cells became a human cell line for cancer research. The book relates that Henrietta Lacks's oldest daughter became a patient at Crownsville and describes how the author and Henrietta's youngest daughter, Deborah, discover what happened to her. Perhaps she was on the roll when Florine worked at Crownsville.

Gerald and Florine Thompson raised their five children—Charles, Douglas, Lorenzo, Gerald, and Claudenia—on Shady Rest Road. Their next-door neighbors were Gerald's brother Calvin and Florine's cousin

Ruth. On Friday evenings the two families piled into their cars to go shopping in Annapolis along the city dock near Susan Campbell Park. The women put their clothes in washers at the laundromat and headed for the A&P to buy groceries, children in tow. Someone would get back to the laundromat to change the clothes over to the dryers, or the lady who worked there would see that they were switched. The men might go to the barbershop on the point of Fleet and Cornhill or visit with friends. Blacks owned 90 percent of the townhouses in the immediate downtown area, and there were three beer joints in the area for blacks. At the end of the evening, the children were taken to the 5-and-10-cent store, where they were allowed to purchase a small toy or treat. The tired children were much quieter on the return trip home to Shady Side.

Mr. Gerald and Mrs. Florine Thompson, named "Betty Crocker" by her brother's college friends, is never too far from a kitchen and food preparation. **Florine Thompson Collection**

CHAPTER 17

"THE LITTLE CHURCH BESIDE
THE ROAD"

" S T. MATTHEW'S GAVE ME a twenty-five dollar scholarship when
that was as much as five thousand dollars is now," said Charles
Coates, Sr. "I went to Morgan State that whole first year with that
money plus work." He washed dishes in the cafeteria, not scheduling
classes during mealtimes. The second year his father's Masonic lodge
gave him a scholarship and he worked. The last two years he worked full
time and graduated in 1938, the year DeWayne Salisbury was born.

DeWayne Salisbury remembered that when he was young all of
the children sat in the front pews. The youngest children were in the
front rows and the bigger kids behind. The potbelly stove was in the
right corner with the Amen Corner, and it was cold if you were too
far away from it. In the summertime the windows were open, but the
sanctuary was hot because there were no ceiling fans or air conditioning.
"Sometimes we would try to duck Sunday school to go over and play at
the school, but someone would come to get us." First was Sunday school,
followed by the 9:00 service. "The morning service seemed like eight
hours at that time," laughed Mr. Salisbury. Families went home to eat
and then returned for the second service at 3:00.

Other church members related memories of how it was for them growing up in the church. First and foremost, a child went to church and behaved. A look from a parent or grandparent was all it took to maintain proper behavior from a child. The child sat upright, looked to the adult to be sure he was in line, and followed along in the hymnal or Bible. A Bible would be handed to the child and the passage to follow pointed out. The adult might give a nod of the head or a sideways glance to show the child where to address her attention. The message was: You were to be seen and not heard. Doris Brown reported that "if I didn't squawk on Sundays about church, my mother didn't make me stay all day, so I could go to my girl friend's 'in the field' to play after Sunday School."

Ron Holland, about age 5, grew up in Franklin and St. Matthews UM churches. **Ron Holland Collection**

In his Sunday school days, Ron Holland remembered that the children were broken up into age groups, with his age group meeting with his aunt, Credella Matthews, in the old multipurpose room, while the other three groups were spaced out in the sanctuary. At that time the adults did not have Sunday school.

The most unusual church memory was that of Sarah Scott Matthews, Ron Holland's grandmother and matriarch of the Matthews family. A memorable event for Shady Side elders was the hurricane of 1933. Miss Sarah explained in her interview, "Now we were at church at Franklin Church, and then we came home. My mother's father's house had split apart."

Julius C. Love was the first pastor of St. Matthew's Methodist Episcopal Church in the Great Swamp. At the time Rev. Love was pastor at Franklin Chapel, the mother church to St. Matthew's. He preached at one church and then preached at the other church. When a church shares the same pastor, it is identified as being on a circuit. The churches continued to share the same minister until 1983. St. Matthew's held church followed by Sunday school, and Franklin had Sunday school followed by church, so the minister could travel between the two churches.

Church Memories

Calvin Cohen Matthews drew a picture of how he remembered the first St. Matthew's A.M.E. church built in 1887; it was remodeled 1911. According to information provided by Calvin Matthews, "The building was 29' in height by 48' in length." The men had to install cables around the rafters to keep the rafters from buckling in the middle. They also built a church steeple. In 1922 Albert Johnson was in charge of the lumber that was brought in and used for the building. Albert Johnson was Jean Yvonne Johnson's great-grandfather. Today she is St. Matthew's delegate to the Annual Conference of the United Methodist Church.

When Charles Coates, Sr., attended St. Matthew's, the church was an ordinary wooden structure, before it was bricked up.

DeWayne Salisbury was a young person when the brick façade was added, but he remembered helping to put up the scaffolding with other churchmen. "George 'Bootie' Crowner worked for a brick company that charged very little for the bricks. Mr. Bootie bricked the church. St. Matthew's men built the scaffolding and mixed the mortar. I helped put up the scaffolding."

A Memorial

Surrounded by shrubs and flowers is a brick sign in front of the church that announces the hours for Sunday services at St. Matthew's Church. The Kendal "K.D." Gross family gave the sign in loving memory of their eighteen-year-old son, Kendal Gross, who died from brain cancer in 1969. His cousin Chuck Gross said that during "Boy's" (Kendal's) illness, Boy's little dog Tiny was always on his lap. The faithful Chihuahua curled up on him when he was in his wheelchair, in bed sleeping, or resting when friends and family came to visit. After Boy passed, "that little dog grieved for him. It wasn't too long after Boy died, maybe a month, and then the dog died."

★   ★   ★

Rev. Richard Herbert, Sister Helen Gorham, and Sister Christolyne Scott organized the first Family Day in 1976. Family Days and rallies are held to raise necessary funds for church expenses in addition to weekly Sunday giving. The women's rally is held in the spring and the men's rally in the fall. For the women's rally and Women's Day, for example, a chairman, theme, monetary goal, and activities were organized, and then all the women were asked to stay after church to discuss the plans and to collect start-up money for food purchases. Another person collected money for those wanting corsages to wear on Women's Day itself. Event jobs were divided, including a yard sale with food available for purchase, a major church dinner, a tea, dinners "to go" from someone's home, and invitations to Sunday afternoon speakers and choirs. In addition, each lady was also asked to give $100 for the Women's Day rally. Culminating at Women's Day, the women dressed in white with the year's selected accent color, usually in the corsages. A guest speaker preached, the women's chorus sang, and the anticipated financial report announced each event's sum and the grand total. A newer sister was alarmed when she overheard an older sister whisper, "We didn't make our goal." Expecting some unforeseen difficulty, the junior woman asked the senior lady, "What is going to happen then?" The reply: "Oh, nothing. We're just disappointed."

Both the women and the men support the rally of the other group in significant ways, so the wellbeing of the church is sustained. It should be noted that other congregations loyally support St. Matthews' events, as do St. Matthews' faithful support other churches' rallies.

Mr. and Mrs. John Fountain pause for a moment after church services. Both were active in every part of church and community. Mr. Fountain's passing in 2011 was a particularly sad time because he had touched and blessed so many lives. **Ann Widdifield Collection**

An October Sunday 2010 at St. Matthews UMC

Earlier in the week, a family group from the congregation cleaned all the rooms of the church in preparation for Sunday. Each "cleaning team" takes this duty seriously, and the church is in readiness. Brother Herb Matthews, Sr., or another trustee, has opened the church by checking that all necessary doors are unlocked, the inside air temperature is satisfactory, and all is welcoming for the day. Cars begin pulling in to drop off passengers and then park on the south side of the church or park across the street at Lula G. Scott School. No ushers or church greeters are stationed at the door, but they will be in place before the worship service.

Sunday school begins at 8:45 a.m. with a fifteen-minute opening in the sanctuary led by Sister Laura (Mrs. DeWayne) Salisbury. Some members are already seated in the pews as others continue to arrive, greet, hug, and exchange pleasantries before Sister Laura calls the gathering to order. She refers to the agenda distributed at the beginning of the month. Reading selected scripture and leading the morning altar prayer are shared responsibilities of Sunday school members. If someone is absent, another person volunteers to substitute.

During construction of the new sanctuary from spring through fall of 2011, the congregation met in the fellowship hall. Acoustics were sometimes challenging, and people sat on folding metal chairs that soon began to be populated by tie-on cushions. Padded chairs with armrests were unofficially reserved for senior ladies of the church, and younger gentlemen immediately saw to the ladies' comfort.

Sister Laura announces the hymn and Sister Credella (Mrs. Alexander Matthews) plays an introduction to the hymn at the piano. Occasionally, she will turn around, smiling sweetly, and say, "Now, you all wait for me," and then the first verse is sung and the singers do wait for her. The scripture reader is announced, and he or she reads the scripture selection. The praying person quietly walks to the altar as all prepare their hearts and minds for prayer. The heavenly father is addressed, gratitude given to God for safety through the night, thanks given for "one more day," and blessings asked for the Sunday school teachers and the pastor and her message, as other needs are expressed. Appreciation and love for God is clear. Closing the prayer through Jesus' name, the prayer ends with an echoed "Amen." Gathering belongings, people head to either of two adult classes as conversations quietly begin again.

One adult class, led by Miss Credella, meets in the fellowship hall or a classroom, and a second class meets with teacher Sister Pickle—Miss Kathleen Hicks—in one of the three classrooms. Both classes study and discuss the same book, but Miss Pickle's group reads the material together and discusses as they go, while the fellowship hall group only discusses the material. Some members have to slip away a little earlier than the others to prepare for choir, or greet, or work as a church officer. By the time Sunday school members reach the sanctuary, it is more than half full.

People tend to sit in the same general area on a particular side of the church, as is true in most churches. Any newcomer is encouraged to have a seat in any spot. "Sit any place you like, or have a seat," motioning to the seat beside them.

We Enter to Worship

The pastor, choir, worship leaders, and Leviticus Praise Team gather in the vestibule for the processional while the pianist plays the prelude. The ushers remain in the vestibule throughout the service to assist with the flow of the service. An acolyte—either a senior, young adult, or junior usher—lights the candles on either side of the pulpit. The pianist begins the chords for the processional, and the choir enters singing their opening hymn. Usually the congregation joins in the singing until all are seated. If latecomers arrive and the processional has started, they wait until everyone is seated and then enter. Ushers help them get situated.

The Praise team of Patricia Matthews, Tyra Dunscomb, and Kathleen Hicks come forward, and one leader greets the church and then asks, "Does anyone have a word from the Lord?" This is the congregation's opportunity to share what God has done for them during the week, give a testimony, or express a particular need in the community. The Praise leaders also share until it is time for the worship leader to begin with the welcome.

All are welcomed and visitors are invited to introduce themselves. This Sunday, a senior gentleman, accompanied by his sister and her grandchild, stands and introduces himself, saying that after church they hope to find out more about their Dennis ancestors. If only "home folk" are in attendance, the worship leader calls on Sister Janet Scott, who highlights announcements, reads any correspondence to the church, refers to information on the bulletin board, and updates information on "shut-ins," those who are hospitalized, and anyone else in need.

The worship leader invites all to stand for a responsive reading of the Call to Worship printed in the bulletin, followed by the printed Prayer of Invocation, each individual's Silent Prayer of Confession, and the congregation's singing of the Lord's Prayer. After the singing of the opening hymn, which is selected from either the Methodist hymnal or Songs of Zion, the children are called forward for Children's Time.

Children's Time is a favorite, relaxed, happy time to see toddlers to high school students face-to-face. Each Sunday a different member prepares a theme to discuss with the children. Children's responses often stimulate the words: "Out of the mouths of babes." Unsurprisingly, the message applies to the adult learners as well. As the children return to their seats, the choir prepares to sing the musical selection.

Different choirs sing each Sunday during the month: the Senior Choir, the Male Chorus, Psalm 95:1, the Women's Choir, Points of Glory, the Combined Choir, and the Children's Choir. Each choir is led by various directors and accompanied by varying pianists and other musicians on percussion. The music is spiritually uplifting, and the church body freely participates in the songs through singing and body movements of hand clapping, swaying, rocking, foot tapping, and personal praise. Call-and-response, known in music terminology as antiphony, is often present in the musical selections that are inclusive and inspiring.

The Reading of the Word

The worship leader announces the reading of the Prayer of Illumination, has the congregation read responsively, and announces who will be reading the Old and New Testament selections from the pulpit. The Affirmation of Faith is said responsively, and the Doxology is sung.

The Church at Prayer

The sister or brother who will be praying the pastoral prayer from the pulpit is announced. All who wish to come to the altar rail come forward for the prayer. Voices coming from the pews or railing might be, "Yes, Lord; My Lord; Please, God," or some sound of agreement with the prayer. The choir and congregation sing another song as worshippers return to their seats.

Proclamation and Response

The worship leader announces the Hymn of Preparation and says that following that will be the voice of the Rev. Theresa A. Robinson, who will bring the message. Rev. Robinson gives the topic of her sermon and preaches from scripture and gives examples of how to apply the passages in the Christian walk. Responses from the pews might be, "Preach, preacher; Amen; Yes," or clapping briefly. A worshipper can just sit and listen, but it is also acceptable to participate. Rev. Robinson closes with, "And this is the word of the Lord," and gives an Invitation to Christian Discipleship. While the choir and congregation sing the Invitational Hymn, those who wish to come forward for prayer do so. Rev. Robinson might anoint someone with oil and pray specifically for that individual.

Presenting the Lord's Tithes and Our Offerings

As worshippers sit down, three ushers bring forward the offering table and a little wooden church on a pedestal. One of the ushers holds up each basket and explains the activity the basket is collecting for. The little model church is for the building fund dedicated to the new sanctuary. The worship leader invites the congregation to pray the offertory prayer in unison, and the choir begins singing the offertory selection. The ushers begin directing the people from the back pews forward to the front so they can put in their tithes and offerings. The children come forward with their families. Those who are unable to go forward remain seated while the able return by another pew to reach their seats.

Once the congregation has finished, one usher leads the choir from the left side of the chancel and another usher leads those seated on the right side of the chancel up the front toward the back of the church. When all are in the main aisle, that group turns to face the front of the church, and they put their tithes and offerings in the collection baskets and return to their seats. The offertory prayer is given. Turning toward the chancel with the baskets in his hands, an usher lifts them, and all sing "All Things Come of Thee." A closing hymn is sung and the congregation sits. An usher/acolyte comes forward to take the light from the candles and extinguishes them in the "Carrying Forth the Light" tradition and returns to the vestibule. The choir leaves in a recessional, followed by Rev. Robinson on the arm of an usher. Rev. Robinson gives the benediction, the Threefold Amen is sung, and the congregation remains seated and silent while the pianist plays the Postlude. Parishioners have the opportunity to greet the pastor and fellow worshippers as they depart for home and the week ahead. The final section at the bottom of the bulletin is: "We Depart to Serve."

Ushers in the Church

The Usher Psalm printed on the back of the Annual Ushers' Day program reads: "The Lord is my light. He is the joy of my salvation, of whom then shall I be afraid? I am a doorkeeper in the house of the Lord. Yea, though I meet with unpleasant conditions, I must keep smiling, for I must enter into His presence with thanksgiving and into His courts with praise. Yea, though I walk through the shadow of unkindness, I must smile, for the beauty of the Lord is upon me; my countenance is filled with light, the light of love, patience and endurance. I shall strive to give joy to the sorrowful, hope to the lost, sunshine to the darkness, and I shall remain a doorkeeper in the house of the Lord as long as I live."

Photographed in the old sanctuary in 2010 are ushers DeWayne Salisbury, Mary Holland, Darlene Matthews and Jessie Smith. **Ann Widdifield Collection**

St. Matthew's United Methodist Church's Usher's Board has been an important functioning group throughout most of the church's history.

Identified by their dress uniforms, gloves, and badges, they welcome and assist arriving churchgoers. Each person arriving at the church doors receives a warm smile and a friendly greeting. Someone is stationed outside the front door to assist those being dropped off or to gather in the newcomers. If there is a question, the usher will have an answer or know whom to ask.

The ushers distribute church bulletins that detail the order of worship, announcements, and information about the life of the church as people take their seats in the pews. An usher enters the sanctuary to light the chancel candles and returns to the sanctuary watching to see what the congregation, choir, musicians, or pastor needs. Throughout the service the ushers rotate the responsibility of standing at the back of the church. The overhead fans might need adjustment, hand fans are given, a message is delivered, the offering is conducted, or, if it is the first of the month, guidance is given in directing the congregation to the communion rail. An usher formally stands and walks with his or her left gloved hand held to the small of the back.

These visible signs of an usher's dress and work do not explain all that is required of an usher. The usher has specific requirements to fulfill in training, in testing, and in rules of conduct in order to become a member of St. Matthew's ushers' unit. The ushers follow "The Universal Church Ushers' Manual," which explains techniques with illustrations and gives questions and answers. When working with trained ushers from other interfaith Christian churches affiliated with the Interdenominational Church Ushers Association (ICUA), he or she follows the same unified system developed by George Grier in 1951. Ushers can attain three certificates in the field of ushering through the National United Church Ushers Association of America, Inc.

Charles H. Dorsey was acknowledged as the father of the Ushers Movement in Philadelphia in 1886. In 1910 Elijah H. Hamilton traveled for the Brotherhood of Ushers of Philadelphia to neighboring states to organize a national group. Maryland joined the national organization in 1920. Besides the church boards, there are the Interdenominational Church Ushers Association (ICUA) of Anne Arundel County (www. annearundel@icuaofmd.com); the ICUA of Maryland (www.icuaofmd. com), organized in 1915; the eastern region (www.easternregionushes. org); and the national association (www.nationalchurchushers.org).

"Today in every Black congregation there is an Usher Board unlike any other organization in another ethnic group. The Usher Board and Ladies Auxiliary in the Black Church is a pivotal and significant organization." (From the 77th Annual Convention 1996 Souvenir Journal, "Charles H. Dorsey," page1.) Baptist, AME, and UMC churches are affiliated with the ICUA.

The National Usher Association of America (NUAA) has had various departments since 1919, and the changes in the departments have reflected the improved economic and social situation of the black community at large. The original departments were: Embroidery/Arts and Crafts, Individual and Domestic Science, Civic, Printing, Education, Social Service, Anti-Lynching, Music, Prohibition, Historian, Business, and National Organizer. The 18 departments of the NUAA reflect the concerns of today such as: Allan Griffith Education, Henry Ballard Music, Historical Society, A.W. Briggs Health Unit, George T. Grier School of Ushering, and Jessie Burnett Arts and Crafts.

In Maryland, the state ICUA Board of Trustees of Maryland, Inc., honored DeWayne Salisbury of St. Matthew's in 1996 for his service as president of the ushers' board for 15 years. He held positions in the Anne Arundel County Unit, and he also served as a marshal for the ICUA of Maryland. He had earned state and national certificates. As a young man, Mr. Salisbury, who always loved church and fellowship, began helping Arnett Scott, now deceased, then head usher at St. Matthew's. It was Mr. Scott who encouraged and invited Mr. Salisbury to become an usher.

St. Matthew's Usher's Day anniversary is usually held in October and planned by the board with the minister's approval. The 2010 program's theme was "Faithfulness: to our God, church and unit." The sanctuary was packed, added chairs in the aisle were full, and the overflow crowd sat and stood in the vestibule. That year Rev. Gregory Nick from Shiloh Baptist Church in Port Royal, Virginia, spoke. Rev. Nick is a homegrown son of the James and Helen Nick family. Grandson of Marion and Irenia Nick, he can trace his Shady Side roots to great-grandparents William and Hattie Nick and great-great-grandparents Henry and Rhoda Nick.

The Shiloh Baptist Male Chorus, United Chorus, and musicians presented several musical selections. Usher Herbert Stevenson from Macedonia United Church gave a response to St. Matthew's welcome, which was given by Usher Brionna Dove. Usher Keith Staton, county president; Usher Mary Holland, St. Matthew's president; and Rev. Theresa Robinson made remarks at the end of the service.

On the Usher Board in 2010 were Mary Holland, president; Ralph Bullock, 1st vice-president; Sylvia Pindell, financial secretary; Darlene Matthews, treasurer; Jesse Smith, chaplain; DeWayne Salisbury, senior member; and Milford Gross, member. Gregory Sharps, Jr., was a young adult and junior ushers were Herbert Matthews, Jr., Bruce Thompson, Jr., Brionna Dove, and Chaunce Ferguson, Jr. Honorary members listed were Eliza Dennis and Ralph Bullock. Although Miss Doll Baby is no longer working the floor, she still tries to attend meetings.

The ushers' board is self-sustaining and raises funds with a walk supported by sponsors in April and their annual fish fry the second Saturday of October.

St. Matthew's ushers have been respected leaders and guides for Sunday worship for generations. On duty before the worshippers arrive, they keep the service running smoothly and finish their responsibilities after the congregation departs. If anyone has a need, the usher is the first person to arrive to assist. The ushers are a vital presence in St. Matthew's UMC as they convey the warmth of Christian fellowship.

Ron and Mary Holland stand in front of St. Matthews after church in 2010.
To her chagrin Ron teases Mary and calls her "the church police."
Ann Widdifield Collection

CHAPTER 18

NEIGHBORING METHODIST CHURCHES

FIRST TIME VISITORS TO Shady Side are often puzzled or curious to know why two United Methodist churches—St. Matthew's and Centenary—sit next to each other. Assumptions have been that (a) the two churches separated after the Civil War; (b) instead of staying in the balcony, Negroes built their own place of worship; (c) the white church, nicknamed the "Frozen Chosen," wanted to be separate; (d) it had to do with socializing—neither congregation would cooperate; (e) all of the above; or (f) none of the above. The correct answer is (f)—none of the above. A reading of St. Matthew's history eliminates the first three choices, and some church records and newspaper articles from the Captain Avery Museum's library indicate that cooperation between the two churches has been ongoing.

Except for Centenary's first two decades, St. Matthew's has been its neighbor since October 22, 1887. Augustus and Martha Lerch gave about one-and-a-half acres for the Centenary church site, but the church itself arrived on oxcart. Originally built by Owensville Episcopalians in 1849, the church served as their chapel. The Shady Side Methodists bought the building, dismantled it, and transported the wood and hardware to a boat in Galesville that carried the materials to Shady Side, where they were off-loaded and brought by oxcart to its location for reconstruction in 1866. According to a taped interview with Glorious Andrews Shenton, "It came into being 100 years after the Methodist Church was established in this country . . . Centenary." The third Centenary church building now sits at the site.

Which church can claim they were first? The earliest existing congregation was probably the group that met in 1831 at the Franklin Meeting House in Churchton.[1] Centenary Methodist Church was deeded in 1867, and twenty years later St. Matthew's Methodist Episcopal Church was deeded its first parcel of land to its trustees: John T. Gross, Joseph Matthews, William (Bill) Nick, James Boyd, and Edward Dennis. According to the handwritten deed signed in the presence of George W. Hyde, justice of the peace, on October 27, 1887, the land was purchased from James and Mary Jane Thompson for thirty-five dollars. The Thompsons each signed their marks (X) to the document. The land was described as "situated in the Great Swamp . . . on the road from Sudley to Parrish's Creek within a hundred yards more or less of Centenary Church and certainly one half acre of land more or less." The deed also stated that Salem Avery had conveyed by deed the same tract of land to James Thompson in January 1887. This land originally came from the Mc Loughlin farm and had been conveyed by deed to Salem Avery.

The second parcel was deeded from William and Mary E. Avery on October 19, 1900, to trustees Henry Scott, Solomon Carter, Joseph Matthews, William (Bill) Nick, and Charles Crowner. St. Matthew's was part of the West River Circuit that included Franklin and Friendship (now Carters) Methodist Churches, but in 1921 Carters was removed from the West River Circuit. Rev. Ely Lofton pastored both Franklin and St. Matthew's. In 1922 during the pastorate of Rev. J. L. Brown, St. Matthews' cornerstone was laid for a new A-frame sanctuary with distinctive varnished ceiling beams and a bell tower. Trustees were Henry Scott, Clifton Scott, and Alexander Dennis.

for that purpose.

Witness the hands and seals This 13th day
of May ___ A.D. Nineteen Hundred and one

      Solomon Cromer   (seal)

      Charles E. Matthews   (seal)

Test —   Henry Scott   (seal)

W. F. Owens   William Nick   (seal)

Justice of the Peace   Joseph Matthews   (seal)

      Selimman Scott   (seal)

      James E. Cromer   (seal)

      John W. Moden   (seal)

      Jas. H. Jenkins   (seal)

State of Maryland } ss.
Anne Arundel County }

I hereby certify that on this 13th day of May
A.D. Nineteen Hundred and one before me the sub-
scriber a Justice of the Peace of the State of Maryland
in and for the aforesaid county, personally appeared
Solomon Cromer, Charles E. Matthews, Henry
Scott, William Nick, Joseph Matthews, Selimon
Scott, James E. Cromer & John Moden and
James H. Jenkins. and acknowledged the
aforegoing plan, agreement and Articles

be disposed of and used in accordance with the provisions of said Discipline thereof ———— Witness the hands and seals of the of the parties of the 1st and 2nd part this 28th day of June in the year Nineteen Hundred and one ————

Joseph Matthews (seal)
Charles + Matthews (seal)
William Nick mark (seal)
Henry Scott (seal)
Charles Crowner (seal)
Joseph Matthews (seal)
William Nick (seal)
Solomon Crowner (seal)
Edward M. Dennis (seal)

Wo. T. Owens JP.

State of Maryland, Anne Arundel County set: I hereby certify that on this 20th day of June in the year Nineteen Hundred and one before me the Subscriber a justice of the Peace of the State of Maryland in and for the county aforesaid personally appeared Joseph Matthews James Boyd Charles Matthews, Edward Dennis, and William Nick and Henry Scott, Solomon Crowner, Joseph Matthews, William Nick and Charles Crowner trustees and did acknowledged the aforgoing instrument and deed to be their respective acts and deeds and further certify that the said named William Nick, Joseph Matthews did on the same occasion and time twice acknowledged this

*By 1922 the mortgage agreement is typed and impression of the seal
can be seen. Familiar surnames appear but some given names change.
Once again Alexander Dennis's name appears on a document.*
St. Matthews UMC Collection

In 1938 Rev. A. T. Middleton was pastor. On the Official Board, the nine trustees were Charles H. Crowner, Jerome Nick, Clifton Scott, Soville Scott, Chesterfield Coates, Jacob Moulden, James Crowner, Pearl Gross, and Rachel Gross. The eight stewards were Marion Nick, Charles Thompson, Myrtle Thompson, Carrie Nick, Daniel Johnson, Ruth Nick, Ada Matthews, and Matiel Carter. Sunday school superintendent was Erma Scott, and Helen Gorham was the assistant.

In 1943 the mortgage of 1922 was paid off and the church celebrated the Burning of the Mortgage Palm Sunday.

After praying and waiting nine months for approval, the congregation's prayers were answered when Maryland National Bank loaned St. Matthew's $9,600, requiring monthly payments of $90 beginning in

June 1963. The church was able to replace the coal stove with an oil furnace, and Brother Leonard Nick added on a small education room, a hall, restrooms, and a furnace room. Sister Daisy Thompson was president, and Brother Clarence Johnson was secretary when the finance committee paid the contractors $9,483.82 in December 1963.

Bishop John Wesley Lord sent a letter dated February 25, 1964, to Mrs. A. W. (Ethel) Andrews, chairman of the Commission on Christian Social Concerns at Centenary Methodist Church. He was "congratulating and praising her for the measure of the Christian witness on the sharing service held on Race Relations Sunday, and what took place both in Centenary Methodist Church and in the Negro Church across the way." A note written at the bottom indicated that this was a beginning of the relationship between the two churches after the Supreme Court struck down the "separate but equal" doctrine in 1954.

However, this was not the first time that blacks and whites worshipped together with the two races attracted to the message of Methodism. As noted in the chapter about Miss Doll Baby Dennis, blacks and whites were worshipping together long before the Civil War. According to Francis Asbury's journal, he first visited Calvert County in 1777. Heading to Calvert again on a Monday, June 4, 1782, he preached to about 100 people at West River, which was then part of the Calvert Circuit.[2] The nascent evangelical churches welcomed both black and white people who even addressed each other as "brother" and "sister."[3] Many embraced the new message of salvation, and worshippers, white and black, free and slave, found salvation in Jesus Christ as a personal savior.

The Methodist Episcopal Church of America became a denomination in Baltimore in December 1784. Black worshippers were denied significant influence in church governance. Seating was separate, black members took communion after white members, and class meetings were divided. Cemeteries also were segregated.

There were black circuit riders that often could not read but had the ability to remember and accurately quote book, chapter, and verse of the Bible. Care had to be taken not to upset plantation owners. Even white preachers never preached about the evils of slavery.[4] Officially, the Methodist Church was opposed to slavery, and a rule remained in place that itinerant preachers could not hold slaves. [5]

Attending a November 1835 Methodist meeting were a preacher in charge, one associate, one preacher for the colored people responsible for the work with one elder, two deacons, one local preacher, eight white exhorters, seven colored exhorters, and 62 class leaders.[6] (Authorized by the minister to do so, an exhorter helped believers' understanding of the message by applying the minister's text or point. Not preaching a sermon of his own, he urged, encouraged, advised, and alerted believers in what the minister had taught. They were present at camp meetings and services and assisted ministers in encouraging Christians. After a year or so he might be given a license to preach on his own.)

In 1837 reports noted that West River Circuit had 923 blacks and 457 whites.[7] Since 1856 the black members had been requesting a division of the two races so they could more actively participate in worship and conduct the services based on their particular needs, ideas, hopes, and methods without white interference. Just before the end of the Civil War, in 1864, the black leaders finally convinced the predominantly white conference to separate into two different divisions. The Washington Conference was formed, which gave the black congregations autonomy. Although black local preachers were often ordained, they were not accepted as full members of the conference until the organization of the Delaware Conference in 1864. [8]

According to Rev. Ed Schell, an authority on Methodist Church history, Anne Arundel churches were always in the Washington Conference. Other than Bishop Burns, who was elected in 1856 to go to Liberia, the first election of two black bishops in America took place in 1920. It took a period of time until there were enough black bishops to complement the white bishops and to have enough black bishops to head the 15 black conferences. The first all-black annual conference, called the Central Jurisdiction, met in 1939. Thus, time passed with the Methodist Church having two separate divisions.

Finally, in 1964 during the General Conference, the Central Jurisdiction was broken apart, and conferences of black and white churches began to be merged, depending on geographical location. The Washington Conference, including Anne Arundel County, merged into the Baltimore Conference in 1965.

In 1965 Brother George Crowner bricked St. Matthew's frame church, and Brother Varnell Nick put a cable through the middle of the church to support the frame.

Two denominations, the Methodists and the Evangelical United Brethren churches, merged nationally in 1968 and became the United Methodist Church, or UMC. Both local churches saw a change in the order of worship, new hymnals, and a name change. No longer St. Matthew's Methodist Episcopal Church, it became St. Matthew's United Methodist, and Centenary became Centenary United Methodist Church. The Baltimore Conference became the Baltimore-Washington Conference in 1992.

In 1984 St. Matthew's hoped to renovate, but they didn't have enough land to accomplish their plans. They looked into the availability of the open field lying between St. Matthew's and Centenary United Methodist churches. After hiring a surveyor, they learned that the land was once owned by John Nick but was later purchased in a tax sale by Benjamin Michaelson.[9] In 1937 Mr. and Mrs. William Thomas purchased two acres of land between the churches and deeded the land to Centenary in 1937. [10]

During John Nick's lifetime, he gave a parcel of land behind the church to St. Matthew's Church where the graveyard is today. He still owned three and a half acres that included the Nick burial ground with seven gravesites. John Nick's home, surrounded by a white picket fence, was behind St. Matthew's cemetery. Because one living descendant of the John and Mary Nick family would not sign papers to allow another sibling or grandchild of John Nick to buy the acreage, the grandchild bought other property. When a grandchild went to the courthouse to see about buying the Nick land, he learned that it had been sold. He also learned a family had 20 years to redeem the land if all living descendants would sign an agreement—but there was no agreement.

Brother Johnny Washington, renovation chairman, arranged a meeting of trustees from St. Matthew's and Centenary to discuss the situation in February 1986. Based on the information about the land purchase and gift, Centenary gave a portion of the land to St. Matthew's for the renovation. Trustees Brother Gerald Thompson and Brother Johnny Washington of St. Matthew's and Brother Richard A. Busch and Brother Howard C. Shenton from Centenary signed the subdivision agreement in April 1987. When the need for land arose again in 1991, Centenary kindly gave the necessary land for St. Matthews' expansion.

An article written about Shady Side by Liz Atwood for the *Baltimore Sun* in 1992 was headlined "Commuters find haven in waterfront refuge: Affordable homes lure newcomers." In a sidebar, among several listed points, was the 1990 census population of 2,983 people, with the average price of a single-family home at $131,509, but the reporter gave the name of only one United Methodist Church—Centenary UMC—as a point of interest. When descendants with old family names were noted, only white surnames were given.

On September 7, 1998, the *Baltimore Sun* ran a lengthy story titled "Segregation separates neighboring churches: Methodists follow traditional paths of worship in Shady Side." This story revealed the observations, concerns, and hopes of the two female pastors of the two churches. The Rev. Roberta Matthews, pastor of all-black St. Matthew's United Methodist Church, and the Rev. Stephanie Vader of all-white Centenary United Methodist Church wondered together if the absolute segregation of the two churches was symbolic of a bigger problem in the community. Noting that churches in Baltimore and Washington, DC, and elsewhere in the country have similar demographics, Rev. Vader said, "But in a town this small, the lines of separation are so much more stark, so much more visible."

Several laypersons from both churches and the community at large all agreed that there was no breakdown of race relations in the community. "Things are good here," was the general sentiment. In 1998, St. Matthew's was in the midst of their $500,000 church renovation, and Centenary had no idea that, within two short years, their church would accidently burn beyond rehabilitation. Rev. Matthews remarked, "It's amazing. We probably could have built a brand-new church to house both congregations for less than we'll end up paying for the two renovations. But there isn't the support to do that." St. Matthew's invited Centenary to use their church, but they accepted Oakland Methodist Church's invitation and worshipped there. Centenary began rebuilding in 2002 and held their consecration service in 2003.

Both ministers agreed that if there had been a forced consolidation of the two congregations at that point in time (1998), it would have destroyed two houses of worship. "The absolute separation of race is not representative of the kingdom of heaven," said Rev. Matthews. Rev. Vader added, "Not at all representative of the body of Christ." Again, they agreed, "Something had to be done." Rev. Vader said, "It really comes down to this: Are people willing to step out of their comfort zones and deal with the race issues surrounding this segregation? . . . For now, I'd say they aren't quite there."

The article concluded that the two congregations had little interest in becoming one because each could lose favorite traditions, worship styles were different, and one sanctuary would not be used. In the meantime, the two churches were becoming increasingly cooperative by having joint Vacation Bible School, a minister exchange for a Sunday, and joint services on occasion. Rev. Vader and Rev. Matthews coordinated people from both church congregations to perform the play "What's That You

Say, Lord?" at Southern High School, in Annapolis at the Maryland Hall for Creative Arts, and at the Lincoln Theatre in Washington, DC. Seven other area churches had participants in the play as well.

Another four years passed and the *Capital* ran a story headlined: "Two churches, one mission: South county churches promote integration with joint services." Rev. Roberta Matthews of St. Matthew's in Shady Side and Rev. Ramon McDonald of Mt. Zion UMC in Lothian are pictured in his church sanctuary, and the story explains that their two congregations, basically one black and one white, were sharing a series of services during the summer of 2002.

The two pastors formed a covenant team of ten members from each church to prepare worship services for the two churches and to show appreciation and respect for one another and to worship God together: "We work, play and go to school in an integrated setting. We should worship together." The first combined service drew about equal numbers of both congregations. The pastors weren't sure where the services would lead, but they were confident there was room for them in the community.

Rev. McDonald received occasional phone calls asking if his church was the white church. (There are two Mt. Zion churches in Lothian.) His cheerful reply: "No, ours is the red brick church."

Shocking to the residents of the Shady Side and Churchton area was the threat and arrival of the Ku Klux Klan from the Frederick-based Invincible Empire, Knights of the Ku Klux Klan. On October 24, 1993, the *Capital* carried the story, headlined: "Churchgoers outnumber KKK members." Shouting "white power" and racial epithets, fifteen KKK members dressed in white robes and army fatigues rallied off Chalk Point Road with about forty onlookers. Forty county police officers were in place to control traffic and prevent trouble and monitor the situation. A disbelieving onlooker said, "You see it in the movies, but you just don't think it's for real." A second group made up of local citizens gathered, holding candles and hand painted "United" signs at Muddy Creek and

Chalk Point Roads. The group's organizer said, "This is not what this neighborhood is about. To ignore it is denial, and we need to make our voice heard."

At the same time, about 250 black and white residents and clergy from the area packed Centenary UMC Church to promote harmony, pray, sing, and speak out strongly against the presence of the Klan in Shady Side.

Four days later the paper ran a story headlined: "KKK rally provokes thoughts of bringing racial groups together." Centenary's pastor, Rev. Peter De Groote, was quoted as saying, "It accelerated our intention to get a joint committee of lay people together to plan how to do things together, to break down the invisible walls between the races." St. Matthew's minister, the Rev. George A. Stansbury, said, "When trouble comes in the community, the black and white come together. I do believe that the message went out to the KKK that they were not wanted in Shady Side."

Then, on November 13, 1993, the *Capital* reported that vandals had trashed St. Matthew's UMC, stealing amplifiers, tools, and a sanctuary microphone. Using a fire extinguisher, the vandals sprayed foam in the minister's office, over church choir robes, and on an electric organ in the sanctuary. Two adults and two teenagers from Shady Side were arrested with the goods in connection to the robbery and vandalism. A police officer was quoted as saying, "I'm at a loss to understand this senseless vandalism." Rev. Stansbury wondered, "Why be malicious? If you want to steal something, take it."

Sixteen years later, two 15-year-old boys took "malicious" one step further in September 2009 by breaking into a bus parked behind St. Matthew's Church and spray-painting seats and windows. The *Capital's* headline: "2 teens charged with hate crime"; it reported that each youth was charged with one count each of destruction of property and hate crime. A detective narrowed his suspects' list because the boys were absent from school the day of the crime, and local students at particular bus stops were interviewed. The two boys first denied but then admitted that they were responsible for the vandalism. Comments from the normally quiet community were: "Deplorable," "Shocking," "I thought we had gotten over this period," and "The teens' bias is not indicative of how the rest of the county's residents feel."

In late October 2010, St. Matthew's moved forward with the long delayed plans of the 1999 renovation with phase 2 to build a badly needed new sanctuary. Economizing to keep the mortgage manageable, the original sanctuary plan was scaled down for approximately 175 people, saving $200,000. Once again, Centenary United Methodist helped by sending a letter giving St. Matthew's permission to use their water tank in case of a fire, which saved an additional $85,000. The service of consecration of the sanctuary was Saturday, February 4, 2012.

Robert Taylor, president of the Methodist Men, took pictures and videos as the church sanctuary was being built in 2011.

The two Methodist churches continue to sit peacefully side by side in Shady Side. Any and all are welcome in either church. Sunday school starts at 8:45 a.m. with worship at 10 a.m. at St. Matthew's UMC and ends around 12:15 to 12:30 p.m. Rev. Theresa Robinson is pastor. Centenary has Bible Study at 9:15 a.m. and the worship service at 10:30 a.m., ending about an hour later. Rev. Merne Crane is pastor.

Shady Side's two Methodist congregations have worshipped God through the name of Jesus Christ in their own traditions for decades with few difficulties in their separateness. Each is respectful of the other, polite in all circumstances, and only makes references to the others' idiosyncrasies in the privacy of their own circles. Alike in doctrine, the two churches and the community maintain a reverential divide. Neither church wants divisiveness and has cooperated to maintain the peaceful status quo. Some people in each church will say that one day the two churches will come together, but probably not soon.

Other Shady Side Churches

George and Gladys Holland and their family attended St. Paul's A.M.E. Chapel. An article from the Maryland Historical Trust stated that the McKail family founded the chapel in Shady Side in 1878, less than twenty years after the Civil War. A small white frame building, it was 20 feet wide and 26 feet long and rested on four brick piers. The cornerstone on the left (south) corner of the building read: "St. Paul's A.M.E. Chapel 1883," and the entrance was in the middle of the gabled south wall. The roof had a double covering of asbestos shingles on the left side and wooden shake shingles on the right. Three oblong four-foot windows were on both the west and east sides of the church. The church burned in 1976, and the remaining eight members united with the Ebenezer Church in Galesville. The building's shell remained until the presiding AME bishop gave permission for the vestrymen to tear it down.

In a 1984 interview, Josephine Tongue, then age 76, said that Verden Denny was her Sunday school teacher at St. Paul's, "where the graveyard is. Mr. Denny lived down Bay Shore near Julius Dennis." She said that after the church burned her family went to the sister church in Galesville. After Sunday school she was often allowed to go and play but was admonished, "Don't let the dark catch you out." She was supposed to "look at the sun to leave in time to come home." She stated that she had a good life coming up.

Across from the entry to Avalon Shores is a sign marking the way to "Ebenezer A.M.E. Church, St. Paul's Cemetery, Shady Side, MD." The maintained cemetery is located along an angled grassy path leading from Shady Side Road near Avalon Boulevard to the graves somewhat behind the gray house that faces the main road. The earliest grave date seen in 2010 was 1912, and the most recent was 1993. Ernest Johnson, a soldier in World War I, several Hollands, and other graves can be seen.

One unique grave is that of Sylvester Brent (1912-1971); the inscription reads: "Bess A legend in his own time."

Why might this inscription appear on a man's tombstone? The answer may lie in the 1984 interview with Charles J. Coates. All Mr. Coates knew about Mr. Brent was that he was big, over six feet tall, and awkward looking. "You didn't see people as tall as Mr. Brent every day. He walked the road most of the time. 'Bess' was his nickname." Mr. Coates recalled seeing Mr. Brent walking to and from the post office whenever he returned to Shady Side. In her interview, Josephine Tongue said that Sylvester, nicknamed "Bess," was her brother. He worked for Leatherbury's all of his days until he became disabled and then died when he was 70. "Leatherbury's put the stone there. He also worked for Jennie Leatherbury. Mother worked for her for years."

The presently empty gray two-story building sitting between the cemetery and Shady Side Road (at the T of Hawthorne Street) has had a variety of uses over the years. It has housed several different businesses, has been a private home, and was the Shady Side post office for over twenty years. That location preceded the present post office at the corner of Shady Side Road and West River Roads.

The white frame Baptist church on the west corner of Avalon Shores and Shady Side Roads was established as a mission church in 1960, and meetings were held in the Avalon Shores Rescue Squad building for the first year. A four-room house and seven lots were purchased, a sanctuary was built, and the First Baptist Church of Shady Side was incorporated and begun with 45 charter members.[11] According to a website of the First Baptist Church of Shady Side, the church's mission began in 1957.

Turning right onto Snug Harbor Road, the brick church to the right is home to the congregation of the Judah Temple Ministries. Earlier called the House of Prayer, the church is located at 1427 Snug Harbor Road, and worship is in the Pentecostal tradition, which emphasizes the Holy Spirit. This congregation bought the church building after their church on Sudley Road burned in 1991. Rev. William A. "J. R."

Pinkney is pastor of the church, which has a predominantly African American membership. Services are at 11 a.m. on Sundays, and Sunday school is at 10:00.

One hundred years earlier, at the turn of the nineteenth century, a new white church was formed on the very spot of the Judah Temple Ministries. There are two stories of how the congregation originated. One is that it was made up of Episcopalians and German Lutherans who decided to follow the Episcopalian tradition. The second story is that there was a dispute over a schoolteacher's being disciplined and fired. For whatever reason, the teacher withdrew from the Methodist church, and those members who supported her also withdrew and formed a new fellowship based on the teacher's original Episcopalian faith.

The first frame structure was built on land given to the parish by Mr. and Mrs. Basil Owings. St. John's Chapel, dedicated in 1892, was located between the road and the cemetery that is seen in front of the brick church today. James Atwell, with assistance from parishioners, built the original church with white oak planks sawed from James Crandell's woods. Surnames of members were Avery, Crandall, Larson, Parrot, Proctor, Trott, Owings, Smith, Wilde, Witt, and Heinrich. [12]

According to a Shady Side native, one grave is that of a mother who died during childbirth delivering twins. The mother and her newborns were buried together, with one child placed in each arm. When the brick church was built in 1954, the grave was reportedly covered by the new structure. Woody Avery said in a 1991 interview that he helped close the burial grounds at St. John's because the ground was too wet. "You go down a few feet and the Lord would abided down and drown them after they die."

The parish had six ministers up to 1976. Finally, the membership declined, and the church dissolved in the 1980s and remained vacant until Judah Temple Ministries bought the church and its land.

CHAPTER 19

SERVING IN THE MILITARY

S HADY SIDE'S AFRICAN AMERICAN men have served in the military since World War I. This research does not address the participation of ancestors of local families in previous wars; however, examining the history of blacks in military service prior to World War I might assist in drawing a conclusion.

The American Revolution, The War of Independence

Boston Patriots, including Samuel Adams, declared Crispus Attucks, son of a black father and Indian mother, to be a martyr of the 1770 Boston Massacre. To this day Attucks is recognized as a symbol of African American patriotism because he perished at the hands of British soldiers. He was not the only African American in that Boston crowd, and the African Americans present that day were not the only black participants in the War for Independence. [1]

In July 1775 George Washington forbade the enlistment of black troops, in spite of the fact that blacks had served well in the earlier battles of Lexington and Concord and Bunker Hill, and several had fought in the French and Indian War.[2] By November of that same year,

Lord Dunmore, the last royal governor of Virginia, offered to liberate slaves who joined the British side as Loyalists.[3] On December 30, 1775, Washington reconsidered and allowed the reenlistment of blacks in the Continental Army. Congress held back, but by the end of 1776 troop shortages forced them to allow blacks to be recruited in the Continental Army and state militias. South Carolina and Georgia refused, but black men from those colonies joined other Patriot units.

Maryland was the only southern colony to grant freedom to black slaves who served. The National Society Daughters of the American Revolution published *Forgotten Patriots: African American and American Indian Patriots in the Revolutionary War.* One hundred ten names are listed for Maryland as serving between 1775 and 1783. Of those listed names, 32 have no residence given; Charles County had 17, Worcester County 13, Anne Arundel 7, and Baltimore 6. Other Maryland counties are represented in descending numbers. Of interest on the list were: one African American man served in the Navy as a sailor on the ship *Baltimore* from 1777 to 1778; an African American boy belonging to Mr. John Henry served; an African American man belonging to David Weem served; "Black Boy Gim" was a drummer; Henry William was born in Anne Arundel County and died in Baltimore, living about 100 years; and one Indian soldier served. [4]

In the majority of the colonies, black patriots served in integrated military units. Black soldiers made up about 17 percent of the Patriot fighters, and two black men crossed the Delaware River with Washington that Christmas night in 1776 to interrupt the Hessian (German) mercenaries' holiday party. [5]

Lord Dunmore, confident in the fighting ability of his African American troops, influenced other Loyalist and British commanders to recruit thousands of black men who worked and fought in exchange for their freedom. From Cornwallis's surrender at Yorktown in 1781 to 1783, the ratification of the Treaty of Paris recognizing the independence of the United States, many of the 20,000 black Loyalists left the country with white Loyalists. Some went first to Nova Scotia and later to Great Britain or to Sierra Leone, the British free black colony on the west coast of Africa founded in 1787. Others went to the British Caribbean islands of Jamaica, Andros, Great Inagua, and Trinidad. Disastrously, some were re-enslaved. [6]

The War of 1812 (1812–1815)

Traditionally in opposition, Britain and France wanted economic and military control of the Atlantic (1793–1815). The fledgling United States wanted to annex Canada, to stop the British from supporting the American Indians in the Old Northwest, and, in particular, to stop British ships from interfering with American ships trading with Europeans. When hostilities blossomed into war, African Americans were again fighting on both sides: British and American.

Northern states were slow in mobilizing black troops during the first two years of the war. Southern states, fearful that armed black men would aid slave revolts, refused to enlist blacks. By 1792 North Carolina was the only state that had not eliminated black participation in its militia. In 1798 the secretary of the Navy ended black service on warships.

Slaves were offered freedom in Canada or the British West Indies in exchange for helping the British. When the British invaded the Chesapeake in 1813, burned Washington, DC, and attacked Baltimore in 1814, African Americans participated. By the time the British were threatening Philadelphia and New York, the American military also offered freedom to enlisting slaves. One hundred black sailors fought on Lake Erie, and at least 600 free black men fought with General Andrew Jackson at the Battle of New Orleans. These men were promised equal pay, benefits, and treatment and Jackson delivered. [7] However, after Jackson was elected president, he had fourteen slaves,

318

six males and eight females, living in the White House as recorded by the 1830 Census. [8]

The Mexican War (1846–1848)

Black soldiers from the Louisiana Battalion of Free Men of Color and blacks on naval vessels such as the *USS Treasure* and the *USS Columbus* participated in the Mexican War.

(http://en.wikipedia.org/wiki/Miitary history of African Americans)

The Civil War (1861–1865)

In the beginning, North and South each believed they would be the victor in a short war to settle the issue of two different objectives. Four years later, 620,000 Americans were dead, and black men made up 40,000 of that number. [9]

Initially, Abraham Lincoln was focused on saving the Union but was not convinced that slavery was the true issue. His Preliminary Emancipation in 1862 was ridiculed in the South, resented by many in the North, opposed by Northern Democrats, but applauded by abolitionists and most black people. On January 1, 1863, Lincoln issued the Emancipation Proclamation, which marked the beginning of the end of slavery. In addition, Congress passed the Militia Act of 1862, which authorized the enlistment of black troops in the Union army. [10]

Black troops immediately faced discrimination and hostilities at every juncture. Blacks were ostracized by many who thought blacks couldn't endure combat and by those who preferred that a black man die rather than a white man; there was to be no integration into the all-white regiments. Black troops had white officers who most often were prejudiced against the men and their fighting ability. Usually black troops worked in construction, in transportation as teamsters, as cooks, or in burial details. Willing and prepared to fight, they were frozen in fatigue duty. Paid less than white soldiers, they disproportionately suffered more casualties by war's end. Although black men had been serving in the U.S. Navy since about 1790, they were paid less than white sailors; they were insulted, called names, and assigned the worst jobs: loading coal, tending boilers, waiting tables. About 20% of the men serving in the Union Navy were black sailors.[11]

In April 1865, General Lee surrendered to General Grant at Appomattox Court House in Virginia. Of the 185,000 black soldiers and sailors who served, 40,000 died in combat and of disease. The Congressional Medal of Honor was awarded to 21 black men for heroism. [12]

After the Civil War, the Army was reduced, but Senator Henry Wilson, a Republican from Massachusetts, managed to keep the military open to black men. Four all-black regiments, two cavalry and two infantry, spent most of the next thirty years on the western frontier and were commanded by white officers. Discrimination was evident in food, housing, and location, but black soldiers recognized that the civilian life offered few opportunities. Plains Indians, impressed with the skills of the black soldiers, displayed respect by naming them "buffalo soldiers." Naval service continued to be restrictive for black sailors. Although a few black men enrolled in the Naval Academy in the 1870s as midshipmen, none graduated, due at least in part to social ostracism. [13]

The Spanish-American War of 1898

Once again thousands of black men served in the military during this April to August conflict, with the final treaty signing in December. Twenty-two black sailors, among 266 men, died when the battleship *USS Maine* blew up in Havana Harbor. Again, white officers commanded all-black units except where some volunteer units refused, saying, "No officers, no fight." For the first time, black men commanded three all-black units coming from Illinois, Kansas, and North Carolina. Most of these volunteer units remained in Florida and didn't see combat, but four regiments of Buffalo Soldiers did go to Cuba, where they fought well. The impressed Spanish troops nicknamed them "smoked Yankees." At the battle of San Juan, two black cavalry regiments and one infantry regiment fought beside white troops, including Theodore Roosevelt's Rough Riders. [14]

Black military units served during the Philippine Insurrection: the regular 24th and 25th Infantry, the 9th Cavalry, and the 48th and 49th Volunteer Regiments. [15]

The Punitive Expedition to Mexico

Elected in 1912, Woodrow Wilson soon disappointed William Monroe Trotter and W.E.B. Du Bois, militant black leaders, who had originally encouraged black voters to support Wilson rather than William Howard Taft or Theodore Roosevelt. When Trotter and a black delegation protested segregation in the Treasury Department and post office in a 1914 meeting, Wilson defended his separation of the races as a means to avoid friction. [16]

In 1916 Francisco "Pancho" Villa and other Mexican rebels attacked territory in New Mexico in an effort to provoke war between the two countries. President Wilson sent 15,000 troops under the command of John J. "Black Jack" Pershing. (His nickname was the result of his having commanded black troops in Cuba during the Spanish-American War.) The black 10th Cavalry was part of the US forces trying to capture Villa in Mexico. Again commanded by a white officer, the 10th Cavalry on this mission had a black officer, Lieutenant Colonel Charles D. Young, who led a black regiment to rescue an element of the white 13th Cavalry. The major supposedly said, "I could kiss every black face out there."

Young, an 1889 graduate of the Military Academy at West Point, served in Cuba, the Philippines, Haiti, and Mexico but was not permitted to command troops during World War I. [17]

World War I Begins in Europe-1914
America Enters 1917
War ends 1918

The Shady Side men who were drafted for World War I entered a rigidly segregated Army. The Army used black servicemen as stevedores, construction workers, cooks, bakers, and laborers, not preparing black soldiers adequately for combat. Only 11.3 percent of black servicemen saw combat. The 369th Regiment proved itself so well that by June 1918 French commanders were requesting as many black troops as possible.

Under pressure from groups such as the NAACP, the War Department created an officer training school at Fort Des Moines, Iowa. More than a thousand black men received commissions, but none was promoted above captain.

In the Navy, black men served as waiters, kitchen attendants, and stokers for the ships' boilers. No black men joined the Marine Corps—only whites were accepted. At war's end, black troops returned on segregated ships, and the famed Jim Europe band was not allowed to join the farewell parade in New York City. [18]

Shady Side's African American World War I Veterans

First Name	Last Name	Branch of service	Rank	Dates of Service
Julius	Dennis	Army		
Jacob	Dennis	Army		
William	Johnson		PFC	
John William	Matthews	Army		Lived 1896-1976
Herman	Nick	Army		
James A.	Nick		CPL	
William G.	Nick	Army	PVT	
E.	Offer		PVT	
Richard Thomas	Scott		PVT	
Octif	Turner, Sr.	Army	E-2	

John Matthews stands between William "Flump" Nick, left,
and an unidentified friend of John's (right). **Jean Matthews Johnson Collection**

World War II Begins in Europe-1939
US enters 1941
War ends 1945

In 1941, under pressure from A. Philip Randolph, president of the Brotherhood of Sleeping Car Porters, and many other groups that threatened to march on Washington, President Franklin D. Roosevelt issued Executive Order 8802, which decreed that there would be no discrimination in the employment of defense workers or government because of race, creed, color, or national origin. The order ended racial exclusion but did not outlaw segregation in the military; however, the Marine Corps now had to accept black men. Black men accepted into the service were sent to a separate training camp in North Carolina under white drill instructors and officers, while white recruits trained in South Carolina. [19]

Although black and white inductees were taken in at the same rate, the War Department's policy continued segregated units, with African Americans serving in noncombatant positions in transportation and engineering corps. Black physicians and nurses could care only for black military personnel. Qualified black nurses fought quotas established by the U.S. Army Nurse Corps that blocked their admission. The Army allowed only a small number of black nurses and the Navy none. Some cared for prisoners-of-war in England.

Clarence Johnson, Sr. is photographed with his mother,
Sarah Johnson Thompson. **Jean Matthews Johnson Collection**

Black uniformed soldiers were harassed, given the least desirable spots, and separated in parades, canteens, church services, and transportation. It was exasperating for African American soldiers to witness German and Italian POWs imprisoned in the United States receiving greater inclusion and better treatment than the country's own black soldiers. African Americans were constantly and consistently reminded of their second-class status in the United States.

Many African Americans did see combat under white officers in Europe and Asia. After the Battle of the Bulge in 1944, 2,500 black volunteers fought in integrated units as an experiment. It only happened once during the war, but the success of the experiment laid the groundwork for expanded opportunities in the military. In January 1945 the Army opened its Nurse Corps to all applicants, and the Navy followed suit five days later. More than 300 black nurses were accepted into the Army Nurse Corps. About 4,000 black women served in the Women's Army Auxiliary Corps (WAACs). [20]

Ira Thompson looked forward to mail call and a letter from Miss Daisy Crowner. Daisy Crowner walked from Cedarhurst Road to the Shady Side post office on Snug Harbor Road and hoped to find a letter from Ira.
Daisy Crowner Thompson Collection

After the December 7, 1941, Japanese attack on Pearl Harbor, the services began to change their position on African Americans. The Navy began accepting black men as sailors and noncommissioned officers and, by 1943, allowed blacks into officer training school. Finally, the historically white Marine Corps opened its arms to include blacks in 1942. Black officers were trained in integrated posts and bases, except in the U.S. Army Air Corps.

An all-black pursuit squadron training program was created by the War Department at Tuskegee Army Air Field in 1941. The Tuskegee Airman, commanded by black officers, flew more than 15,500 sorties and completed 1,578 missions, destroyed 409 enemy aircraft, sank an enemy destroyer, knocked out ground installations, and never lost a heavy bomber they escorted deep into Germany. General Benjamin O. Davis, Jr., who had graduated from West Point in 1936, commanded the 332nd Group when it was deployed to Italy in January 1944. "The 332nd participated in campaigns in Italy, France, Germany, and the Balkans." [21]

Jumping forward to June 2011, Leroy Battle, an original Tuskegee Airman and recipient of the Congressional Gold Medal, was invited and honored with other Tuskegee Airmen at the Italian Embassy in Washington, DC. Leroy Battle is well known, respected, and admired in Shady Side because of his military and music careers, but he is also recognized as the man who won the heart of Alice Holt, Shady Side's beloved teacher and principal at Lula G. Scott School and first principal of today's Shady Side Elementary School. Mr. Battle has written two books: *Easier Said* and *And the Beat Goes On . . .* , which tell of his life, his career in music, and his dedication to family and education.

In *And the Beat Goes On . . .* , Mr. Battle told about "his most severe encounter with racism," when he and his air group were moved to Freeman Field in Seymour, Indiana, for additional training in 1945. A disgruntled colonel assigned the group illegally, immediately closed down the officers' club in defiance of a 1940s Army Regulation, and assigned armed guards to keep the all-black air group out. Second Lieutenant LeRoy Battle and 18 other black officers attempted to enter the club and were arrested. In all, 104 black officers were placed under barracks arrest, and three officers were held to be court-martialed. The rest of the men, including Leroy Battle, received Letters of Reprimand that remained in their records until August 1995, when the Air Force overturned the court-martial and expunged the Letters of Reprimand. The incident was referred to as "The Freeman Field Munity." [22]

Dr. Lisa Battle Singletary embraces her father, Tuskegee Airman Mr. LeRoy Battle, who holds his Congressional Gold Medal that he received in 2007. The first Congressional Gold Medal was awarded to George Washington in 1776. **Ann Widdifield Collection**

Shady Side's World War II Veterans

First Name	Last Name	Branch of service	Rank	Dates of Service
Ralph	Bullock	Navy Air Force	E-7	1944-1946 1953-1971
Charles Franklin	Crowner	Army		
James Melvin	Crowner	Army	TECH 5	
Robert Cornelius	Dennis	Army	Sgt.	1943-1946
William	Gorham	Army		
Melvin Garfield	Gross	Army	PVT	
James E.	Gross	Army	SSGT	
Clarence Elsworth	Johnson			1943-1946
Ernest	Johnson		PFC	

James Edward	Nick	Army		1946
Earl Arthur	Nick	Army		1946
Marshall	Nick	Army		
James E.	Nick	Army Air Force		1946
William C.	Smith	Army	PVT	
Ira	Thompson	Army		1942-1945
Thomas	Turner	Navy	Petty Officer 3rd Class	

The National Association for the Advancement of Colored People (NAACP) honored more than a dozen Anne Arundel black veterans at the county branch's 52nd anniversary dinner in 1996. Clarence Johnson, Sr., and Ira Thompson were among those honored. During the presentations, Mr. Johnson told how the Germans had spread leaflets saying that the men should lay down their arms because back in the United States they would be second-class citizens. Mr. Johnson said that they figured America was the best place to be and it was "our country." Another man found Army life as segregated as civilian life. He said, "The only place where black soldiers came first was in boarding lines for troop ships—so they could be given the lowest bunks in the hold."

Mr. Clarence E. Johnson, Sr.

Jean Yvonne Johnson Collection

Executive Order 9981

President Harry Truman reinstated the draft in March 1948 because of the possibility of war with the Soviet Union and the February communist coup in Czechoslovakia. A. Philip Randolph had formed the League for Non-Violent Civil Disobedience Against Military Segregation, and the military realized that black men and women were *not* going to take Jim Crow any longer. When the Soviet Union imposed the blockade on West Berlin in June 1948, President Truman issued Executive Order 9981, officially desegregating the armed forces, in July 1948. Randolph disbanded his organization and called off marches planned for Chicago and New York. [23]

Although integration of the services took years to effectively complete, the national cemeteries adopted the policy immediately and disbanded burial segregation in 1948, ending the 80-year-old practice. (www.arlingtoncemetery.mil/ historic information/black history)

Korean Conflict (1950-1953)

The North Koreans, backed by the Soviet Union, invaded South Korea in 1950, so with UN sponsorship the United States intervened. In 1951 the Army authorized the formal integration of its units in Korea. In 1952 Colonel Benjamin O. Davis was appointed commander of the 51st Fighter Interceptor Wing in Korea. [24] The armed services were one of the first American institutions to bar racism. ("Separate but equal" was negated in 1954 with the *Brown vs. Board of Education* decision.)

First Name	Last Name	Branch of service	Rank	Dates of Service
Clarence Elsworth	Johnson, Jr.	Air Force		
Marshall	Nick	Army		
Monroe W.	Scott	Army	Corporal	1949-1952
George Ollie	Thompson	Army	SGT	
Josh	Thompson	Army Band		1952
Earl	Turner	Army	Corporal, E-4, Military Police	1953-1956?
Octif	Turner, Jr.	Army	Staff Sgt. E-7	1951-1955___
Hughward	Crowner	Army		1956

Monroe Wilson Scott (right) relaxes with a buddy in Korea.
Olivia Scott Gray Collection

Vietnam

(America sends aid and advisors to South Vietnam, War escalates under President Johnson—1965-1975)

As the numbers of American soldiers in Southeast Asia increased, the Vietnam War became more unpopular and polarized the nation. African Americans were overrepresented among the U.S. troops in Vietnam, because of the disproportionate issuing of draft deferments for white middle class college students and graduate students. Some black men and women entered (not as draftees) the military because the military offered education and vocational opportunities. Project 100,000 accepted applicants who would otherwise have been rejected because of lack of skills or criminal records.[25] Black casualty rates were slightly higher than their percentage of the total population. Twenty African Americans received the Medal of Honor for their actions. (Wikipedia. org/ Military_ history_ of_ African_ Americans)

First Name	Last Name	Branch of service	Rank	Dates of Service
Walter L.	Austin	Marines	E-4	1965-1969
Marshall	Baker	Army		
Ralph	Bullock	Navy Air Force	E-7	1944-1946 1953-1971
Calvin	Crowner	Army		
Eugene T.	Gray	Army	E-4	1966-1968
Chuck	Gross	Army		
Harold	Hudson	Army		
Gilbert A.	Nick	Army		
Gilbert	Turner	Army	E-4	1967-1969
Sterling	Turner	Army	E-5, Airborne	1966-1969

Others who served:

First Name	Last Name	Branch of service	Rank	Dates of Service
Alvin	Coates	Army	E-4	1978-1981
Charles	Coates, Sr.	Navy		
Carroll Hinton	Crowner	Army	SP4	
Dale	Crowner, Jr.	Navy		
Hughward	Crowner			

Ty Ron	Crowner	Air Force		
Cornelius	Dennis, Jr.	Army		1978-
Cornelius	Dennis, Sr.	Army		
Steve	Dennis	Army		
Robert	Dennis	Army Reserves		1978-1986
Ronnie	Dove	Army	Staff Sgt.	1979-1991
Odell	Dove	Army	PFC	1994-1996
C.J	Harros	Navy		1993-1997
Arthelbert	Holland	Army	E-4	1953-1956
Alexander	Holland	Army	Sgt. 1st class, E-5	1951-1953
Clarence	Johnson, Jr.	Air Force	Sgt. 1st class, E-5	1996-1970
Clarence	Johnson, Jr.	Army Reserves	E-7	1970-2002
James	Lindsey	Army		
Larry	Lindsey	Army		
Norman	Matthews	Army		1977-1981
John William	Matthews	Army		Lived 1896-1976
William	Matthews			
John T. (Tommy)	Nick	Army		26 years
Troy	Nick	Army	Sgt. 1st class, E-5	
Jerry	Smith	Air Force		
Calvin	Thompson	Army	PVT	
Smack	Thompson	Army	E-4	
Bruce	Thompson, Sr.	Air Force		1974-1978
Calvin	Thompson			1929-1977
Josh	Thompson	Army		

Thomas L.	Thompson	Army		
Wilson	Thompson			
Clifton	Tongue, Jr.			
Wilson	Turner	Army	Sp. E-4	1956-1958
Anita	Tyler	Army		
Guy	Washington	Army		1969-1972

The Foreign Service

Wendell Matthews, son of Credella and Alexander Matthews, chose a less known career to serve his country but an equally challenging one. He joined the Foreign Service, which comes under the Department of State. Googling "foreign service officer," one reads: "We look for motivated individuals with sound judgment and leadership abilities that can retain their composure in times of great stress, or even dire situations, like a military coup or a major environmental disaster." There are five career tracks, and once an individual selects a track it is not possible to change during the Foreign Service Officer Test registration.

Born July 17, 1950, in Shady Side, Wendell graduated from Southern High School in 1968 and Morgan State University in 1972 and went on for his master's degree in educational psychology at Northwestern University, a private research university in Evanston, Illinois. After working in Prince George's and Montgomery Counties' boards of education and teaching psychology at Prince George's Community College, Wendell joined the Foreign Service in about 1980. He was interested in people and fluent in French and German. "He was the mirror of his grandfather, John Matthews, only a shade taller," said one cousin, "and he loved photography. He had really nice cameras, and I liked to visit with him every chance I could. He had a thick moustache and straight hair and was a loving, affectionate son."

Wendell Matthews
Jean Yvonne Johnson Collection

Another cousin exchanged letters with him and knew he could be in a dangerous spot but was told not to tell his parents because they would worry. "Of course, he could never reveal his mission. He loved photography. He and his sister Sandy had a drawling type of voice like their mother. He was well versed and dressed meticulously but casually rather than in church clothes. He was intelligent, humble and a giving person. He sent for his parents to see the Holy Land, to visit the Greek Islands and to visit him in Athens, Greece. Wendell was awesome." He spent a second assignment in Amman, Jordan.

Family and friends looked forward to seeing him on his furloughs, which occurred every two years. When stateside he lived in an apartment building in Washington, DC, where the family visited him, but he also came home to Shady Side. Then, ready for a new two-year assignment, he said good-bye and was off again, this time to Bangui, Central African

Republic, to serve as the administrative officer at the U.S. Embassy. He hadn't been gone too long when his parents received a devastating phone call telling them that Wendell had drowned in the Ubangi River. Shock raced through the community as the terrible news spread. Later, State Department representatives came to express their condolences. Wendell would be buried honorably.

The hearse was driven past Wendell's home place on Scott Town Road enroute to St. Matthew's United Methodist Church, where the funeral and burial took place. One of his cousins remembered feeling such a loss of not only a kind person, but also a loving, giving, and wonderful individual. Filled with sorrow, she felt so much pride in how he had served his country with dedication and dignity.

Twenty years later, Wendell's sister Sandy was taking a normal drive home from Franklin United Methodist Church when she had to stop behind a car that was making a turn near Brown's Way. Someone advancing behind her wasn't watching and slammed into Sandy's car, forcing it into the oncoming traffic. Sandy was killed.

Psychologists and grief counselors say that the most difficult pain and loss come from losing a child. It is unimaginable to know how to survive such grief. "Our trust is in the Lord," said Miss Credella. "Through the grace of God we move on. God is in charge; all power is in His hands. We can't dwell on the past. We have done the best that we can and leave the rest to God. We pray and know life goes on. Thank the Lord, His grace is sufficient."

The U.S. Naval Academy

Victor Smith grew up about seven years behind Wendell Matthews, so their paths didn't cross much except at church. Vic is the first African American from Shady Side to graduate from the U.S. Naval Academy. In 2011, two black midshipmen with Shady Side connections, John Booth and Cory Dennis, are fourth classmen, better known as plebes, and Dale Crowner, Jr., an Academy graduate, now teaches at the Academy.

Vic spent his earliest years living in Shady Side, but later the family moved to Severna Park, where he entered segregated schools. Integration came as Vic entered third grade, and he and his two brothers were the minority in a white school, but it went smoothly for them. Very strong athletically and academically, Vic was the teacher's pet, and he loved his teacher. One of nine children, Vic was ever so happy to return to Shady Side alone for the summers at his Grandmother Thompson's house on Shady Rest Road. He attended a week of church camp at West River Camp, and then his grandmother picked Vic up for the rest of the summer. In Shady Side, Vic played sports with John and Beebe Castro's teams.

In Severna Park, Vic's dad had to work all the time and couldn't get his sons to practices, so people in the local sports organization picked up Vic and later his brothers to get them back and forth to the practices and games. He and his brothers were the only black kids in the organization, and Vic was the quarterback from the start. After a little resentment over Vic's position wore off and people recognized the brothers were athletic and could play well, the ice was broken and their teammates were inviting them to their homes. They were a team and all was well until a celebratory day ended in the ugliness of racism. A bull roast for the team was being held at a Yacht Club, and as the brothers were getting out of the car to joined their buddies, their father called out to his sons, "Hey, you all go on, and I'll be back later to pick you up." Not until their father returned did his sons learn that he had been told to leave because he was black. Their father had been minimized, disenfranchised, and dismissed while they were unaware and celebrating with the team.

Once a successful black businessman was asked if he had had any roadblocks in his life, and he replied in a mild tone, "Well, I've been black all my life." At first the response seemed obvious, even a little facetious, but on further thought, in historical context, the poignancy of his statement registered powerfully.

Because of Vic's academic and football capabilities, the Green Hornets Organization succeeded in getting him an extraordinary scholarship to Severn School, a private prep school, for high school. His family moved back to Shady Side, but Vic, in ninth grade, and his older brother, Gil, a senior, lived across the street from each other with two different sets of relatives in Severna Park. Every weekend Vic rushed home to be with his family and friends in Shady Side and lugged himself back to school after the weekend. Much to his father's chagrin ("People put a lot of time and effort getting you that scholarship. I think you should go back."), Vic said, "No," because he wanted to be with his friends and attend Southern High School. From his sophomore year forward, he was at home, with friends, and played basketball and football for Southern's Bulldogs until he graduated. (His nickname was "Supe," short for Super.) He hoped for scholarships but none came. He always knew he wanted to go to college, and he would be the first in his family if he could go.

After graduation at age eighteen, Vic enlisted in the Navy in 1975, packed the family's only suitcase—an old alligator one—and had his first airplane flight to Rhode Island to attend prep school in hopes of making it into the Naval Academy. With his math, science, and technical skills, he did become a midshipman at the Naval Academy the next year and played basketball all four years. After a rigorous four years on campus and summers of on-site military training, he received his commission, tossed his hat in the air, and became an ensign (an officer and a gentleman).

Dressed in the winter mess dress uniform, Pleb Vic Smith heads to classes at the Naval Academy. **Victor Smith Collection**

Vic Smith, number 14, scores again for Navy. For good reason, a 1978 Academy magazine cover page superimposed "Sports Illustrated" to highlight a victory. **Victor Smith Collection**

Vic's Grandma Margie Thompson (left) Ensign Smith and his parents,
Augustine and Clayton Smith, stand outside Bancroft Hall on the porch off
Memorial Hall. **Victor Smith Collection**

When he was growing up, he knew the Academy as a "place behind those walls." Within the walls, he looked forward to coming home to Shady Side whenever he could. Often he brought other midshipmen happily in tow. They loved being invited and even came without Vic, because they loved the people and got treated so well. Frank Hopkins, a taxi driver from Shady Side, was a dependable ride home and took care of Vic. "Whenever I needed to go home, I called the taxi switchboard and Mr. Frank came and picked me up." His aunt Pickle was living in Annapolis at that time, so he could visit there as well.

Finally outside the Academy walls, he spent eight years on active duty and followed that with thirteen years in the Naval Reserves, from which he retired in 2000. What was the best part about the military? "The discipline," Vic said. He now serves on the screening committee for Academy applicants and is impressed with the focus of today's young people who are applying and interviewing to attend the Academy.

Vic's father, Clayton Ashley Smith, taught him to do his best. "Whatever you do [in life], think beyond the present situation, understand your opportunities and focus on those." Besides his father, Vic's champions included Purnell Crowner, "who was a very instrumental person with the youth at our time, just a fantastic person"; Cordell Salisbury, "my godfather, who was one of the best quarterback Bates High School ever had, always encouraged me to go do something"; Rev. Johnnie Washington, who "was a wise man and teacher"; and his older brother, Gil, "who always let me tag along with him."

Vic is a grandson of Margie Matthews Scott Thompson, whose first husband, John Scott, drowned in 1929 and who later married George Thompson. He was the first son of Clayton and Augustine Thompson Smith and has been married to Tamara "Tammy" Wallace Smith for thirty years. They have three children and one grandchild. Vic was the first president of the Shady Side Boys and Girls Club, and he coached and tutored kids while he worked full-time jobs. He has been the chairman of St. Matthew's Building Committee for fourteen years, sings with Psalm 95:1, a men's performing group, and is a member of the St. Matthew's United Methodist Men.

CHAPTER 20

APRIL 2011

W HY DO PEOPLE COME to Shady Side? It's at the end of a road, so
no one is just passing through. In a 2009 interview, longtime
Churchton resident, 105-year-old Titus Blunt, said, "Shady Side? Why
would anyone want to go to Shady Side?" His point was well taken,
because people taking the Shady Side Road have a definite reason for
going.

People live there because of family roots, or because they want a
rural setting close to water. It offers a quiet place to raise a family, lower
housing prices without packed apartment buildings, and it is within an
hour's drive of several large cities and jobs. These pages have given
glimpses of several African American residents who have walked and
driven the road. If their deceased family members could come back,
they might be temporarily disoriented at the intersection of Routes 468
and 256.

Residents of Shady Side often say they live in Columbia Beach,
Cedarhurst, Avalon Shores, Westelee, West Shady Side, Idlewild, Felicity
Cove, or Snug Harbor, but they all share the same zip code, and all of
the children go to the same public schools. Most people are likeable,
they are usually friendly, and the majority are kind and helpful, but

people no longer know everybody in the village. Residents sometimes hunker down in their own development or social circles and miss out on opportunities just off the main road or within a mile of their homes.

The traditional Fourth of July parade is probably the best example of community participation during the year, but in April 2011 the Shady Side communities had several opportunities to participate in local events. The first was the opening of an exhibit at the Captain Avery Museum called Memories and Mementos: A History of Shady Side Schools. The second was the "Shake Your Groove Thing" dinner and dance commemorating the life of Everett "Chuck" Gross, held at the Kiwanis Club. The third was the long-anticipated ground breaking on April 17, 2011, for St. Matthew's United Methodist Church's new sanctuary.

April 3, 2011

An advisory committee chaired by Beth Denniston began working on the schools project in the fall of 2010 for the opening on April 3, 2011. Since the exhibit was showing Shady Side's two schools during segregation, it was important to have advisory committee members who grew up in Shady Side and attended the two public schools. Bobby Bast, Marge Calhoun, Elaine Catterton, Tyra Dunscomb, Carmelia Hicks, Jean Yvonne Johnson, and Mary Kitchen were asked, and they actively participated. Yvonne Holland Matthews had a wide range of knowledge and experiences, having attended Churchton elementary school as a student and taught at the Shady Side segregated school and both integrated schools; she also agreed to work on the committee. Susy Smith, chairman of the Shady Side Rural Heritage Society Board of Directors, Jennifer Sturgell, third grade teacher at present-day Shady Side Elementary, Karl Graham, June Hall, and Ann Widdifield were also on the committee. The schools exhibit was made possible with the support of the Maryland Historical Trust, the Maryland Humanities Council, and the Chaney Foundation, from whom the museum had received grants.

Additional board members and staff came along to get the exhibit up and running and continued working up to minutes before the opening.

Visitors attending the exhibit opening view the 1+1=1 Documentary.
The schools' exhibit appears in the background.
Ann Widdifield Collection

The exhibit featured a sample schoolroom, a wall banked with more than 50 class pictures from both Lula G. Scott and Shady Side Elementary Schools, showcases with surviving school days mementos, three teaching principals' photos made into window blinds, and interactive outdoor games in front of a mural depicting black and white children playing during a late spring recess. Allison King was the mural artist. A sign above an old classroom desk built for two students invited visitors to sit down to write their memories in a book available for collecting additional stories. During opening day, one visitor identified several unknown children in a school picture.

Sisters Sylvia Turner Pindell (left) and Nina Turner Bullock sit at the desk for two as they look through a memory book. Janet George (far left) is in charge of the Miss Ethel Andrews' Memorial Library at the museum.
Ann Widdifield Collection

Youth from St. Matthew's United Methodist Church, under the guidance of Tyra Dunscomb, and students from Shady Side Elementary School, under the guidance of Jennifer Sturgell, interviewed and audio recorded senior Shady Side residents who had attended the segregated schools. Their findings can be read in the schools' memories book in the same section. They asked identical school day questions selected by the advisory board.

The "1+1=1" documentary playing on a flat screen television attracted a lot of attention and viewer interest. The script was written and narrated by Terence Smith, a volunteer who is a retired print and TV journalist, and it was produced by Wayne Shipley. Participants interviewed were Jennifer Neiman Sturgell, a current teacher at Shady Side Elementary School, and retired teachers Yvonne Matthews and Doris Brown, who taught at the segregated and integrated schools. Former students Jean Yvonne Johnson and Carmelia Hicks, who attended

Lula G. Scott, and Bobby Bast and Richard Neiman, who attended the white Shady Side School, were also interviewed. Beebe Castro, a former physical education instructor in the newly integrated schools, said that her husband had integrated sports teams in Shady Side before the local schools integrated.

Carmelia Nick Hicks and Jean Yvonne Johnson, members of the advisory committee, pose in front of the mural of the playground. **Ann Widdifield Collection**

Shady Side Elementary Chorus sang several selections under the direction of Kristen Witmer in the museum's packed great room. Some of the children stood on the stairs leading to the second floor. Bobby Bast read his poem "Shady Side Memories," which touched the hearts of children and adults. Out on the screened porch of the museum were refreshments for all—including a huge platter of peanut butter and jelly sandwiches! Junior docents Vanessa Petersen and Daisy Youngmann and senior docent Ann Sparrough provided tours of the Captain Avery house.

The following Sunday, the Spiritual Vibrations, a local gospel group of family and friends that have been singing together for 22 years, performed for the "Memories and Mementos" exhibit. Attendance was excellent for both opening days, and many who had never visited the museum in the past discovered one of Shady Side's most delightful treats.

April 16, 2011

More than 150 tickets were purchased before the April 16th "Shake Your Groove Thing" dance at the Kiwanis Club of Shady Side to celebrate the life of Everett "Chuck" Gross, but more than 200 attended. Chuck's only child, Chantal Gross Banks, with assistance from her mother, Carla Gross, and other family and friends, hosted the event. DJ Robert Taylor provided the music, and sponsors were Renno's Market, Deale Food Rite, Chick-fil-A in Edgewater, the Party Place in Deale and members of Hope United Methodist Church on Muddy Creek Road. They volunteered to cook and serve a hearty meal during the event. Chuck's brother OT Turner donated the drinks.

Nearing the first-year anniversary of life without her dad, Chantal decided to turn the family's heartache from the waves of grief and take a heading toward a positive response to the inevitable day. During the past year, Chantal had worked hard daily to push her way through the ever-present pain and sadness from her sudden, tragic loss. Her planning helped make the approaching days more constructive for her and encouraging for the family and friends who also missed Chuck.

The day of the dance the clouds opened up, and Shady Side once again had full ditches of water. Chantal was uneasy because of the steady drumming and usual lowland spots filling with water. Joanne Riley of Joanne's Touch in Churchton said, "It was a torrential rain." She was there early and feared that people might stay away because of the nasty weather, but a little later people began pouring in to counterbalance the pouring rain.

The dinner and dance was an intergenerational gathering of genders and races. A four-year-old won the dancing contest. Seeing many of the community joining together and having family fun, one of Chantal's aunts said that something good was coming from the tragedy. The casual evening was a great success, and $2,600 was raised for the American Foundation for Suicide Prevention.

Chantal Gross Banks has been asked to share her experiences and strategies in living life after a suicide to help others recently struck with such a loss. She wanted people to know it is okay to talk about suicide, depression, and mental illness. Very few would have known or even guessed that her dad was fighting a battle with depression and post-traumatic stress disorder. His outgoing, energetic, generous, cheerful ways masked what was going on inside. Perhaps it became just too hard to keep the two selves operating. The one truth about a suicide is that there is never an answer to the question, "Why?" No one will ever truly know.

In the fall of 2010, friends and family had joined Chantal and her team for the Annapolis Out of Darkness walk put on by the American Foundation for Suicide Prevention (www.AFSP.org). With additional donations from caring people, her team came in first in money raised for Maryland's Out of Darkness walks. She gave much credit to the Hospice of the Chesapeake in Annapolis and the AFSP for helping her through many rough days and nights. Wanting to raise awareness of suicide prevention and education, Chantal was interviewed for "Valentine's Day Increases Feeling of Loss," which appeared in the *Severn Patch* on February 11, 2011. She was interviewed for an educational, multipurpose video about her feelings of being left behind after a suicide and how she is dealing with the pain and loss. Doctors, psychologists, and educators can use the video in helping families facing suicide or to use in seminars and conventions.

April 17, 2011

After much anticipation, setbacks, financial discussions, and decisions between two options for building a new sanctuary, St. Matthew's broke ground for the sanctuary construction on April 17, 2011.

Left to right are Vic Smith, Carmelia Hicks, Gerald Thompson and Ralph Bullock, members of the 1993 building committee. **Doris Crowner Brown Collection**

During a 1993 groundbreaking in construction that included the multipurpose room, kitchen, and three classrooms, an elderly lady had predicted to a senior gentleman that the sanctuary would not be built during her or his lifetime. The elderly lady was only half right, because the gentleman is still living. Locals and the bank were equally impressed when they learned that the earlier construction was paid off ahead of time. Congregations wanting to build churches or additions have been faced with financial challenges and bankers unwilling to loan money in the struggling economy.

There was a big turnout of church members to watch the old sanctuary come down. People were seated in chairs, walking about taking pictures, or parked in cars at various viewing spots. Donna Brown Hicks brought her daycare children over to see some of the excitement.

Before they return to their day care center, Mrs. Donna Brown Hicks's children sit together while the old sanctuary behind them continues to be removed.
Ann Widdifield Collection

The church held its Service of Consecration of the Sanctuary on February 4, 2012

Doris Crowner Brown stands between friends from childhood Jean Matthews Johnson (left) and Jean's sister Sarah Matthews Thompson (right). Builder David Ward made the large center cross (background) from beams saved from the previous sanctuary. Communion stewards (background left) prepare the altar for the communion service.
Jean Yvonne Johnson Collection

Before the Consecration service begins, builder David Ward of Taurus Enterprises and his wife, Gail, sit behind and chat with Dorothea Dennis (left), Joyce Powell and Deborah Thompson (standing).
Jean Yvonne Johnson Collection

Mr. and Mrs. Alexander Matthews take part in the consecration service. Communions stewards (right foreground) and service participants (background) listen. Jean Yvonne Johnson Collection

July 4, 2011

Every July 4 since 1976, America's Bicentennial, the road into Shady Side has closed for a few hours, so the Shady Side community can enjoy its traditional parade. In 1976 there were floats from different housing areas, an outdoor program presented in front of the Kiwanis Club, displays and games, and fireworks at the end of the day. Because of the expense, the fireworks have sputtered out. And sadly, each year some beloved viewers and participants have departed. But in the circle of life, new folks find a place among the regular families staking out spots along the edges, hopping over a ditch, to watch the pageantry of an honest to goodness, down home, old-fashioned American parade in Shady Side.

Mohan Grover—also is known as the unofficial mayor of Shady Side—wears an Uncle Sam's hat as he walks past the lead parade team.
Ann Widdifield Collection

Shady Side people reach for candy being tossed by parade folks. Seated (from far left) is DeWayne Salisbury and Teresa Fountain. Yvonne Johnson, Laura Salisbury, Jean Johnson, and Doll Baby Dennis capture some treats, while Jant Tompson (right of the Lula G. Scott sign), Alexander Matthews with his camera and Vic Smith in ball cap, (furthest right) watch the parade.
Ann Widdifield Collection

Surprised, Darnita Gross Baker and her dog Muffin finish the parade at the Kiwanis Club on Snug Harbor Road. Judah Temple Ministries Church (background). **Ann Widdifield Collection**

Heading south from St. Matthew's UMC and Shady Side, cars now travel on a decent road that has improved over its history. From a sucking muddy road, it has had its ditches improved and roadbed widened. Those taking the road have experienced life in different ways and changing times.

Mohan Grover's daughter, Monica Grover Fitzgerald, resident of Washington, D.C., decorates her dad's car that always signals the end of the parade.
Ann Widdifield Collection

BIBLIOGRAPHY

Andrews, E. N. (Ed.). (1952). *Discovering our school community: Shady Side Elementary School.* Shady Side, MD: Shady Side Elementary School.

Andrews, F. E. (1991). *Miss Ethel remembers.* Shady Side, MD: Shady Side Rural Heritage Society.

Battle, L. (1995). *Easier said.* Annapolis, MD: Annapolis.

Battle, L. (2008). *And the beat goes on . . .* Southport, ME: Cozy Harbor.

Bradford, J. C. (Ed.). (1977). *Anne Arundel County Maryland a bicentennial history 1649-1977.* Annapolis, MD: Anne Arundel County and Annapolis Biventennial Committee.

Brown, P. L. (1988). *A century of "separate but equal" education in Anne Arundel County.* New York, NY: Vantage.

Culp, E. W. (1942, July). *West River circuit 1836-1942.* Paper presented at Consecration of Centenary Methodist Church, Shady Side, MD.

Dennis, J. (n.d.). *Jacob Dennis will.* Unpublished manuscript.

Fitz, V. W. (1984). *Spirit of Shady Side peninsula life 1664-1984.* Shady Side, MD: Shady Side Peninsula Association.

Fitz, V. W. (1991). *Captain Salem Avery House: It's History 1860-1990.* Shady Side, MD: Shady Side Rural Heritage Society.

Gates, H. L.,Jr. (2009). *In search of our roots: How 19 extraordinary African Americans reclaimed their past.* NewYork, NY: Crown.

Grundset, E. G., Diaz, B., Gentry, H., & Strahan, J. (Eds.). (2008). *Forgotten patriots: African American and American Indian patriots in the Revolutionary War, A guide to service, sources and studies.* National Society Daughters of the American Revolution.

Hine, D., Hine, W., & Harrold, S. (2008). *The African-American odyssey.* Upper Saddle River, NJ: Pearson Education.

Holt, A., Smith, J. S., & Jones, S. V. (Eds.). (1952-1953). *Discovering our school community: Lula G. Scott School.* Shady Side, MD: Shady Side School and Churchton School.

Hynson, J. M. (2000). *Maryland freedom papers Volume 1 Anne Arundel County.*

Lippson, A. J., & Lippson, R. (1984). *Life in the Chesapeake Bay.* Baltimore, MD: Johns Hopkins University Press.

Moore, W. (2011). *The other Wes Moore: One name, two fates.* NewYork, NY: Spiegel & Grau.

Redford, D. S. (1988). *Somerset homecoming: Recovering a lost heritage.* NewYork, NY: Bantam Doubleday Dell.

Rice, C. (2010). *Extraordinary, ordinary people.* NewYork, NY: Crown.

Shady Side Elementary PTA Committee (Ed.). (1975-1976). *Shady Side past and present.* Shady Side, MD: Shady Side School PTA.

Skloot, R. (2010). *The immortal life of Henrietta Lacks.* NewYork, NY: Crown.

The committee on history and records. (1982). *The Franklin years: The committee on history and records presents the history of Franklin United Methodist Church.* Unpublished manuscript, Franklin United Methodist Church, Franklin, MD.

The Records & History Task Force Committee, & Brown, D. (2003). *Celebrating: Remembering the past and inspiring the future 116 years.* Unpublished manuscript, St. Matthews United Methodist Church, Shady Side, MD.

Walsh, K. T. (2011). *Family of freedom: Presidents and African Americans in the White House.* Boulder, CO: Paradigm.

Whitaker, M. (2011). *My long trip home.* New York, NY: Simon & Shuster.

Wilkerson, I. (2010). *The warmth of other suns: The epic story of America's great migration.* New York, NY: Random House.

Williams, J. P., Jr. (1993). *Chesapeake almanac: Following the bay through the seasons.* Centerville, MD: Tidewater.

ENDNOTES

Chapter 1—Location and Place

1. Lippson, A. J., & Lippson, R. (1984). *Life in the Chesapeake Bay.* Baltimore, MD: Johns Hopkins University Press, pp. 4-5.
2. Fitz, V. W. (1984). *Spirit of Shady Side peninsula life 1664-1984.* Shady Side, MD: Shady Side Peninsula Association, pp.7-11.
3. Ibid. p. 7
4. Hine, D., Hine, W., & Harrold, S. (2008). *The African-American odyssey.* Upper Saddle River, NJ: Pearson Education, p. 57.
5. Ibid. p. 58.
6. Ibid. p. 59.
7. Ibid. pp. 29-33.
8. Ibid. p. 23.
9. Gates, H. L., Jr. (2009). *In search of our roots: How 19 extraordinary African Americans reclaimed their past,* New York, NY: Crown Publishing Group, p. 17.
10. Hine, D., Hine, W., & Harrold, S. (2008). *The African-American odyssey.* Upper Saddle River, NJ: Pearson Education, pp.62-63.
11. Ibid. p. 70.
12. Ibid. p.61.

13. Bradford, J. C. (Ed.). (1977). *Anne Arundel County Maryland a bicentennial history 1649-1977.* Annapolis, MD: Anne Arundel County and Annapolis Biventennial Committee, p.11.

14. Fitz, V. W. (1984). *Spirit of Shady Side peninsula life 1664-1984.* Shady Side, MD: Shady Side Peninsula Association, p. 24.

15. Ibid. p.26.

16. Ibid. p. 24.

17. Ibid. pp. 3,4,11,28.

18. Ibid. pp.13,15.

19. Hine, D., Hine, W., & Harrold, S. (2008). *The African-American odyssey.* Upper Saddle River, NJ: Pearson Education, p. 94.

20. Bradford, J. C. (Ed.). (1977). *Anne Arundel County Maryland a bicentennial history 1649-1977.* Annapolis, MD: Anne Arundel County and Annapolis Biventennial Committee, p.14.

21. Fitz, V. W. (1984). *Spirit of Shady Side peninsula life 1664-1984.* Shady Side, MD: Shady Side Peninsula Association, pp.28,29.

22. Bradford, J. C. (Ed.). (1977). *Anne Arundel County Maryland a bicentennial history 1649-1977.* Annapolis, MD: Anne Arundel County and Annapolis Biventennial Committee, pp. 13,15.

23. Hynson, J. M. (2000). *Maryland freedom papers Volume 1 Anne Arundel County,* p.1.

24. Bradford, J. C. (Ed.). (1977). *Anne Arundel County Maryland a bicentennial history 1649-1977.* Annapolis, MD: Anne Arundel County and Annapolis Biventennial Committee, p.15.

25. Fitz, V. W. (1991). *Captain Salem Avery House: It's History 1860-1990.* Shady Side, MD: Shady Side Rural Heritage Society, p.14.

26. Bradford, J. C. (Ed.). (1977). *Anne Arundel County Maryland a bicentennial history 1649-1977.* Annapolis, MD: Anne Arundel County and Annapolis Bicentennial Committee, p.14.

27. Ibid. p.14.

28. Fitz, V. W. (1984). *Spirit of Shady Side peninsula life 1664-1984.* Shady Side, MD: Shady Side Peninsula Association, p. 29.

29. Hynson, J. M. (2000). *Maryland freedom papers Volume 1 Anne Arundel County,* p. 1.

30. Ibid. p.ii.

31. Bradford, J. C. (Ed.). (1977). *Anne Arundel County Maryland a bicentennial history 1649-1977.* Annapolis, MD: Anne Arundel County and Annapolis Bicentennial Committee, p. 14.

32. Ibid. p. 19.

33. Ibid. p. 17.

34. Fitz, V. W. (1984). *Spirit of Shady Side peninsula life 1664-1984.* Shady Side, MD: Shady Side Peninsula Association, p.35.

35. Fitz, V. W. (1991). *Captain Salem Avery House: It's History 1860-1990.* Shady Side, MD: Shady Side Rural Heritage Society, pp. 9-10.

36. Bradford, J. C. (Ed.). (1977). *Anne Arundel County Maryland a bicentennial history 1649-1977.* Annapolis, MD: Anne Arundel County and Annapolis Bicentennial Committee, p. 15.

37. Hine, D., Hine, W., & Harrold, S. (2008). *The African-American odyssey.* Upper Saddle River, NJ: Pearson Education, p. 95.

38. Fitz, V. W. (1984). *Spirit of Shady Side peninsula life 1664-1984.* Shady Side, MD: Shady Side Peninsula Association, p.26.

39. Fitz, V. W. (1991). *Captain Salem Avery House: It's History 1860-1990.* Shady Side, MD: Shady Side Rural Heritage Society, p. 11.

40. Bradford, J. C. (Ed.). (1977). *Anne Arundel County Maryland a bicentennial history 1649-1977.* Annapolis, MD: Anne Arundel County and Annapolis Bicentennial Committee, p.19.

41. Fitz, V. W. (1984). *Spirit of Shady Side peninsula life 1664-1984.* Shady Side, MD: Shady Side Peninsula Association, p. 32.

42. Bradford, J. C. (Ed.). (1977). *Anne Arundel County Maryland a bicentennial history 1649-1977.* Annapolis, MD: Anne Arundel County and Annapolis Bicentennial Committee, p.22.

43. Gates, H. L., Jr. (2009). *In search of our roots: How 19 extraordinary African Americans reclaimed their past,* New York, NY: Crown Publishing Group, p.8.

44. Wilkerson, I. (2010). *The warmth of other suns: The epic story of America's great migration.* New York, NY: Random House, p.391.

45. Battle, L. (2008). *And the beat goes on . . .* Southport, ME: Cozy Harbor, p. 36.

46. Wilkerson, I. (2010). *The warmth of other suns: The epic story of America's great migration.* New York, NY: Random House, p. 390.

47. Bradford, J. C. (Ed.). (1977). *Anne Arundel County Maryland a bicentennial history 1649-1977.* Annapolis, MD: Anne Arundel County and Annapolis Bicentennial Committee, pp. 20-21.

48. Ibid. p. 20.

49. Ibid. p. 19.

50. Hine, D., Hine, W., & Harrold, S. (2008). *The African-American odyssey.* Upper Saddle River, NJ: Pearson Education, p.412.

51. Ibid. p. 416.

52. Wilkerson, I. (2010). *The warmth of other suns: The epic story of America's great migration.* New York, NY: Random House, p. 39.

53. Ibid. pp. 41-42.

54. Hine, D., Hine, W., & Harrold, S. (2008). *The African-American odyssey.* Upper Saddle River, NJ: Pearson Education, p. 66.

55. Ibid. p. 493.

56. Ibid. p. 626.

Chapter 3–Eliza Dennis, Miss Doll Baby

1. Hine, D., Hine, W., & Harrold, S. (2008). *The African-American odyssey.* Upper Saddle River, NJ: Pearson Education, p.303.

2. The Records & History Task Force Committee, & Brown, D. (2003). *Celebrating: Remembering the past and inspiring the future 116 years.* Unpublished manuscript, St. Matthews United Methodist Church, Shady Side, MD, Part I.

3. Ibid. p.2.

4. Battle, L. (2008). *And the beat goes on* . . . Southport, ME: Cozy Harbor, p.22.

5. Dennis, J. (n.d.). *Jacob Dennis will*. Unpublished manuscript.

6. Bradford, J. C. (Ed.). (1977). *Anne Arundel County Maryland a bicentennial history 1649-1977*. Annapolis, MD: Anne Arundel County and Annapolis Bicentennial Committee, p.22.

Chapter 4–Shady Side School Stories

1. Hine, D., Hine, W., & Harrold, S. (2008). *The African-American odyssey*. Upper Saddle River, NJ: Pearson Education, p.414 and 2005 Shady Side Rural Heritage Society Newsletter.

2. Brown, P. L. (1988). *A century of "separate but equal" education in Anne Arundel County*. New York, NY: Vantage, pp. 33-35.

3. Ibid. pp. 105-108.

4. Ibid. p. 114.

5. Ibid. p. 116.

6. Ibid. pp. 117, 118

7. Ibid. p.119.

8. Ibid. p. 132

9. Ibid.pp.103-134.

Chapter 5—Boarding Houses and Post Offices

1. Holt, A., Smith, J. S., & Jones, S. V. (Eds.). (1952-1953). *Discovering our school community: Lula G. Scott School*. Shady Side, MD: Shady Side School and Churchton School, p.5.

2. Ibid. p 6.

3. Shady Side Elementary PTA Committee (Ed.). (1975-1976). *Shady Side past and present*. Shady Side, MD: Shady Side School PTA, p. 28.

4. Andrews, F. E. (1991). *Miss Ethel remembers.* Shady Side, MD: Shady Side Rural Heritage Society, p.121.

Chapter 6—The Nicks
Chapter 7—Watermen and Water Stories

1. Lippson, A. J., & Lippson, R. (1984). *Life in the Chesapeake Bay.* Baltimore, MD: Johns Hopkins University Press, pp.168, 199.
2. Shady Side Elementary PTA Committee (Ed.). (1975-1976). *Shady Side past and present.* Shady Side, MD: Shady Side School PTA, p.3.
3. Andrews, E. N. (Ed.). (1952). *Discovering our school community: Shady Side Elementary School.* Shady Side, MD: Shady Side Elementary School, p.6.
4. Ibid. p. 6.
5. Ibid. p. 5.

Chapter 8—Chuck Gross
Chapter 9—Stores and Businesses

1. Andrews, E. N. (Ed.). (1952). *Discovering our school community: Shady Side Elementary School.* Shady Side, MD: Shady Side Elementary School, p. 48.
2. Ibid. p. 8.
3. Ibid. p.18.
4. Ibid. p. 18.
5. Ibid. p. 48.
6. Ibid. p. 48.
7. Ibid. p. 49.

Chapter 10 Crowner Families

1. Fitz, V. W. (1991). *Captain Salem Avery House: It's History 1860-1990.* Shady Side, MD: Shady Side Rural Heritage Society, pp. 14, 15.

2. Walsh, K.T. (2011). Family of freedom: Presidents and African Americans in the White House. Boulder, CO: Paradigm, p. 8.

3. Wilkerson, I. (2010). *The warmth of other suns: The epic story of America's great migration.* New York, NY: Random House, p. 43.

4. Ibid. p. 221

Chapter 11—Buddy Holland

1. Fitz, V.W. (1984). Spirit of Shady Side peninsula life 1664-1986. Shady Side, MD: Shady Side Peninsula Association. p. 99.

Chapter 12—Hog Stories

1. Shady Side Elementary P.T.A. Committee (Ed.). (1975-1976). Shady Side past and present. Shady Side, MD: Shady Side School PTA, p. 16.

Chapter 13—Shady Side Neighborhoods

1. Holt, A., Smith, J. S., & Jones, S. V. (Eds.). (1952-1953). *Discovering our school community: Lula G. Scott School.* Shady Side, MD: Shady Side School and Churchton School, p.4.

2. Andrews, F. E. (1991). *Miss Ethel remembers.* Shady Side, MD: Shady Side Rural Heritage Society, p. 7.

3. Shady Side Elementary PTA Committee (Ed.). (1975-1976). *Shady Side past and present.* Shady Side, MD: Shady Side School PTA, p. 22.

4. Ibid. p. 21.

5. Ibid. p. 27.

6. Ibid. p. 21.

7. Ibid. p. 20.

8. Ibid. p. 20.

Chapter 14—Athletics and Recreation in Shady Side

1. Battle, L. (1995). *Easier said*. Annapolis, MD: Annapolis, p.161.
2. Ibid. p. 163.

Chapter 15—Matthew Families
Chapter 16—Thompson Families
Chapter 17—The Little Church at the Side of the Road
Chapter 18—Neighboring Churches

1. The committee on history and records. (1982). *The Franklin years: The committee on history and records presents the history of Franklin United Methodist Church*. Unpublished manuscript, Franklin United Methodist Church, Franklin, MD, p 1.
2. Ibid. Part I
3. Hine, D., Hine, W., & Harrold, S. (2008). *The African-American odyssey*. Upper Saddle River, NJ: Pearson Education, p. 68.
4. The Records & History Task Force Committee, & Brown, D. (2003). *Celebrating: Remembering the past and inspiring the future 116 years*. Unpublished manuscript, St. Matthews United Methodist Church, Shady Side, MD, p. 4, Part I.
5. Ibid. p.3.
6. Culp, E. W. (1942, July). *West River circuit 1836-1942*. Paper presented at Consecration of Centenary Methodist Church, Shady Side, MD, p.9.
7. Ibid. p.8
8. The Records & History Task Force Committee, & Brown, D. (2003). *Celebrating: Remembering the past and inspiring the future 116 years*. Unpublished manuscript, St. Matthews United Methodist Church, Shady Side, MD, p.24.
9. Ibid. 1983-1989 section.
10. Shady Side Elementary PTA Committee (Ed.). (1975-1976). *Shady Side past and present*. Shady Side, MD: Shady Side School PTA, p.51.
11. Ibid. p.56.

12. Ibid. p.55.

Chapter 19—Serving in the Military

1. Hine, D., Hine, W., & Harrold, S. (2008). *The African-American odyssey.* Upper Saddle River, NJ: Pearson Education, p. 85.
2. Ibid. pp. 91-94.
3. Ibid. p. 95.
4. Grundset, E. G., Diaz, B., Gentry, H., & Strahan, J. (Eds.). (2008). *Forgotten patriots: African American and American Indian patriots in the Revolutionary War, A guide to service, sources and studies.* National Society Daughters of the American Revolution, pp.461-463.
5. Hine, D., Hine, W., & Harrold, S. (2008). *The African-American odyssey.* Upper Saddle River, NJ: Pearson Education, p. 94.
6. Ibid. pp. 93,97,101.
7. Ibid. pp. 125-126.
8. Walsh, K. T. (2011). *Family of freedom: Presidents and African Americans in the White House.* Boulder, CO: Paradigm p. 33.
9. Hine, D., Hine, W., & Harrold, S. (2008). *The African-American odyssey.* Upper Saddle River, NJ: Pearson Education, p. 268.
10. Ibid. pp. 272-278.
11. Ibid. pp. 279-284.
12. Ibid. p. 292.
13. Ibid. pp. 390-392.
14. Ibid. pp. 393-395.
15. Ibid. p. 396.
16. Ibid. p. 246
17. Ibid. p. 428
18. Ibid. pp. 428-430.
19. Ibid. pp. 542-543.
20. Ibid. pp. 545-548.
21. Ibid. p. 549.

22. Battle, L. (2008). *And the beat goes on* . . . Southport, ME: Cozy Harbor, p. 39.

23. Hine, D., Hine, W., & Harrold, S. (2008). *The African-American odyssey*. Upper Saddle River, NJ: Pearson Education, p. 559.

24. Ibid. pp. 559-561.

25. Ibid. 616-617.

Chapter 20—April 2011

ANN WIDDIFIELD EARNED MASTER'S degrees from Ball State University in 1970 and the University of Virginia in 1984. She taught in elementary schools for 37 years. She and her husband, Noel, live in Shady Side, Maryland, and have five granddaughters between their daughter, Julie, and son, David.